Liberty
Versus the Tyranny of
Socialism

Liberty
Versus the Tyranny of
Socialism

Controversial Essays

WALTER E. WILLIAMS

HOOVER INSTITUTION PRESS
Stanford University   Stanford, California

www.hoover.org

Hoover Institution Press Publication No. 564

The Hoover Institution Press acknowledges Creators Syndicate, Inc., and also the Foundation for Economic Education (publisher of *The Freeman*), for their permission and cooperation in the reprinting of Walter E. Williams's columns and articles in this collection.

First printing, 2008
16 15 14 13 12 11 10 09 08   9 8 7 6 5 4 3 2 1
Manufactured in the United States of America
The paper used in this publication meets the minimum requirements of the American National Standard for Information Sciences— Permanence of Paper for Printed Library Materials, ANSI Z39.48-1992. ∞

Library of Congress Cataloging-in-Publication Data
Williams, Walter E. (Walter Edward), 1936–
Liberty versus the tyranny of socialism / by Walter E. Williams
       p.   cm. — (Hoover Institution Press publication ; no. 564)
ISBN 978-0-8179-4912-9 (pbk. : alk. paper)
1. Social sciences. I. Title. II. Hoover Institution Press publication ; 564.
H85.W55 2008
320.52092—dc22   2008016376

Contents

Preface   xi
Acknowledgments   xiii
Education   1
  A Donor with Backbone   4
  The Shame of Higher Education   6
  Murder at VPI   8
  Academic Cesspools   10
  Academic Cesspools II   12
  Academic Slums   14
  Indoctrination of Our Youth   16
  What's With GMU?   18
  Who's to Blame?   20
  College Stupidity   22
  Are Academic Elites Communists?   24
  Anti-Intellectualism among the Academic Elite   26
  Education Ineptitude   28
  Education Ineptitude II   30
  Believe It or Not   32
  School Violence Toleration   34
  Higher Education in Decline   36
  Higher Education in Decline II   38
  What's Wrong with Education?   40
  Fiddling whilst Rome Burns   42
Environment and Health   45
  Busybodies or Tyrants?   48
  Global Warming Heresy   50
  Trans Fat Ban   52
  Fearmongering   54
  Do We Want Socialized Medicine?   56
  Phony Science and Public Policy   58
  FDA: Friend or Foe?   60
  Health Care: Government vs. Private   62
  Deadly Environmentalists   64
  Global Warming Hysteria   66

Silencing Dissent   68
Do We Want This?   71
Destructive Western Policy   73
Envirobamboozled   75
Is This the America We Want?   77
Weak-Kneed Corporate CEOs   79
Killing People   81
They're Coming after You   83

Government   85
Competition or Monopoly   88
Stupid, Ignorant or Biased?   90
Congressional Constitutional Contempt   92
Bitter Partisan Politics   94
Attacking Lobbyists Wrong Battle   96
Is There a Federal Deficit?   98
Click It or Ticket   100
The Slippery Slope   102
The Pretense of Knowledge   104
Why We Love Government   106
The FairTax Book   108
Are We a Republic or a Democracy?   110
Not Yours to Give   112
Social Security Deceit   114
Stupid Airport Security   116
Stupid Airport Security II   118
Stupid Airport Security III   120
Is It Permissible?   122
Congressional Miracles   124
Minimum Gasoline Prices   126
Dangers of No Tax Liability   128
National Sales Tax   130

Income   133
Should We Save Jobs?   136
The Tempermental Minimum Wage   138
Economists on the Loose   140
Are the Poor Getting Poorer?   142
Income Mobility   144
The Poverty Hype   146

Minimum Wage, Maximum Folly   148
Are CEOs Overpaid?   150
How Not to Be Poor   152
Dead-End Jobs   154
Income Inequality   156
From Whence Income?   158
The Morality of Markets   160
The Politics of Envy   162
International   165
Goodies Cost   167
The Seen and Unseen   169
The Anti–Free Trader's True Enemy   171
Nonsense Ideas   173
Trade Deficits: Good or Bad?   175
World Poverty   177
Creating Effective Incentives   179
Rules of Engagement   181
The Pope Sanctions the OECD Thugs   183
How to Create Conflict   185
Disappearing Manufacturing Jobs   187
Foreign Aid to Africa   189
Will the West Defend Itself?   191
Foreign Trade Angst   193
Should We Trade at All?   195
Should We Copy Europe?   197
Our Trade Deficit   199
Aid to Africa   201
Sweatshop Exploitation   203
Self-Inflicted Poverty   205
The Appeasement Disease   207
Economic Stupidity   209
Poverty Myths   211
Do Peace Treaties Produce Peace?   213
Congressional and Leftist Lies   215
Law and Society   217
Constitution Day   219
Rules More Important Than Personalities   221
Property Rights   223

Democracy or Liberty   225
The Law versus Orders   227
Economic and Property Rights   229
Bogus Rights   231
Results versus Process   233
The Law or Good Ideas?   235
Ignorance or Contempt   237
American Contempt for Rule of Law   239
Liberty's Greatest Advocate   241
Corporate Courage   243
Confiscating Property   245
Attacking Western Values   247
Immigration vs. Gate-Crashing   249
The Greatest Generation   251

Potpourri   253
Illegal Immigration   254
Straight Thinking 101   256
Things to Think About   258
Historical Tidbits   260
Running Out of Oil?   262
Passing of a Giant   264
The Productive vs. the Unproductive   266
Making Intelligent Errors   268
Economic Lunacy   270
Do We Really Care about Children?   272
Why We're a Divided Nation   274
What's Inflation?   276
Basic Economics   278
U.S. Atrocities in Iraq   280
Will the West Survive?   282
Economics 101   284
Economic Lunacy   286
Attack on Decency   288
Profiling Needed   290
A Dynamite Economics Department   292
Who May Harm Whom?   294
Too Much Safety   296
There's No Free Lunch   298

Dopey Ideas and Expressions   300
Different Visions, Different Policy   302
My Organs Are for Sale   304
Parting Company Is an Option   307
Honesty and Trust   310

Race   313

Regrets for Slavery   316
Do People Care?   318
Liberal Views, Black Victims   320
Insulting Blacks   322
Betrayal of the Civil Rights Struggle   324
Racial Hoaxes and the NAACP   326
What's Discrimination?   328
What's Prejudice?   330
Discrimination or Prejudice   332
Discrimination, Prejudice, and Preferences   334
How Much Does Politics Count?   336
Racial Profiling   338
Victimhood: Rhetoric or Reality   340
Betrayal of the Struggle   342
Racial Profiling   344
Price Discrimination   346
Three Cheers for the Cos   348
A Usable Black History   350
Does Political Power Mean Economic Power?   352
Stifling Black Students   354

Economics for the Citizen   357

Preface

This book contains a selected collection of newspaper columns I have written over the past few years. Writing a weekly column for nearly thirty years is one of the loves of my life and the fruition of an admonition given to me by Professor Armen Alchian, one of my tenacious mentors during my graduate years at UCLA, who told me that the true test of whether one knows his subject comes when he can explain it to someone who knows nothing about it. If there is one glaring dereliction of economists, it is making our subject accessible to the ordinary person. The most important thing to be said about economics is that economics, more than anything else, is a way of thinking. As such, the tools of economics can be applied to topics commonly thought to be in the realm of economics, such as international trade, regulation, prices of goods and services, and costs and choice. The same economic tools can be usefully applied in areas not commonly thought to be in the realm of economics, such as racial discrimination, national defense and marriage.

The reader should be aware of a bias that underlies much of what I write. That bias is an unyielding defense of personal liberty that is a necessary consequence of the initial premise I make about humans. That initial premise that is each of us owns himself. Stated another way: I am my private property and you are yours. The institution of private property is the right held by the owner of property to keep, acquire, dispose, and exclude from use. The premise of self-ownership determines what human acts are moral or immoral and consistent with that premise. For example, rape, murder, slavery, fraud, and theft are immoral because they violate private property.

Americans articulate respect for private property rights, but their actions indicate otherwise. For example, although most Americans find slavery offensive, they do not find the essence of slavery offensive, which is a set of circumstances whereby one person is forcibly used to serve the purposes of another. Casual examination of the federal budget demonstrates that forcibly using one person to serve the purposes of another is now the primary function of the federal government in the forms of programs such as Social Security, Medicare, food stamps, farm and business subsidies, foreign aid, and the like. Americans, through the tax code, are forcibly used to serve the purposes of another, the recipient of government largesse.

Our founders feared government. Thomas Jefferson said, "I consider the foundation of the Constitution as laid on this ground that all powers not delegated to the United States, by the Constitution, nor prohibited by it to the states, are reserved to the states or to the people. To take a single step beyond the boundaries thus specially drawn around the powers of Congress, is to take possession of a boundless field of power not longer susceptible of any definition." Many of my columns focus on the growth of government and our loss of liberty, but many other columns demonstrate how the tools of economics can be used in ways that ordinary people can understand.

Acknowledgments

In 1958, as a taxicab driver in Philadelphia, Pennsylvania, I had the good fortune to meet Connie Taylor. In 1960, having received orders to ship out to Korea for a thirteen-month tour of duty in the army, I made the wisest decision of my life: I married Connie. A few days after Christmas 2007, having been married nearly forty-eight years, Mrs. Williams passed away. I have never had so much sorrow or been as lonely.

In my less sorrowful moments, I console myself by saying, "We had a good ride." We lived up to the vow our minister read to us: "To have and to hold, from this day forward, for better, for worse, for richer, for poorer, in sickness or in health, to love and to cherish 'till death do us part." When we married, neither one of us had much to speak of except determination and a willingness to make the kind of sacrifices that ultimately enabled us to have a good life with luxuries that would have been only a dream in 1960. Topping that, Mrs. Williams blessed me with a lovely daughter, Devyn, who became the apple of both of our eyes.

No one makes the progress that Mrs. Williams and I made without a lot of help. People, more experienced than we, gave us advice along the way and assisted us in financial tight spots. Professors at California State University, Los Angeles, and at UCLA, where I completed my doctorate, went beyond the call of duty to teach me economics. Much of that extra effort came in the form of extensive office hours, gifts of books and articles, and staying late into the evening to help me learn statistical techniques.

Writing columns is a tremendous learning experience. Readers often write saying, "here's an example," "did you ever look at it this way?" or "that's not true because." Thanks to readers of my columns for the many things that I have learned and also to my editor Karen Duyrea at Creators Syndicate, who saved me grief by catching errors before they caused me embarrassment.

Finally, thanks to Mrs. Spolarich, my assistant for some sixteen years who has helped keep my professional life in order.

Education

Without question American primary and secondary education is in shambles. According to the National Center for Education Statistics, in 2006, American students ranked 33rd among industrialized countries in math literacy; in science literacy, they ranked 27th. Dramatic evidence of poor-quality high school education is the fact that, at many colleges, more than 50 percent of incoming freshmen require some sort of re-medial education, costing billions of dollars. All of this is in the face of rising high school grade point averages that increasingly tell little about the student's academic proficiency.

The education that white students receive is nothing to write home about, but that received by black students is nothing short of gross fraud. Washington, D.C., is typical of many cities. At twelve of its nineteen high schools, more than 50 percent of the students test below basic in reading; at some of those schools the percentages approach 80 percent. At fifteen schools, more than 50 percent test below basic in math; in twelve of them 70 to 99 percent did so. (Below basic is the category the National Assessment of Education Progress uses for students unable to display even partial mastery of the knowledge and skills fundamental for proficient work at their grade level.) In the face of these deficiencies, each year more than 80 percent, and up to 96 percent, of high school students are fraudulently promoted to the next grade.

Politicians and those in the public education establishment argue that more money is needed to improve education. Minnesota and Iowa rank first and second in terms of student academic achievement; yet their per student education expenditures in 2004 were $8,000 and $8,600, respectively, whereas Washington, D.C., spent $13,000 per student.

In 2002, a Zogby poll found that contemporary college seniors scored on average little or no higher in literature, music, science, geography and history than the high school graduates of a half-century ago. A 1990 Gallup survey for the National Endowment of the Humanities, given to a representative sample of seven hundred college seniors, found that 25 percent did not know that Columbus landed in the Western Hemisphere *before the year 1500; 42 percent could not place the Civil War in the correct half century; and 31 percent thought Reconstruction came after World War II. A 1993 Department of Education survey found that, among college graduates, 50 percent of whites and more than 80 percent of blacks couldn't state in writing the argument made in a newspaper column, use a bus schedule to get on the right bus, that 56 percent could not calculate the right tip, that 57 percent could not figure out how much change they should get back after putting down $3.00 to pay for a 60-cent bowl of soup and a $1.95 sandwich, and that more than 90 percent could not use a calculator to find the cost of carpeting a room. But a 1999 survey taken by the American Council of Trustees and Alumni of seniors at the nation's top 55 liberal arts colleges and universities found that 98 percent could identify rap artist Snoop Doggy Dogg and Beavis and Butt-Head but that only 34 percent knew George Washington was the general at the Battle of Yorktown.*

Diversity, instead of academics, has become the concern. Our institutions of higher learning not only take diversity seriously but make it a multimillion-dollar operation. Juilliard School has a director of diversity and inclusion; Massachusetts Institute of Technology has a manager of diversity recruitment; Toledo University, an associate dean for diversity; the universities of Harvard, Texas A&M, California at Berkeley, Virginia, and many others boast of officers, deans, vice-presidents, and perhaps ministers of diversity. Diversity wasn't the buzzword back in the 1970s, '80s, and '90s. Diversity is the response by universities, as well as corporations, to various court decisions holding racial quotas, goals, and timetables unconstitutional. Offices of diversity and inclusion are simply substitutes for yesterday's offices of equity or affirmative action. It's simply a matter of old wine in new bottles, but it is racial discrimination just the same. Diversity is based on the proposition, without any evidence whatsoever, that having some sort of statistical racial representation is a necessary ingredient to a good education.

Out of the diversity movement has come speech codes. Martin Gross, in his book The End of Sanity, *reported that up to 383 colleges had some form of speech code. Under the ruse of ending harassment, some universities created speech codes, such as Bowdoin College's ban on jokes and stories "experienced by others as harassing." Brown University has*

banned "verbal behavior" that "produces feelings of impotence, anger or disenfranchisement" whether "unintentional or intentional." The University of Connecticut has outlawed "inappropriately directed laughter." Colby College has banned any speech that could lead to a loss of self-esteem. "Suggestive looks" are banned at Bryn Mawr College and "unwelcomed flirtations" at Haverford College. Fortunately for students, the Foundation for Individual Rights in Education (FIRE) has waged a successful war against such speech codes.

Then there's proselytizing of students. An ethnic studies professor at Cal State Northridge and Pasadena City College teaches that "the role of students and teachers in ethnic studies is to comfort the afflicted and afflict the comfortable." UC Santa Barbara's School of Education e-mailed its faculty asking them to consider classroom options concerning the Iraq war, suggesting they excuse students from class to attend antiwar events and give them extra credit to write about it. An English professor at Montclair State University in New Jersey tells his students, "Conservatism champions racism, exploitation, and imperialist war." A Massachusetts School of Art professor explains that his concern is to do away with whiteness "because whiteness is a form of racial oppression." He adds, "There cannot be a white race without the phenomenon of white supremacy." A Bucknell professor agrees saying, "A lot of our students, I think, are unconsciously racist."

If undergraduate education is not to assume the quality of primary and secondary education, immediate action must be taken. A good start might be for generous donors to withhold funds to colleges and universities who have forsaken their academic mission. The columns in this section focus on these and other education issues.

A Donor with Backbone

Wednesday, March 21, 2007

James W. McGlothlin, chairman and CEO of The United Company of Bristol, Va., and a former member of The College of William & Mary's Board of Visitors and a longtime donor, withheld his pledge of $12 million to the college. He made his decision because of the actions taken by Gene Nichol, the college president, who ordered the removal of the cross from Wren Chapel. The cross had been displayed on the chapel altar since around 1940. Nichol's justification was that he wanted to make the chapel welcoming to non-Christians.

That's a lie. President Nichol was a chapter president of the American Civil Liberties Union (ACLU) for North Florida, and an ACLU board member in North Carolina and Colorado. The ACLU has maintained an attack on religious symbols for decades, but usually through the courts. President Nichol's actions simply spared them a costly court battle to remove the religious symbol from William & Mary's Wren Chapel.

Nichol's actions caused a storm of controversy that he probably didn't anticipate. Caving in to the pressure, on March 6th, he agreed to return the cross to Wren Chapel. The ACLU has enjoyed phenomenal success in attacking our religious values. Unless they are stopped, I guarantee you they won't be satisfied until they get some judge to order the removal of crosses from the graves at Arlington and other military cemeteries.

The College of William & Mary's Wren Chapel cross issue is simply the tip of a much larger problem. For decades, college administrators and professors have sanctioned or participated in an attack on traditional American values. They've denied campus access to military recruiters, promoted socialism and attacked capitalism, and instituted race and sex quotas in admissions and in the awarding of scholarships. They've used their positions of trust to indoctrinate students with anti-Americanism. Despite this attack, taxpayers and private donors have been extremely generous, pouring billions upon billions of dollars into institutions that often hold a generalized contempt for their values.

Mr. McGlothlin is to be congratulated for his courage in taking a stand against this liberal attack on American values. Other wealthy donors ought to emulate Mr. McGlothlin's courage by withholding their donations to colleges that foster or sanction attacks on traditional American values and decency. While it's a bit more difficult, since their money is taken from them, taxpayers ought to rebel as well by pressuring their legislators.

Many college benefactors fondly recall their experiences at their alma maters some 20, 30 or 40 years ago. Often, what they remember bears little or no resemblance to what goes on at campuses today. With relatively little effort, benefactors can become more informed simply by visits to the college's website to discover whether there are activities offensive to their values. If there's an office of diversity, it strongly suggests the college is practicing some form of race or sex discrimination.

The Foundation for Individual Rights in Education (FIRE) provides information about colleges that have "politically correct" speech codes that suppress debate. The Young America's Foundation (YAF) publishes information about inane courses at some of our colleges, such as UCLA's "Queer Musicology" or Johns Hopkins' "Mail Order Brides."

Some colleges have brazenly violated donor intent. Princeton University has been taken to court by the Robertson family for misuse of $207 million of a gift estimated at $700 million in today's prices. Because they violated donor intent, Boston College, USC, UCLA, Harvard and Yale have been forced to return multimillion-dollar gifts. It's high time that donors large and small summon some of Mr. McGlothlin's courage and hold colleges accountable to standards of decency and honesty.

The Shame of Higher Education

Wednesday, April 4, 2007

Many of our nation's colleges and universities have become cesspools of indoctrination, intolerance, academic dishonesty and the new racism. In a March 1991 speech, Yale President Benno Schmidt warned, "The most serious problems of freedom of expression in our society today exist on our campuses. . . . The assumption seems to be that the purpose of education is to induce correct opinion rather than to search for wisdom and to liberate the mind."

Writing in the fall 2006 issue of Academic Questions, Luann Wright, in her article titled "Pernicious Politicization in Academe," documents academic dishonesty and indoctrination all too common today. Here are some of her findings:

- An ethnic studies professor, at Cal State Northridge and Pasadena City College, teaches that "the role of students and teachers in ethnic studies is to comfort the afflicted and afflict the comfortable."
- UC Santa Barbara's School of Education e-mailed its faculty asking them to consider classroom options concerning the Iraq War, suggesting they excuse students from class to attend anti-war events and give them extra credit to write about it.
- An English professor at Montclair State University in New Jersey tells his students, "Conservatism champions racism, exploitation and imperialist war."

Other instances of academic dishonesty include professors having their students write letters to state representatives protesting budget cuts. Students enrolled in cell biology, math and art classes must sit through lectures listening to professorial rants about unrelated topics such as globalism, U.S. exploitation of the Middle East and President Bush.

Wright is also the founder of NoIndoctrination.org, a website containing hundreds of reports of similar academic bias and dishonesty.

Anne D. Neal, president of The American Council of Trustees and Alumni, wrote a companion article titled "Advocacy in the College Classroom." She says that campuses across the nation have cultivated an atmosphere that permits the disinviting of politically incorrect speakers; politicized instruction; reprisals against or intimidation of students who speak their mind; political discrimination in college hiring and retention; and campus speech codes.

On most college campuses, there's the worship of diversity. The universities of Harvard, Texas A&M, UC Berkeley, Virginia and many others boast of officers, deans and vice presidents of diversity. Many academics make the mindless argument, with absolutely no evidence to back it up, that racial representation is necessary for academic excellence. For them, getting the right racial mix requires racial discrimination.

Diversity wasn't the buzzword back in the 1970s, '80s and '90s. Diversity is the response by universities, as well as corporations, to various court decisions holding racial quotas, goals and timetables unconstitutional. Offices of diversity and inclusion are simply substitutes for yesterday's offices of equity or affirmative action. It's simply a matter of old wine in new bottles, but it's racism just the same.

In an open letter titled "To the President of My University," Carl Cohen, professor of philosophy at the University of Michigan, summarizes, "Diversity is a good thing—but the claim that the need for diversity is so compelling that it overrides the constitutional guarantee of civic equality is one we swallow only because, by holding our nose and gulping it down, we can go on doing what our feeling of guilt demands."

Until parents, donors and taxpayers shed their unwillingness to investigate what's sold to them as higher education, what we see today will continue and get worse. Just as important is the recognition of the fact that boards of trustees at our colleges and universities bear the ultimate responsibility, and it is they who've been grossly derelict in their duty.

Murder at VPI

April 25, 2007

The 32 murders at Virginia Polytechnic Institute (VPI) shocked the nation, but what are some of the steps that can be taken to reduce the probability that such a massacre will happen again? A large portion of the blame can be laid at the feet of the VPI administration and its campus security personnel, who failed to warn students, faculty and staff.

Long before the massacre, VPI administration, security and some faculty knew Cho Seung-Hui, the murderer, had mental problems. According to The New York Times, "Campus authorities were aware 17 months ago of the troubled mental state of the student. . . ." More than one professor reported his bizarre behavior. Campus security tried to have him committed involuntarily to a mental institution. There were complaints that Cho Seung-Hui made unwelcome phone calls and stalked students. Given the university's experiences with Cho, at the minimum they should have expelled him, and their failure or inability to do so is the direct cause of last week's massacre.

But there is something else we might want to look at. There's a federal law known as the Family Educational Rights and Privacy Act of 1974 (FERPA). As VPI's registrar reports, "Third Party Disclosures are prohibited by FERPA without the written consent of the student. Any persons other than the student are defined as Third Party, including parents, spouses, and employers." College officials are required to secure written permission from the student prior to the release of any academic record information.

That means a mother, father or spouse who might have intimate historical knowledge of a student's mental, physical or academic problems, who might be in a position to render assistance in a crisis, is prohibited from being notified of new information. Alternatively, should the family member wish to initiate an inquiry as to whether there have been any reports of mental, physical or academic problems, they are prohibited from access by FERPA. Of course, the student can give his parent written permission to have access to such information, but how likely is it that a highly disturbed student will do so?

FERPA is part of a much broader trend in our society where parental authority is being usurped. Earlier this year, San Francisco Bay Area Assemblywoman Sally Lieber introduced a bill that would prosecute parents for spanking their children. Because of widespread opposition, the assemblywoman withdrew her bill. Schools teach children sex material that many parents would deem offensive. Texas Gov. Rick Perry issued an executive order mandating that every 11- and 12-year-old girl be given Gardisil HPV vaccination as a guard against a sexually transmitted disease that can cause genital warts and even cervical cancer.

Last February, the Commonwealth of Virginia's legislature unanimously passed a law, the first of its kind in the country that bans universities from expelling suicidal students. Such a law suggests that the Commonwealth's legislature is more concerned about the welfare of a suicidal potential murderer than the lives of his innocent victims. As such, those legislators might consider themselves in part culpable for VPI's 32 murder victims.

There is a partial parental remedy for governmental and university usurpation of parental rights through the power of the purse. Prior to writing out a check for a child's college tuition, have a legal document drawn up where the child gives his parents full and complete access to any mental, physical and academic records developed during the child's college career. While such a strategy might not be necessary for every parent, it should at least be considered by parents whose child has an unstable mental or physical history.

Academic Cesspools

Wednesday, October 17, 2007

The average taxpayer and parents who foot the bill know little about the rot on many college campuses. "Indoctrinate U" is a recently released documentary, written and directed by Evan Coyne Maloney, that captures the tip of a disgusting iceberg. The trailer for "Indoctrinate U" can be seen at www.onthefencefilms.com/movies.html.

"Indoctrinate U" starts out with an interview of Professor David Clemens, at Monterey Peninsula College, who reads an administrative directive regarding new course proposals: "Include a description of how course topics are treated to develop a knowledge and understanding of race, class, and gender issues." Clemens is fighting the directive, which applies not to just sociology classes but math, physics, ornamental horticulture and other classes whose subject material has nothing to do with race, class and gender issues.

Professor Noel Ignatiev, of the Massachusetts School of Art, explains that his concern is to do away with whiteness. Why? "Because whiteness is a form of racial oppression." Ignatiev adds, "There cannot be a white race without the phenomenon of white supremacy." What's blackness? According to Ignatiev, "Blackness is an identity that can be plausibly argued to arise out of a resistance to oppression." Bucknell professor Geoff Schneider agrees, saying, "A lot of our students, I think, are unconsciously racist." Both Ignatiev and Schneider are white.

The College of William & Mary and Tufts and Brown universities established racially segregated student orientations. At some universities, students are provided with racially segregated housing, and at others they are treated to racially separate graduation ceremonies.

Under the ruse of ending harassment, a number of universities have established speech codes. Bowdoin College has banned jokes and stories "experienced by others as harassing." Brown University has banned "verbal behavior" that "produces feelings of impotence, anger or disenfranchisement" whether "unintentional or intentional." University of Connecticut has outlawed "inappropriately directed laughter." Colby College has banned any speech that could lead to a loss of self-esteem. "Suggestive looks" are banned at Bryn Mawr College and "unwelcomed flirtations" at Haverford College. Fortunately for students, the Foundation for Individual Rights in Education (FIRE) has waged a successful war against such speech codes.

Central Connecticut State College set up a panel to discuss slavery reparations. All seven speakers, invited by the school, supported the idea. Professor Jay Bergman questioned the lack of diversity on the panel. In response, two members of the African Studies department published a letter criticizing Bergman, saying, "The protests against reparations stand on the same platform that produced apartheid, Hitler and the KKK." Such a response, as Professor Bergman says, is nothing less than intellectual thuggery.

For universities such as Columbia and Yale, military recruiters are unwelcome, but they welcome terrorists such as Columbia University's invitation to Colonel Mohammar Quadaffi and Mahmoud Ahmadinejad. Yale admitted former Taliban spokesman Sayed Rahmatullah Hashemi as a student, despite his fourth-grade education and high school equivalency degree.

On other campuses, such as Lehigh, Central Michigan, Arizona, Holy Cross and California Berkeley universities, administrators banned students, staff and faculty from showing signs of patriotism after the 9/11 attacks. On some campuses, display of the American flag was banned; the pledge of allegiance and singing patriotic songs were banned out of fear of possibly offending foreign students.

Several university officials refused to be interviewed for the documentary. They wanted to keep their campus policies under wraps, not only from reporters but parents as well. When college admissions officials make their recruitment visits, they don't tell parents that their children will learn "whiteness is a form of racial oppression," or that they sponsor racially segregated orientations, dorms and graduation ceremonies. Parents and prospective students are kept in the dark.

The Intercollegiate Studies Institute (isi.org) has published "Choosing the Right College," to which I've written the introduction. The guide provides a wealth of information to help parents and students choose the right college.

Academic Cesspools II

Wednesday, November 7, 2007

In last month's column "Academic Cesspools," I wrote about "Indoctrinate U," a recently released documentary exposing egregious university indoctrination of young people at prestigious and not-so-prestigious universities (www.onthefencefilms.com/movies.html). I said the documentary only captured the tip of a disgusting iceberg.

The Philadelphia-based Foundation for Individual Rights in Education (FIRE), a frontline organization in the battle against academic suppression of free speech and thought, released information about what's going on at the University of Delaware, and probably at other universities as well, that should send chills up the spines of parents of college-age students. The following excerpts are taken from the University of Delaware's Office of Residence Life Diversity Facilitation Training document. The full document is available at www.thefire.org.

Students living in the University's housing, roughly 7,000, are taught: "A racist: A racist is one who is both privileged and socialized on the basis of race by a white supremacist (racist) system. The term applies to all white people (i.e., people of European descent) living in the United States, regardless of class, gender, religion, culture or sexuality. By this definition, people of color cannot be racists, because as peoples within the U.S. system, they do not have the power to back up their prejudices, hostilities or acts of discrimination. (This does not deny the existence of such prejudices, hostilities, acts of rage or discrimination.)" This gem of wisdom suggests that by virtue of birth alone, not conduct, if you're white, you're a racist.

If you're white and disagree with racial quotas, preferences and openly racist statements made by blacks to whites, and you call it reverse racism or reverse discrimination, here's the document's message for you: "Reverse racism: A term created and used by white people to deny their white privilege. Those in denial use the term reverse racism to refer to hostile behavior by people of color toward whites, and to affirmative action policies, which allegedly give 'preferential treatment' to people of color over whites. In the U.S., there is no such thing as 'reverse racism.'" I agree with the last sentence. Racism is racism irrespective of color.

A white University of Delaware student might not have an ounce of ill will toward any race. According to the university's document, he's a racist anyway. "A non-racist: A non-term. The term was created by whites to deny responsibility for systemic racism, to maintain an aura of innocence in the face of racial oppression, and to shift responsibility for that oppression from whites to people of color (called 'blaming the victim'). Responsibility for perpetuating and legitimizing a racist system rests both on those who actively maintain it, and on those who refuse to challenge it. Silence is consent."

Then the document asks, "Have you ever heard a well-meaning white person say, 'I'm not a member of any race except the human race?' What she usually means by this statement is that she doesn't want to perpetuate racial categories by acknowledging that she is white. This is an evasion of responsibility for her participation in a system based on supremacy for white people."

I doubt whether this racist nonsense is restricted to the university's housing program. Students are probably taught similar nonsense in their sociology, psychology and political science classes. FIRE's outing of the University of Delaware's racist program elicited this official response from Vice President Michael Gilbert, "The central mission of the University, and of the program, is to cultivate both learning and the free exchange of ideas." (According to thefire.org, as a result of public exposure, and without condemning this racist program, on Nov. 2 President Patrick Harker ordered the mandatory re-education halted pending a review.)

It's a safe bet the university did not highlight this kind of learning experience to parents and students in its recruitment efforts. Nor were generous donors and alumni informed that they are racists by birth. I'd also guess that this kind of "education" was kept under wraps from the state legislators who use taxpayer money to fund the university.

Academic Slums

Wednesday, December 19, 2007

Every three years, the Organisation for Economic Co-operation and Development (OECD) conducts its Programme for International Student Assessment (PISA). PISA is a set of tests that measure 15-year-olds' performance in mathematics, science and reading.

The National Center for Education Statistics summarized the findings in "Highlights From PISA 2006" (http://nces.ed.gov/pubs2008/2008016.pdf). American students ranked 33rd among industrialized countries in math literacy, and in science literacy, they ranked 27th. Reading literacy was not reported for the U.S. because of an error in the test instruction booklets.

How do we get out of this mess of abysmal student performance? Presidential hopeful Barack Obama has proposed an $18 billion increase in federal education programs. That's the typical knee-jerk response—more money. Let's delve a bit, asking whether higher educational expenditures explain why secondary school students in 32 industrialized countries are better at math and science than ours. In 2004, the U.S. spent about $9,938 per secondary school student. More money might explain why Swiss and Norwegian students do better than ours because they, respectively, spent $12,176 and $11,109 per student. But what about Finland ($7,441) and South Korea ($6,761), which scored first and second in math literacy? What about the Slovak Republic ($2,744) and Hungary ($3,692), as well as other nations whose education expenditures are a fraction of ours and whose students have greater math and science literacy than ours?

American education will never be improved until we address one of the problems seen as too delicate to discuss. That problem is the overall quality of people teaching our children. Students who have chosen education as their major have the lowest SAT scores of any other major. Students who have graduated with an education degree earn lower scores than any other major on graduate school admissions tests such as the GRE, MCAT or LSAT. Schools of education, either graduate or undergraduate, represent the academic slums of most any university. As such, they are home to the least able students and professors with the lowest academic respect. Were we serious about efforts to improve public education, one of the first things we would do is eliminate schools of education.

The inability to think critically makes educationists fall easy prey to harebrained schemes, and what's worse, they don't have the intelligence to recognize that the harebrained scheme isn't working. Just one of many examples is the use of fuzzy math teaching techniques found in "Rethinking Mathematics: Teaching Social Justice by the Numbers." Among its topics: "Sweatshop Accounting," "Chicanos Have Math in Their Blood," "Multicultural Math" and "Home Buying While Brown or Black." The latter contains discussions on racial profiling, the war in Iraq, corporate control of the media and environmental racism.

If you have a fifth-grader, his textbook might be "Everyday Math." Among its study questions are: If math were a color, it would be (blank) because (blank). If it were a food, it would be (blank) because (blank). If it were weather, it would be (blank) because (blank). All of this is sheer nonsense, and what's worse is that the National Council of Teachers of Mathematics sponsors and supports much of this nonsense.

Mathematics, more than any other subject, is culturally neutral. The square root of 16 is 4 whether you're Asian, European or African, or even Plutonian or Martian. While math and science literacy among white 15-year-olds is nothing to write home about, that among black 15-year-olds is nothing less than a disaster.

Few people appreciate the implications of poor math preparation. Mathematics, more than anything else, teaches one how to think logically. As such, it is an important intellectual tool. If one graduates from high school with little or no preparation in algebra, geometry and a bit of trigonometry, he is likely to find whole areas of academic study, as well as the highest paying jobs, hermetically sealed off from him for his entire life.

Indoctrination of Our Youth

Wednesday, February 22, 2006

Let's start off with a few quotations, then a question. In reference to the president's State of the Union: "Sounds a lot like the things Adolf Hitler used to say." "Bush is threatening the whole planet." "[The] U.S. wants to keep the world divided." Then the speaker asks, "Who is probably the most violent nation on the planet?" and shouts "The United States!"

What's the source of these statements? Were they made in the heat of a political campaign? Was it a yet-to-be captured leader of al Qaeda? Was it French Prime Minister Dominique de Villepin? Any "yes" answer would miss the true source by a mile. All of those statements were made by Mr. Jay Bennish, a teacher at Overland High School in Aurora, Colo.

During this class session, Mr. Bennish peppered his 10th-grade geography class with other statements like: The U.S. has engaged in "7,000 terrorist attacks against Cuba." In his discussion of capitalism, he told his students, "Capitalism is at odds with humanity, at odds with caring and compassion and at odds with human rights."

Regardless of whether you're pro-Bush or anti-Bush, pro-American or anti-American, I'd like to know whether there's anyone who believes that the teacher's remarks were appropriate for any classroom setting, much less a high school geography class. It's clear the students aren't being taught geography. They're getting socialist lies and propaganda. According to one of the parents, on the first day of class, the teacher said Karl Marx's "Communist Manifesto" was going to be a part of the curriculum.

This kind of indoctrination is by no means restricted to Overland High School. School teachers, at all grades, often use their classroom for environmental, anti-war, anti-capitalist and anti-parent propaganda. Some get their students to write letters to political figures condemning public policy the teacher doesn't like. Dr. Thomas Sowell's "Inside American Education" documents numerous ways teachers attack parental authority. Teachers have asked third-graders, "How many of you ever wanted to beat up your parents?" In a high school health class, students were asked, "How many of you hate your parents?"

Public education propaganda is often a precursor for what youngsters might encounter in college. UCLA's Bruin Standard newspaper documents campus propaganda. Mary Corey, UCLA history professor, instructed her class, "Capitalism isn't a lie on purpose. It's just a lie," she continued, "[Capitalists] are swine. . . . They're bastard people." Professor Andrew Hewitt, chairman of UCLA's Department of Germanic Languages, told his class, "Bush is a moron, a simpleton, and an idiot." His opinion of the rest of us: "American consumerism is a very unique thing; I don't think anyone else lusts after money in such a greedy fashion." Rod Swanson, economics professor, told his class, "The United States of America, backed by facts, is the greediest and most selfish country in the world." Terri Anderson, a sociology professor, assigned her class to go out cross-dressed in a public setting for four hours. Photos or videotape were required as proof of having completed the assignment.

The Bruin Alumni Association caused quite a stir when it offered to pay students for recordings of classroom proselytizing. The UCLA administration, wishing to conceal professorial misconduct, threatened legal action against the group. Some professors labeled the Bruin Alumni Association's actions as McCarthyism and attacks on academic freedom. These professors simply want a free hand to proselytize students.

Brainwashing and proselytization is by no means unique to UCLA. Taxpayers ought to de-fund, and donors should cut off contributions to colleges where administrators condone or support academic dishonesty. At the K–12 schools, parents should show up at schools, PTAs and board of education meetings demanding that teachers teach reading, writing and arithmetic and leave indoctrination to parents. The most promising tool in the fight against teacher proselytization is the micro-technology available that can expose the academic misconduct.

What's with GMU?

Wednesday, April 5, 2006

George Mason University's basketball team broke into national prominence, going all the way to the NCAA Final Four matchup but losing to the red hot University of Florida Gators. The Patriots' stellar performance this season is emblematic of the entrepreneurship and risk taking that long has been a feature of the University.

In 1980, when I left Temple University to join George Mason University's Economics Department, it was a little known school in northern Virginia. Dr. George Johnson, also from Temple University, was president. In an early meeting, to settle my dispute with one of the deans, I learned that Dr. Johnson was an entrepreneur with a vision. In 1983, Dr. Jim Buchanan, a former mentor during my doctoral student days at UCLA, was enticed to join our economics department, bringing with him several members of the Center for Study of Public Choice that he founded at Virginia Polytechnic Institute. In 1986, Dr. Buchanan won the Nobel Prize in Economics.

In 1986, Henry Manne was offered the deanship at our law school. At the time, the law school was less than nondescript, with most of the faculty having only a tangential academic relationship with the school. Mr. Manne was given complete control over hiring and firing. He hired legal scholars, established the Law & Economics Center and laid the groundwork for GMU Law School to become a first-rate law school. Today, GMU Law School is in the nation's top tier of law schools. According to the latest U.S. News & World Report's "America's Best Graduate Schools 2007," GMU Law School ranks 37th among 193 law schools. One uniqueness of our law school is that its professors revere and respect the U.S. Constitution.

In 1995, my colleagues asked me to become department chairman, and I reluctantly accepted. Our department was under siege by a hostile administration because we all shared characteristics that don't go over well in today's academy; we are libertarian-leaning free market economists. My confrontational stance as chairman didn't endear me to the administration. I decided that the only way to improve our department was to "privatize" it—go out and raise money. With the help of my colleagues, generous donors and a new dean, we built a first-rate department. In 2001, the last year of my term as chairman, Dr. Vernon Smith and six of his colleagues at the University of Arizona's Economic Science Laboratory joined our department. A year later, Dr. Smith became GMU's second Nobel Prize-winner.

You say, "What's up, Williams? I thought we're talking about GMU basketball!" For GMU's basketball team, knocking off several of the nation's top-ranked teams is in itself a stellar performance. Going from no one's guess to being in the Final Four is indicative of some of George Mason University's entrepreneurship. Coach Jim Larranaga and his staff used what my colleagues, Professors Peter Boettke and Alexander Tabarrok, in their Slate.com article "The Secret of George Mason," called the Moneyball model of recruitment. Larranaga knows that he can't compete for freshmen players with the likes of UCLA, Duke, Wake Forest and other top-ranked teams. Boettke and Tabarrok say he overcame that obstacle by hunting "for the undervalued players—the ones who everyone else thought were too short, too thin, or too fat—and then building them into a team. In its astonishing defeat of UConn, GMU's players were giving away 4 inches at nearly every position."

After this season, it's just possible that the GMU Patriots will be able to hold its own against top schools, as does the economics department and law school, in recruiting basketball players. Singer Ray Charles pointed to the problem in his hit song, "Them That's Got," which says, "That old saying them that's got is them that gets is something I can't see. If you got to have something before you can get something, how you get your first is still a mystery to me." George Mason University basketball, as well as law and economics, has solved Ray Charles' mystery. We have something.

Who's to Blame?

Wednesday, July 5, 2006

Let's look at the recent "Nation's Report Card," published annually by the U.S. Department of Education's National Center for Education Statistics. Nationally, in reading, only 13 percent of black fourth graders, and 11 percent of black eighth graders score as proficient. Twenty-nine percent achieve a score of "basic," which is defined as having a partial knowledge and skills necessary to be proficient in the grade. Fifty-nine percent score below basic, not having any of the necessary knowledge and skills. It's the same story for black eighth graders, with 40 percent scoring basic and 49 percent below basic.

In math, it's roughly the same story. For black fourth graders, 12 percent score proficient, 47 percent score basic and 40 percent below basic. For black eighth graders, 8 percent score proficient, while 33 percent score basic and 59 percent score below basic; however, one percent of black fourth graders and eighth graders achieved an advanced score in math. Teachers and politicians respond to this tragic state of affairs by saying that more money is needed. The Washington, D.C. school budget is about the nation's highest with about $15,000 per pupil. Its student/teacher ratio, at 15.2 to 1, is lower than the nation's average.

Despite this, black academic achievement in Washington, D.C. is the lowest in the nation. Reading scores for Washington, D.C.'s fourth-grade black students are: 7 percent proficient, 21 percent basic and 71 percent below basic. For eighth-graders, it's 6 percent proficient, 33 percent basic and 58 percent below basic. It's the same sad tale in math. For fourth-graders, it's 5 percent proficient, 35 percent basic and 59 percent below basic. For eighth-graders, it's three percent proficient, 23 percent basic and 73 percent below basic. With these achievement levels, one shouldn't be surprised that the average black high school graduate, depending upon the subject, has the academic achievement level of the average white sixth, seventh or eighth grader.

Racial discrimination has nothing to do with what's no less than an education meltdown within the black community. Where black education is the very worst, often the city mayor is black, city council dominated by blacks, and often the school superintendent is black, as well as most of the principals and teachers, and Democrats have run the cities for decades. I'm not saying there's a causal connection, just that one would be hard put to chalk up the rotten education to racial discrimination.

There's enough blame for this sorry state of affairs for all participants to have their share: students who are hostile and alien to the education process, parents who don't care, teachers who are incompetent or have been beaten down by the system, and administrators who sanction unwarranted promotions and issuance of fraudulent diplomas that attest that a student has mastered 12th-grade material when in fact he hasn't mastered sixth- or seventh-grade material.

No one can solve the educational problems that black people confront except black people themselves. First, it's foolhardy, and black people cannot afford to buy into the idea that no black child should be saved from the education morass until all black children can be saved. That means we must find a way to permit the escape from rotten schools for as many black children who want to be educated and have supportive parents as we can. Educational vouchers or tuition tax credits would provide such a mechanism.

At one time in black history, there was a high value placed on education, so much so that blacks risked punishment to acquire education in areas of our country where black education was prohibited. Being 70 years old, I know there was a time when schools and black parents cooperated with one another to see to it that children behaved in school and did their work. In principle, the solution to black education problems is not rocket science. The problem is summoning the will.

College Stupidity

Wednesday, August 2, 2006

Colleges and universities will start their fall semester soon. You might be interested in what parents' and taxpayers' money is going for at far too many "institutions of higher learning."

At Occidental College in Los Angeles, a mandatory course for some freshmen is "The Unbearable Whiteness of Barbie." It's a course where Professor Elizabeth J. Chin explores ways in "which scientific racism has been put to use in the making of Barbie [and] to an interpretation of the film 'The Matrix' as a Marxist critique of capitalism." Johns Hopkins University students can enroll in a course called "Sex, Drugs, and Rock 'n' Roll in Ancient Egypt." Part of the course includes slide shows of women in ancient Egypt "vomiting on each other," "having intercourse" and "fixing their hair."

Harvard University students can take "Marxist Concepts of Racism," which examines "the role of capitalist development and expansion in creating racial inequality." You can bet there's no mention of the genocide in Africa and former communist regimes like Yugoslavia. Young America's Foundation and Accuracy in Academia publish lists of courses like these, at many other colleges, that are nothing less than student indoctrination through academic dishonesty.

Parents are paying an average tuition of $21,000, and at some colleges over $40,000, to have their children exposed to anti-Americanism and academic nonsense. According to a 2000 American Council of Trustees and Alumni study, "Losing America's Memory: Historical Illiteracy in the 21st Century," not one of the top 50 colleges and universities today requires American history of its graduates.

A survey conducted by the Center for Survey Research and Analysis at the University of Connecticut gave 81 percent of the seniors a D or F in their knowledge of American history. The students could not identify Valley Forge, or words from the Gettysburg Address, or even the basic principles of the U.S. Constitution. A survey released by the McCormick Tribune Freedom Museum found that American adults could more readily identify Simpson cartoon characters than name freedoms guaranteed in the First Amendment.

The academic dishonesty doesn't end with phony courses and lack of a solid core curriculum; there's grossly fraudulent grading, euphemistically called grade inflation. For example, Harvard's Educational Policy Committee found that some professors award A's for average work. A *Boston Globe* study found that 91 percent of Harvard seniors graduated with honors, that means all A's and a few B's.

I doubt whether these "honor" students could pass a 1950 high school graduation examination. According to the Department of Education's 2003 National Assessment of Adult Literacy, only 31 percent of college graduates were proficient in prose, only 25 percent proficient in reading documents and 31 percent proficient in math.

Who's to blame for the increasingly sad state of affairs at America's colleges and universities? It's tempting to blame professors and campus administrators, and yes, they share a bit of the blame for shirking their academic duty. But the bulk of the blame rests with trustees, who bear the ultimate responsibility for what goes on at the college.

Unfortunately, trustees know little detail about what goes on at their institutions. Most of them have their time taken up by their non-college obligations. As such, they are simply yes-men who, in making decisions, must rely on information, often incomplete or biased, given to them by the president and the provost.

A good remedy would be for boards of trustees to hire a campus ombudsman and staff that's accountable only to the trustees. During my brief tenure as a trustee of a major East Coast university, I made this suggestion only to be asked by the president whether I trusted him. My response was yes I trusted him, but I wanted verification.

Are Academic Elites Communists?

Wednesday, August 16, 2006

Grove City College publishes an excellent newsletter titled "Visions and Values." Its July 2006 edition features an interview with Dr. Richard Pipes, acclaimed Russian historian and Harvard University professor of Sovietology. The interview was conducted by Grove City College professor of political science Dr. Paul Kengor.

Dr. Pipes, who served on the National Security Council during the Reagan administration, explained that there are actually only a few communists among academics. At first glance, that's a puzzling observation, given the leftist bias at most college campuses. Drs. Pipes and Kengor explain the puzzle in a way that makes perfect sense.

While academic leftists, and I'd include their media allies, are not communists, they are anti-anti-communists. In other words, they have contempt for right-wingers, conservatives or libertarians who are anti-communists. Why? Academic leftists, and their media allies, are in agreement with many of the stated goals of communism, such as equal distribution of wealth, income equality and other goals spelled out in Karl Marx and Friedrich Engels' "Manifesto of the Communist Party." Leftist elites love the ideas of communism so much that they are either blind to, or tolerant of, its many shortcomings.

In practice, communism is nothing less than sheer barbarism that makes even the horrors of Nazism pale in comparison. Professor Rudolph J. Rummel of the University of Hawaii outlines that barbarism in his book "Death by Government," a comprehensive detailing of the roughly 170 million people murdered by their own governments during the 20th century. From 1917 to its collapse in 1991, the Soviet Union murdered about 62 million of its own people. During Mao Zedong's reign, 35,236,000, possibly more, Chinese citizens were murdered. By comparison, Hitler's Nazis managed to murder 21 million of its citizens and citizens in nations they conquered. Adding these numbers to the 60 million lives lost in war makes the 20th century mankind's most brutal era.

At home and abroad, leftists have done a thorough and commendable job documenting and condemning the horrors and crimes of Hitler and his fascist Nazi regime, but when have you heard them direct similar condemnation of Joseph Stalin, his successors and Mao Zedong? By and large, they've chosen to overlook the horrors of communism.

The reason for their reluctance to condemn the barbarism of communism is simple. Dr. Pipes says, "Intellectuals, by the very nature of their professions, grant enormous attention to words and ideas. And they are attracted by socialist ideas. They find that the ideas of communism are praiseworthy and attractive; that, to them, is more important than the practice of communism. Now Nazi ideals, on the other hand, were pure barbarism; nothing could be said in favor of them."

Often, when people evaluate capitalism, they evaluate a system that exists on Earth. When they evaluate communism, they are talking about a non-existent Utopia. What exists on Earth, with all of its problems and shortcomings, is always going to fail miserably when compared to a Utopia. The very attempt to achieve the utopian goals of communism requires the ruthless suppression of the individual and an attack on any institution that might compromise the loyalty of the individual to the state. That's why one of the first orders of business for communism, and those who support its ideas, is the attack on religion and the family.

Rank nations according to whether they are closer to the capitalism end or the communism end of the economic spectrum. Then rank nations according to human rights protections. Finally, rank nations according to per capita income. Without question, citizens of those nations closer to capitalism enjoy a higher standard of living and a far greater measure of liberty than those in nations closer to communism.

Anti-Intellectualism among the Academic Elite

Wednesday, February 2, 2005

Dr. Lawrence Summers, president of Harvard University, has been excoriated for suggesting that innate differences between men and women might be one of the reasons fewer women succeed in the higher reaches of science and math. Adding insult to injury, he also questioned the role of sex discrimination in the small number of female professors in science and engineering at elite universities.

Professor Nancy Hopkins, an MIT biologist, attended the National Bureau of Economic Research conference titled "Diversifying the Science and Engineering Workforce" where Dr. Summers gave his lecture. She had to leave the lecture, explaining to a *Boston Globe* (Jan. 17, 2005) reporter, "I would've either blacked out or thrown up." In today's campus anti-intellectualism, it's acceptable to suggest that genetics explains some outcomes, but it's unacceptable to use it as an explanation for other outcomes. Let's try a few, and guess whether Professor Hopkins would barf.

Suppose a speaker said that sickle cell anemia is genetically determined and occurs almost exclusively among blacks. Would Professor Hopkins stomp out of the room, charging racism? What if it were said that a person's chances of being a carrier of the gene for Tay-Sachs disease, a disease without a cure, is significantly higher if he is an Eastern European (Ashkenazi) Jew? Would Professor Hopkins barf and charge the speaker with anti-Semitism?

Jon Entine, in his book "Taboo: Why Black Athletes Dominate Sports And Why We're Afraid to Talk About It (1999)," says, "All of the 32 finalists in the last four Olympic men's 100-meter races are of West African descent." The probability of such an outcome by chance is all but zero. The genetic physiological and biomechanical characteristics that cause blacks to excel in some sports—basketball, football and track—spell disaster for those who have aspirations to be Olympic-class swimmers. Entine says, "No African American has ever qualified for the U.S. Olympic swim or dive team. Indeed, despite a number of special programs and considerable funding that have attracted thousands of aspiring black Olympians, there were only seven blacks who could even qualify to compete against the 455 swimmers at the 1996 Olympic trials."

Do you suppose Professor Hopkins would charge Entine with racism? The only behavioral genetic explanation that campus anti-intellectuals unquestioningly accept is that homosexuality has genetic origins.

What about women in the professions? In my colleague Thomas Sowell's 1984 book "Civil Rights: Rhetoric or Reality," there's a chapter titled "The Special Case of Women." He says, "The economic ramifications of marriage and parenthood are profound, and often directly opposite in their effects on men and women." Marriage increases male labor-force participation and reduces that of women. Marriage increases career interruption for women but not men. That's important for career advance and selection. If you're a good computer technician, engineer or specialist in the higher reaches of science and technology, and you leave your job for a few years, much of your skills and knowledge will be obsolete when you return. The same obsolescence is virtually absent in occupations such as editor, librarian and schoolteacher. This factor, instead of sex discrimination, might explain some of the career choices made by women.

But what about the flap over Dr. Summers' suggestion that genetics or innate differences might play a role in the paucity of women in science and engineering? It's not that important whether Dr. Summers is right or wrong. What's important is the attempt by some of the academic elite to stifle inquiry. Universities are supposed to be places where ideas are pursued and tested, and stand or fall on their merit. Suppression of ideas that are seen as being out of the mainstream has become all too common at universities. The creed of the leftist religion is that any difference between people is a result of evil social forces. That's a vision that can lead to the return to the Dark Ages.

Educational Ineptitude

March 1, 2004

What passes for educational enlightenment these days boggles the mind. Matt Gouras, of the Associated Press, writing in the *Seattle Times* (1/5/04) tells a story about Tennessee schools. The success of some students has made other students feel badly about themselves. What're the schools' responses? Public schools in Nashville have stopped posting honor rolls. Some are considering a ban on posting exemplary school work on bulletin boards. Others have canceled academic pep rallies while others might eliminate spelling bees. Nashville's Julia Green Elementary School principal, Steven Baum, agrees thinking that spelling bees, and publicly graded events are leftovers from the days of ranking and sorting students. He says, "I discourage competitive games at school. They just don't fit my world view of what a school should be."

This is a vision all too common among today's educationist but there's a good reason for it: too large a percentage of teachers represent the very bottom of the academic achievement barrel and as such fall easy prey to mindless and destructive fads.

Retired Indiana University (of Pennsylvania) physics professor, Donald E. Simanek has assembled considerable data on just who becomes a teacher (www.lhup.edu/dsimanek/decline1.htm). Freshman college students who choose education as a major "are on the average, one of the academically weakest groups." Those choosing non-teaching physics and math are one of the academically strongest groups. Some of the more capable who initially chose teaching will find the teacher-preparation curriculum to be boring and intellectually empty, and shift to curricula that are academically more challenging and rewarding. Professor Simanek adds "that on tests such as the Wessman Personnel Classification Test of verbal analogy and elementary arithmetical computations, the teachers scored, on average, only slightly better than clerical workers. A rather low score was enough to pass. Yet half the teachers failed."

There are other causes for the sorry state of today's primary and secondary education. There's been the politicizing of education. Teachers have recruited students to write letters to the President protesting the war and participate in demonstrations against school budget cuts. Very often good teachers and principal are faced with the impossible having to deal with administrators and school boards who are intellectual inferiors and motivated by political considerations rather than what's best for children.

One of the very best things that can be done for education is to eliminate schools of education. There's little in the curriculum that contributes directly to the development of the mind. Professor Simanek says that "Most teachers have learned 'methods and skills' of teaching, but don't have a solid understanding of the subject they teach. So they end up 'teaching' trivia, misinformation, and intellectual garbage, but doing it with 'professional' polish. Most do not display love of learning, nor the ability to do intense intellectual activity of any kind. Lacking these qualities they cannot possibly inspire and nourish these qualities in their students."

According to a recent study by the North Central Regional Education Laboratory titled, "Effective Teacher Recruitment and Retention Strategies in the Midwest," 75% to 100% of the teachers that leave the profession are ranked as either "effective" or "very effective."

To improve teaching we must attract people of higher intellectual ability and we must make teacher salaries related to ability and effectiveness. We must ensure that teachers have more academic freedom, better working conditions, and a suitable environment for teaching. An important component of that environment is the capacity to remove students who are alien and hostile to the education process. Finally, we should consider curriculum changes that eliminate courses that have little, if anything, to do with reading, writing and arithmetic.

The low academic quality of many of our teachers is neither flattering nor comfortable to confront but confront it we must if we're to do anything about our sorry state of education.

Educational Ineptitude II

March 8, 2004

Several weeks ago my column, "Teacher Ineptitude," was about the sorry state of teacher quality concluding that while teacher ineptitude is neither flattering nor comfortable to confront but confront it we must if we're to do anything about our sorry state of education.

The situation is not pretty. Philadelphia schools are typical of poor quality big-city schools. Susan Snyder, *Philadelphia Inquirer* staff writer, in her article, "District to help teachers pass test" (3/24/04), reported "that half of the district's 690 middle school teachers who took exams in math, English, social studies and science in September and November failed." Other test results haven't been released; Pennsylvania Governor Ed Rendell said he understands "concerns that releasing the data could subject teachers to humiliation. . . ." The unflattering fact that we must own up to is that many, perhaps most, of those who choose teaching as a profession represent the very bottom of the academic barrel. Let's look at it.

The National Center for Education Statistics (NCES) compiles loads of statistics on education. The NCES "Digest of Education Statistics" Table 136 shows SAT average score by student characteristics for 2001. Students who select education as their major have the lowest SAT scores of any other major (964). Math majors have the highest (1174). It's the same story when education majors finish college and take tests for admission to graduate schools. In the case of the Graduate Record Examination (GRE), education majors have an average score that's the second lowest (467) of any other major except sociology majors (434). Putting this in perspective, math majors score the highest (720) followed closely by economics in third place (625). It's roughly the same story for students taking the LSAT for admission to law schools where the possible scores range between 120 and 180. Out of 29 majors, education majors ranked 26th averaging a score of 148. Physics/math majors came in first with a 158 score and economics majors third with 155. Readers can readily obtain this information by a "Google" search using the words "GRE major" and "LSAT major."

Though my column criticized teachers, I was pleasantly surprised and encouraged by the responses. Many teachers sent letters saying their experiences mirrored exactly what I reported. Quite a few wrote of horror stories dealing with incompetent colleagues and administrators. There were also some fairly angry letters accusing me of "bashing teachers" and demanding an apology for doing so. The fact of the matter is that there are many excellent, competent and dedicated teachers often working in systems that reward incompetence and slovenliness and penalize excellence and dedication.

Our nation has a serious education problem that easily threatens our future well-being. Corrective action requires that we acknowledge and correct deficiencies no matter how painful and embarrassing they might be. A good start in that direction is to examine successful teacher training programs and if we have the guts imitate them.

Hillsdale College manages Hillsdale Academy, a K–12 primary and secondary school. At Hillsdale no students major in education. Students major and minor in the subjects they will be teaching, specifically art, biology, chemistry, English, French, German, history, Latin, mathematics, music, physical education, physics, science and Spanish. To be admitted to Hillsdale's Teacher Education Program, a student must have and maintain a GPA of 3.0 and higher.

Needless to say teacher incompetency isn't the only explanation for our education malaise. Parents who don't give a damn and students with minds and attitudes alien and hostile to the education process figure in as well. There's not much politicians and the education establishment can do about these factors; however, it's entirely within their power to take measures such as those practiced at Hillsdale to ensure teacher competency.

Believe It or Not

May 17, 2004

Benedict College, Columbia, South Carolina enforces an academic policy that defies belief. Say I'm a freshman taking your class in biology. I learn little from your lectures, assigned readings and homework. I do attend class every day; take notes and manage to average 40 percent on the graded work for the semester. What grade might you give me? I'm betting that all but the academic elite would say, "Sorry, Williams, but no cigar," and I'd earn an F for the course. But, if you're a professor at Benedict College, you'd be fired.

That's exactly what happened to Professors Milwood Motley, Chairman of Benedict's Biological and Physical Sciences Department, and Larry Williams of the same department, both of whom refused to go along with the college's Success Equals Effort (SEE) policy. SEE is a policy where 60 percent of a freshman's grade is based on effort and the rest on academic performance. In their sophomore year, the formula drops to 50-50 and isn't used at all for junior and senior years. In defense of his policy, Benedict's president, Dr. David H. Swinton said that the students "have to get an A in effort to guarantee that if they fail the subject matter, they can get the minimum passing grade. I don't think that's a bad thing."

According to the Associated Press story, carried in TheState.com (8/20/04), Professor Motley said the policy compromises the integrity of Benedict. Students are being passed to increase student retention by falsely boosting academic performance. When Professors Motley and Williams began assigning grades based upon academic performance, Professor Motley said the administration "told us to go back and recalculate the grades, and I just refused to do it." At that point Dr. Swinton fired both for insubordination. Dr. William Gunn, a faculty member for 40 years and president of Benedict College's chapter of the American Association of University Professors, is dead set against the policy and believes most other faculty are as well. Writing in TheState.com (9/22/04), Dr. Gunn says the SEE policy not only harms today's student but as well Benedict graduates who will see their degrees come under suspicion.

Dr. Winton's policy borders on lunacy. Imagine a freshman gets an A for effort in his algebra class but has virtually no grasp of the material, earning him an F grade. Under the college's SEE policy, the student would be assigned a C for the course. What can we expect when the student takes Algebra II and later takes a course where algebra is a tool? He'll fall further and further behind because he hasn't grasped the material from the earlier courses. He'll graduate only if the fraudulent grading continues and his job prospects will depend upon racial preferences.

Here's my question to you: Can you think of a more effective way to discredit and cast doubt on the degrees of all students who graduate from Benedict? How would you like people to be certified in any activity that way—your doctor, your tax accountant, your mechanic or anybody upon whom you depend for reliable proficient service?

Whatever academic handicaps Benedict's students have when they enter—their median SAT score is 803—are disguised and exacerbated by the school's SEE policy. Harvard-educated Dr. Swinton acknowledged he would not implement such a policy at a more selective institution and does not know of a similar policy at any other college.

The blame for this academic madness cannot wholly be placed at its president's feet. Benedict's Board of Trustees bear the blame for either enacting or tolerating this policy. Also culpable are those as taxpayers and donors whose funds make it possible for this madness to continue. While I know it's probably not the case, I wouldn't be surprised if it turned out that the South Carolina Ku Klux Klan were Benedict's largest contributors.

School Violence Toleration

October 4, 2004

I'm wondering just when parents, especially poor minorities, will re-fuse to tolerate day-to-day school conditions that most parents wouldn't dream of tolerating. Lisa Snell, director of the Education and Child Welfare Program at the Los Angeles-based Reason Foundation, has a recent article about school violence titled, "No Way Out," in the October 2004 edition of Reason On Line (www.reason.com).

Ashley Fernandez, a 12-year-old, attends Morgan Village Middle School, in Camden, New Jersey, a predominantly black and Hispanic school that has been designated as failing under state and federal standards for more than three years. Rotten education is not Ashley's only problem. When her gym teacher, exasperated by his unruly class, put all the girls in the boys locker room, Ashley was assaulted. Two boys dragged her into the shower, held her down and fondled her for 10 minutes. The school principal refused to even acknowledge the assault and denied her mother's transfer request to another school. Since the assault, Ashley has received numerous threats and boys fre-quently grope her and run away. Put yourself in the place of Ashley's mother. The school won't protect her daughter from threats and as-sault. The school won't permit a transfer. What would you do? Ash-ley's mother began to keep her home. The response from officials: she received a court summons for allowing truancy.

Then there's Carmen Santana's grandson Abraham who attended Camden High School. After two boys hit him in the face, broke his nose and chipped his teeth, Abraham was afraid to go to school. Guess what. His grandmother was charged with allowing truancy when she kept him home while she sought permission for him to complete his senior year studies at home. Lisa Snell reports that "more than 100 parents have removed their children from Camden schools because of safety concerns. The school district's response: a truancy crackdown."

Nationwide there were approximately 1,466,000 violent incidents that occurred in public schools in 1999–2000. Violent incidents, according to the U.S. Department of Education, National Center for Education Statistics, include rape, sexual battery other than rape, physical attack or fight with a weapon, threat of physical attack with a weapon, and robbery with or without a weapon. Most school violence occurs in inner city schools. During the 1999–2000 school year, 7 percent of all public schools accounted for 50 percent of the total violent incidents and 2 percent of public schools accounted for 50 percent of the serious violent incidents.

Students aren't the only victims of school violence. Between 1996 and 2000, teachers were the victims of approximately 1,603,000 nonfatal crimes at school. There were 1,004,000 thefts from teachers and 599,000 incidents of rape, sexual assault, robbery, aggravated assault, and simple assault.

I'm sorry if I'm out of touch with modern times but this kind of student behavior is completely intolerable. Moreover, there are no signs on the horizon that things are going to get any better. Psychobabblers try to lay the violence at the feet of poverty, single-parenthood and discrimination. That's nonsense. Years ago, when I attended predominantly black schools (1942–1954), there were single-parent households, gross poverty and societal discrimination. During those times, today's school violence would have been unimaginable. Even to curse a teacher was unthinkable.

Today's school violence occurs because it's tolerated. I'm betting that a punishment like caning or six months incarceration at hard labor would bring it to a screeching halt. You say, "Williams, that's cruel and unreasonable!" I say it's cruel and unreasonable to permit school thugs to make schools unsafe and education impossible for everyone else. Short of measures to immediately end school violence, at the minimum parents should be able to transfer their children out of unsafe failing public schools. Or, do you believe, as the education establishment does, that parents and children should be held hostage until they come up with a solution?

Higher Education in Decline

October 11, 2004

College costs have risen dramatically over the last several decades. In many cases, it's difficult to find a college where per-student costs are under $20,000. Most often tuition doesn't measure the true cost because taxpayer and donor subsidies pay part of the expenses. While costs are rising, education quality is in precipitous decline, particularly at the undergraduate level. Part of the reason is the political climate on college campuses where professors use their classrooms for proselytization and indoctrination and teach classes that have little or no academic content. Let's look at some of it.

In a study, to be published in Academic Questions, sociologist Charlotta Stern and economist Daniel Klein found in a random national sample of 1,678 university professors that Democrat professors outnumber Republican professors 3 to 1 in economics, 28 to 1 in sociology and 30 to 1 in anthropology. As George Will said in his *Washington Post* column, "Academia, Stuck to the Left," (11/29/04): "Many campuses are intellectual versions of one-party nations."

That strong campus leftist bias goes a long way to explain mindless university courses like: "Canine Cultural Studies" (UNC, Chapel Hill), "I like Ike, but I Love Lucy" (Harvard), "History of Electronic Dance Music" (UCLA), "Rock and Roll" (University of Massachusetts), "Hip-Hop: Beats, Rhyme and Culture" (George Mason University). There are many other examples documented by Accuracy in Academia (academia.org).

A Zogby survey was commissioned by the National Association of Scholars (NAS) to compare the general cultural knowledge of today's college seniors to yesteryear's high school graduates. The questions for the survey were drawn from those asked by Gallup in 1955 covering literature, music, science, geography, and history. The results were reported in a NAS publication "Today's College Students and Yesteryear's High School Grads." It concludes that "Contemporary college seniors scored on average little or no higher than the high-school graduates of a half-century ago on a battery of 15 questions assessing general cultural knowledge."

A 1990 Gallup survey for the National Endowment of the Humanities, given to a representative sample of 700 college seniors, found that 25 percent did not know that Columbus landed in the Western Hemisphere before the year 1500; 42 percent could not place the Civil War in the correct half-century; and 31 percent thought Reconstruction came after World War II.

In 1993, a Department of Education survey found that among college graduates 50 percent of whites and more than 80 percent of blacks couldn't state in writing the argument made in a newspaper column, use a bus schedule to get on the right bus, 56 percent could not calculate the right tip, 57 percent could not figure out how much change they should get back after putting down $3.00 to pay for a 60-cent bowl of soup and a $1.95 sandwich, and over 90 percent could not use a calculator to find the cost of carpeting a room. But not to worry. A 1999 survey taken by the American Council of Trustees and Alumni of seniors at the nation's top 55 liberal-arts colleges and universities found that 98 percent could identify rap artist Snoop Doggy Dogg and Beavis and Butt-Head, but only 34 percent knew George Washington was the general at the battle of Yorktown.

Americans as donors and taxpayers have been exceedingly generous to our universities. Given our universities' gross betrayal of trust, Americans should rethink their generosity as well as rethink who serves on boards of trustees who in dereliction of duty permit universities to become hotbeds of political activism and academic fraud. There are a few universities where there's still integrity and academic honesty, plus they don't cost an arm and a leg. Among them are: Grove City College, Hillsdale College, Franciscan University and others listed at the web page of Young America's Foundation (www.yaf.org).

Higher Education in Decline II

December 6, 2004

Last week's column discussed the sad and tragic state of affairs in higher education. According to loads of letters received in response to that column, it's worse than I thought. Let me share just a few of them.

One person wrote that he knows an elementary school teacher and said, "She believed, until just this past summer, that the state of Alaska was an island because it is so often shown as an inset on many U.S. maps, appearing somewhat like an island."

A professor said that while he was trying to help a student with a problem, he asked her, "What is 20,000 minus 600?" He went on to say, "She literally could not answer without the calculator." He rhetorically questioned, "Should a person receive a college degree that cannot answer that in their head?"

An English professor wrote, "One of the items that I assigned was a two-page essay that described a favorite vacation or holiday. One student turned in two pictures drawn with crayon depicting the beach. When I gave her a failing grade, she was indignant and said that she put a great deal of work into the pictures. When I told her that she did not do the assignment and that she was supposed to write an essay, she said, 'But I don't know what an essay is!'"

Such students are academic cripples and don't belong in college in the first place. Recently released findings of the Program for International Student Assessment (PISA) ranked U.S. high school students 24th out of 29 countries. American 15-year-olds demonstrate less math proficiency than their counterparts in Hungary and the Slovak Republic. With those findings, we shouldn't be surprised by a recent U.S. Department of Education study finding that nearly half of all college students must take remedial courses in math and reading. According to National Center for Education Statistics, in 2000 close to 80 percent of colleges offered remedial services. Several devastating consequences result when colleges admit unprepared students. First, it lets high schools off the hook by allowing them to continue to confer fraudulent diplomas. Second, it leads to a dumbing down of the academic curricula and the creation of Mickey Mouse courses for students who can't make it in more challenging courses. Academic departments, or professors, who don't dumb down their classes and participate in grade inflation risk declining enrollment and administrative threats to their budgets. Finally, hiring faculty to staff remedial courses inflates college costs to parents and taxpayers.

The nation's primary and secondary education is a national disgrace; will we allow our undergraduate education to become so as well? If we continue down our present course, the answer is an unambiguous yes. To change course, we need to start examining the incentive structure that college administrators face.

To a large extent, college budgets are determined by enrollment size. More students mean higher budgets and therefore incentive to admit students unprepared for college. Colleges should not admit students requiring remedial education. That's not to say youngsters shouldn't receive remedial education, but let them get it elsewhere— maybe at the high school that awarded them a fraudulent diploma.

We might rethink the financing of higher education, particularly at government-owned colleges, so as to introduce competition that might improve quality and drive down costs. High school graduates meeting academic criteria for college admission should be awarded a voucher in the amount of the per capita college cost paid by state taxpayers. The voucher could be used at any college, an idea similar to the GI Bill. There was a time when we could have prevented the K–12 slide to mediocrity, but we didn't seize the moment. Now's our chance with higher education. Will we let the moment pass us by again?

What's Wrong with Education?

October 14, 2001

Here are some test questions. Question 1: Which of the following is equal to a quarter of a million? (a)40,000 (b)250,000 (c)2,500,000 (d)1/4,000,000 or (e)4/1,000,000? Question 2: Martin Luther King, Jr. [insert the correct choice] for the poor of all races. (a) spoke out passionately (b) spoke out passionate (c) did spoke out passionately (d) has spoke out passionately or (e) had spoken out passionate. Question 3: What would you do if your student sprained an ankle? (a) Put a Band-Aid on it, (b) Ice it, (c) Rinse it with water.

Having reviewed the questions, guess which school grade gets these kind of test questions: sixth grade, ninth grade, or twelfth grade. I'm betting that the average reader guesses: sixth grade. You'd be wrong. How about ninth grade? You'd still be wrong. You say, "Okay, Williams, I can't believe they're twelfth grade test questions!" Wrong again. According to a *School Reform News* (9/01) article "Who Tells Teachers They Can Teach?," those test questions came from tests for prospective teachers. The first two questions are samples from Praxis I test for teachers and the third is from the 1999 teacher certification test in Illinois. And guess what. Thirty-one percent of New York City public school teachers fail teacher certification tests. According to the *Chicago Sun-Times* (9/6/01), 5,243 Illinois teachers failed their teacher certification tests.

The *Chicago Sun-Times* also reported that, "One teacher failed 24 of 25 teacher tests—including 11 of 12 Basic Skills tests and all 12 tests on teaching learning-disabled children." Yet, that teacher was assigned to teach learning-disabled children in Chicago. That's classic the blind leading the blind.

Most of these inept teachers are graduates of the nation's schools of education. Unfortunately, for the most part, schools of education, either graduate or undergraduate, are home to students who have the lowest academic achievement test scores when they enter college and they score the lowest among college graduates taking tests, such as

GRE, MCAT, or LSAT, to enter professional schools. If we're really serious about improving public education, we'd shut down schools of education. There is absolutely no relationship between teacher quality and having graduated from a teacher's college and being teacher certified. There may even be a negative relationship as suggested by the fact that students who are home-schooled by parents who've had no teacher training have achievement scores higher than 85 percent of all other students.

Another serious education problem is the fact that many teachers have little or no training in the subjects they teach. According to the U.S. Department of Education, 36 percent of public school teachers—972,000 teachers out of 2.7 million nationwide—didn't major or minor in the core subjects they teach. In other words, there are teachers teaching math and science who might not have taken a single class in those subjects.

The long-term solution to our education problem is to break the education monopoly by introducing the kind of competition that can come from school vouchers, tuition tax credits, and other school choice programs. Of course the powerful education establishment fights tooth and nail against anything that even smacks of competition. There are some shorter term measures that can help stem the decline in education quality. State legislators and school boards have it in their power to eliminate standard certification requirements. As it stands now, a Nobel Laureate in physics wouldn't meet teacher qualifications in most school districts.

Finally, my education question to the NAACP, Urban League, the Black Congressional Caucus, black mayors and city councilmen who walk lockstep with the teaching establishment and do their bidding: In which schools do you think you find the absolutely worst teacher quality?

Fiddling Whilst Rome Burns

December 23, 2002

Casey Lartigue, policy analyst for the Washington, D.C.-based Cato Institute, has written a report that constitutes a devastating indictment of public education. The title is, "The Need for Education Freedom in the Nation's Capitol," Policy Analysis (12/10/02). The title suggests the solution, namely, education reform must be more than simply spending more money to prop up schools that are little more than holding pens. Washington politicians must create a climate where education entrepreneurs can flourish and thereby produce education competition. Parents must have control over the education of their children. Tuition tax credits or education vouchers would facilitate both objectives.

"That's not the answer, Williams, you say. More money and smaller class sizes are what's needed." That's what the education establishment would have us believe; however, if money were the answer, Washington public schools would be the best in the nation if not the world. Per student expenditures are $10,500 a year, second highest in the nation. With a student/teacher ratio of 15.8, they have smaller than average class size. What is the result?

In only one of the city's nineteen high schools do as many as fifty percent of its students test as proficient in reading and at no school are 50 percent of the students proficient in math. At nine high schools, only five percent or fewer of its students test proficient in reading and in eleven high schools only five percent or less are proficient in math. The story gets worse when we look at the percentages for "below basic" performance which means that the student has little or no mastery of subject skills.

At 12 of 19 high schools more than 50 percent of the students test below basic in reading and at some of those schools the percentage approaches 80 percent. At 15 of these schools over 50 percent test below basic in math and in 12 of them 70 to 99 percent do so. But that's not the worst of the story: Each year more than 80 percent, and up to 96 percent, of high school students are promoted to the next grade. That is nothing but fraud, dishonesty and deception, plain and simple. While the education establishment can rightfully point to education problems beyond their control, irresponsible parents, students with alien and hostile minds and rotten teaching conditions, they bear the sole responsibility for fraudulent promotions and fraudulent diplomas.

The bottom line is that if one didn't know better he'd think that Washington's predominantly black public school system was being run by the Grand Dragon of the Ku Klux Klan hell-bent on a mission to sabotage black academic excellence. Instead, it's a system being run by blacks for blacks. As such it means generation after generation of blacks will not be able to measure up academically. Calls for racial quotas and preferences will exist in perpetuity. And, in a world of increasing technology many blacks are condemned to near uselessness in the job market.

But what about Senator Trent Lott? You say, "What in the world does Trent Lott have to do with rotten education received by blacks in D.C?" I'd say nothing but judging by the time and political capital spent by black politicians and civil rights groups attacking Trent Lott you'd think that he was the number one black problem, followed closely by the Confederate Battle Flag.

The attachment of black politicians and civil rights groups to spending resources on symbolism rather than substance is equivalent to Nero's fiddling while Rome burns. I'm sure that if the outrage directed toward Lott's indiscreet remarks were instead directed at fraudulent education delivered to black youngsters across the nation solutions might be found.

Environment and Health

Health care is one of those thorny issues generating a lot of heat but little light. Many Americans and their political leaders have called for what amounts to nationalization of our health-care industry. Before buying in to this siren song, we would do well to examine the delivery of health-care services in countries that have already nationalized their health-care industry, such as Canada, the United Kingdom, and Sweden. The Vancouver, British Columbia–based Fraser Institute has a yearly publication titled "Waiting Your Turn." Its 2006 edition gives waiting times, by treatment, from a person's referral by a general practitioner to treatment by a specialist. The shortest waiting time was for oncology (4.9 weeks). The longest waiting time was for orthopedic surgery (40.3 weeks), followed by plastic surgery (35.4 weeks) and neurosurgery (31.7 weeks).

Canadians also face significant waiting times for various diagnostics, such as computed tomography (CT), magnetic resonance imaging (MRI), and ultrasound scans. The median wait for a CT scan across Canada was 4.3 weeks, but in Prince Edward Island, it's 9 weeks. A Canadian's median wait for an MRI was 10.3 weeks, but in Newfoundland, patients waited 28 weeks. Finally, the median wait for an ultrasound was 3.8 weeks across Canada, but in Manitoba and Prince Edward Island it was 8 weeks.

London's Observer *carried a story saying that an "unpublished report shows some patients are now having to wait more than eight months for treatment, during which time many of their cancers become incurable." The* Observer *also reported, "A recent academic study showed National Health Service delays in bowel cancer treatment were so great that, in one in five cases, cancer which was curable at the time of diagnosis had become incurable by the time of treatment." Another* Observer *article read, "According to a World Health Organisation report to be published later this year, around 10,000 British people die unnecessarily from cancer each year—three times as many as are killed on our roads."*

According to European think tank Health Consumer Powerhouse's

Euro-Canada Health Consumer Index 2008: "Waiting times for care, long a problem in Sweden and too often deadly wherever they're found, are now the longest on the Continent."

There's a cure for our health-care problems. That cure is not to demand more government but less government. I challenge anyone to identify a problem with health care in America that is not caused or aggravated by federal, state, and local governments.

Considerable evidence suggests that the earth's temperature has increased about one degree Celsius over the past century. Environmentalists have seized on this to argue that mankind's activities are creating a global climate disaster. In 2006, sixty prominent scientists signed a letter saying that "observational evidence does not support today's computer climate models, so there is little reason to trust model predictions of the future. . . . Significant [scientific] advances have been made since the [Kyoto] protocol was created, many of which are taking us away from a concern about increasing greenhouse gases. If, back in the mid-1990s, we knew what we know today about climate, Kyoto would almost certainly not exist, because we would have concluded it was not necessary."

False concerns about this pending disaster has and will lead to loss of lives and a reduced standard of living. American deaths due to environmental activist callousness pale in comparison to other countries. How about a few statistics? In 1972, the activist-controlled Environmental Protection Agency banned DDT, a pesticide once considered a "miracle" for all of the lives it saved by killing the mosquitoes that carried malaria. The ban went into effect despite evidence that with proper use it posed no health hazard to humans and only little harm to animals. The EPA ban led to diminished DDT production, making the pesticide less available to the world.

What were the effects? In what is now Sri Lanka there were 2,800,000 malaria cases and 7,300 malaria deaths in 1948; with the use of DDT there were only seventeen cases and no deaths in 1964. After DDT use was discontinued, Sri Lankan malaria cases rose to 500,000 in 1969. Worldwide malaria's devastating effects all but disappeared during the time DDT use was widespread, roughly 1950 to 1970. DDT was seen as such a miracle that it earned its inventor, Dr. Paul Muller, the Nobel Prize in Medicine in 1948. In 1970, a committee of the Na-

tional Academy of Sciences wrote, "To only a few chemicals does man owe as great a debt as to DDT. In a little more than two decades, DDT has prevented 500 million deaths due to malaria that otherwise would have been inevitable."

The environmental extremists' true agenda has little or nothing to do with climate change. Their true agenda is to find a means to control our lives. The kind of repressive human control, not to mention government-sanctioned mass murder, seen under communism, has lost any measure of intellectual respectability. So people who want that kind of control must come up with a new name; that new name is environmentalism.

There's a much more important issue that poses an even greater danger to mankind. That's the effort by environmentalists to suppress disagreement with their view. According to a March 11, 2007, article in London's Sunday Telegraph, *Timothy Ball, a former climatology professor at the University of Winnipeg in Canada, has received five death threats since he started questioning whether mankind was affecting climate change. Richard Lindzen, professor of atmospheric science at MIT, said, "Scientists who dissent from the alarmism have seen their funds disappear, their work derided, and themselves labeled as industry stooges." Nigel Calder, a former editor of* New Scientist, *said, "Governments are trying to achieve unanimity by stifling any scientist who disagrees. Einstein could not have got funding under the present system."*

The columns that follow lay out the dangers we face allowing government to have greater control over our lives in the name of health care and saving the environment.

Busybodies or Tyrants?

Wednesday, March 22, 2006

Some call the people behind the Washington, D.C.–based Center for Science in the Public Interest (CSPI) busybodies, but I call them wannabe tyrants. Let's look at their agenda, which seeks greater control over our lives.

Last year, CSPI filed a lawsuit against the Food and Drug Administration (FDA) to reduce the amount of salt in packaged foods. They also called for the FDA to mandate warning labels on non-diet soft drinks that consumption increases the risk of obesity, tooth decay and osteoporosis. Earlier this year, CSPI announced its intent to sue Viacom Inc. and Kellogg Company for marketing junk food to children.

CSPI has long called for excise taxes on fatty foods, cars and TV sets. Their justification is that obesity adds to Medicare and Medicaid health costs. They want some of the tax revenue used to fund exercise facilities and government fitness campaigns.

There's no end to CSPI's consumer control agenda. They say, "Caffeine is the only drug that is widely added to the food supply." Therefore, they've called for caffeine warning labels. To deal with teenage and adult overconsumption of alcohol, they've called for doubling the tax on beer. According to them, "The last thing the world needs is more drinkers, even moderate ones."

To fight obesity among young people, CSPI calls for a fast-food advertising ban on TV programs seen by children. CSPI's director, Michael Jacobson, said, "We could envision taxes on butter, potato chips, whole milk, cheeses, [and] meat," adding that "CSPI is proud about finding something wrong with practically everything."

I'm guessing that most Americans, except politicians, find this control agenda offensive. Politicians might not find it offensive because controlling lives is their stock in trade, plus there's the promise of the higher revenues from food taxes. Most Americans who might find the CSPI agenda offensive are not motivated by principle. It's a matter of whose ox is being gored.

You say, "What do you mean, Williams?" CSPI tyrants are following almost to the letter the template created by the nation's anti-smoking zealots. Their fellow traveler, New York University professor Marion Nestle, says that the food industry "can't behave like cigarette companies. . . . Yet there are a lot of people who benefit from people being fat and sick, and the whole setup is designed to make people eat more. So the response to the food industry should be very similar to what happened with the tobacco companies."

The anti-smoking zealots started out with "reasonable" demands, such as warning labels on cigarette packs and no smoking sections on airplanes. They made exaggerated claims about the cost that smokers were imposing on the health care system. Then cigarette manufacturers faced multimillion-dollar lawsuits and multibillion-dollar local, state and federal extortion, not to mention confiscatory taxes, all of which are passed on to smokers in the form of higher prices.

Just recently, the City of Calabasas, Calif., adopted an ordinance that bans smoking in virtually all outdoor areas. Partial justification is to protect children from bad influences—seeing adults smoking. Had the anti-smoking zealots revealed their entire agenda back in the '60s and '70s, they wouldn't have gotten much. By using the piecemeal approach, they've been successful beyond their dreams, and the food zealots are following their example.

I'd be interested to know just how many Americans would like to see done to our food industry what was done to the tobacco industry: massive multibillion-dollar lawsuits against food companies; massive suits against restaurants that serve too large a serving, and confiscatory taxes levied on foods and snacks deemed non-nutritious.

Consumers will pay for all of this in the form of higher food prices and fewer choices. There's also the possibility that food zealots in some cities, emboldened by the success of the anti-smoking zealots in Calabasas, who are concerned about smokers passing on bad habits to our youth, might call for an ordinance banning public appearance of obese people so as not to pass bad eating habits on to our children.

Global Warming Heresy

Wednesday, March 28, 2007

Most climatologists agree that the earth's temperature has increased about a degree over the last century. The debate is how much of it is due to mankind's activity. Britain's Channel 4 television has just produced "The Great Global Warming Swindle," a documentary that devastates most of the claims made by the environmentalist movement. The scientists interviewed include top climatologists from MIT and other prestigious universities around the world. The documentary hasn't aired in the U.S., but it's available on the Internet (http://www.youtube.com/watch?v=XttV2C6B8pU).

Among the many findings that dispute environmentalists' claims are: Manmade carbon dioxide emissions are roughly 5 percent of the total; the rest are from natural sources such as volcanoes, dying vegetation and animals. Annually, volcanoes alone produce more carbon dioxide than all of mankind's activities. Oceans are responsible for most greenhouse gases. Contrary to environmentalists' claims, the higher the Earth's temperature, the higher the carbon dioxide levels. In other words, carbon dioxide levels are a product of climate change. Some of the documentary's scientists argue that the greatest influence on the Earth's temperature is our sun's sunspot activity. The bottom line is, the bulk of scientific evidence shows that what we've been told by environmentalists is pure bunk.

Throughout the Earth's billions of years there have been countless periods of global warming and cooling. In fact, in the year 1,000 A.D., a time when there were no SUVs, the Earth's climate was much warmer than it is now. Most of this century's warming occurred before 1940. For several decades after WWII, when there was massive worldwide industrialization, there was cooling.

There's a much more important issue that poses an even greater danger to mankind. That's the effort by environmentalists to suppress disagreement with their view. According to a March 11 article in London's *Sunday Telegraph*, Timothy Ball, a former climatology professor at the University of Winnipeg in Canada, has received five death threats since he started questioning whether man was affecting climate change. Richard Lindzen, professor of Atmospheric Science at MIT, said, "Scientists who dissent from the alarmism have seen their funds disappear, their work derided, and themselves labeled as industry stooges." Nigel Calder, a former editor of *New Scientist*, said, "Governments are trying to achieve unanimity by stifling any scientist who disagrees. Einstein could not have got funding under the present system."

Suppressing dissent is nothing new. Italian cosmologist Giordano Bruno taught that stars were at different distances from each other surrounded by limitless territory. He was imprisoned in 1592, and eight years later he was tried as a heretic and burned at the stake. Because he disagreed that the Earth was the center of the universe, Galileo was ordered to stand trial on suspicion of heresy in 1633. Under the threat of torture, he recanted and was placed under house arrest for the rest of his life.

Today's version of yesteryear's inquisitors include people like the Weather Channel's Dr. Heidi Cullen, who advocates that the American Meteorological Society (AMS) strip their seal of approval from any TV weatherman expressing skepticism about the predictions of manmade global warming. Columnist Dave Roberts, in his Sept. 19, 2006, online publication, said, "When we've finally gotten serious about global warming, when the impacts are really hitting us and we're in a full worldwide scramble to minimize the damage, we should have war crimes trials for these bastards—some sort of climate Nuremberg."

There are literally billions of taxpayer dollars being handed out to global warming alarmists, not to mention their dream of controlling our lives. Their agenda is threatened by dissent. They have the politician's ear; not we, who will suffer if they have their way.

Trans Fat Ban

Wednesday, January 10, 2007

In the wake of New York City's ban on restaurant use of trans fat, Mayor Michael Bloomberg said the ban is "not going to take away anybody's ability to go out and have the kind of food they want, in the quantities they want. . . . We are just trying to make food safer."

That, my friends, is tyrannical double-talk. Let's look at it. Trans fats are derived from partially hydrogenated vegetable oils. They can raise blood levels of LDL, the "bad cholesterol." According to Dr. Elizabeth Whelan, president of American Council on Science and Health, trans fats are about two percent of our daily caloric intake, while saturated fats, which also raise LDL blood levels, make up 10 to 15 percent.

Naturally, we might ask, why the attack on restaurants using trans fats and not saturated fats? The answer's easy; we just need a historical reference. When the anti-smoking zealots started out, they too went after a relatively small target by demanding non-smoking sections on airplanes. That success emboldened them to demand no smoking on planes at all and in airports as well. Then came laws against smoking in restaurants.

Today, in Calabasas, Calif., smoking is prohibited outside, and several California cities have banned beach smoking. Had the anti-smoking zealots revealed their full agenda when they started out, they wouldn't have been nearly as successful. They would have encountered too much resistance.

The nation's food zealots have taken a page from their anti-smoking counterparts. They've started out with a small target—a ban on restaurant use of trans fats. Here's what I predict is their true agenda: If banning a fat that's only two percent of our daily caloric intake is wonderful, why not ban saturated fats, the intake of which is much higher? Then there's the size of restaurant servings. Instead of a law simply requiring restaurants to label the calories in a meal, there will be laws setting a legal limit on portions.

There's a Washington, D.C., organization, Center for Science in the Public Interest, that some call busybodies, but they are more accurately described as petty tyrants. They've made a list of foods you shouldn't eat. Among them are: Dove and Haagen-Dazs ice cream, Mrs. Field's cookies and McDonald's Chicken McNuggets. If they are successful, you shouldn't be surprised to see a ban on these and similar foods.

Food zealots, who share the mindset of Mayor Bloomberg and are ". . . just trying to make food safer," will not be satisfied controlling restaurant menus. After all, most eating is done at home. So why wouldn't the food zealots enact bans on what can and cannot be sold in supermarkets? Nine chances out of ten, most of a person's saturated fat intake occurs during the family dinner.

You say, "Williams, that's ridiculous! They would never tell us what we can eat at home." That's precisely what you might have said when the anti-smoking zealots started out. Belmont, Calif., has recently enacted a law not only banning smoking in apartments and other attached dwellings, but also on the street, in a park and even in one's own car.

Smokers have been relatively passive and have allowed the anti-smoking zealots to run roughshod over them. The question is whether those of us who wish to eat as we please will allow the food zealots to do the same. These people are cowards, and here's why: If Mayor Bloomberg and other food zealots think I'm eating too many trans fats, let them personally come and take fatty foods off my plate or remove them from my shopping cart. Since they don't have the guts to do that, they correctly deem it safer to use the brute force of the state to control what I eat.

Fearmongering

Wednesday, January 24, 2007

Political commentator Henry Louis Mencken (1880–1956) warned that "The whole aim of practical politics is to keep the populace alarmed—and hence clamorous to be led to safety—by menacing it with an endless series of hobgoblins, all of them imaginary." The Weather Channel has taken up that task with its series "It Could Happen Tomorrow."

The Weather Channel started its "It Could Happen Tomorrow" series in January 2006. The program includes episodes where a tornado destroys Dallas, a tsunami destroys the Pacific Northwest, Mount Rainier erupts and destroys nearby towns, and San Diego is devastated by wildfires.

They omitted a program showing a meteor striking my house, for it, too, could happen tomorrow. Of course, any one of these events could happen tomorrow, but I'm reminded of a passage in Shakespeare's *Macbeth*, where after Macbeth listens to the predictions of the witches, Banquo warns him that "Oftentimes, to win us to our harm, the instruments of darkness tell us truths, win us with honest trifles, to betray us in deepest consequence." That is, gain our confidence with trifle truths to set us up for the big lie.

The big lie, conceived by the Weather Channel in cahoots with environmental extremists, is to get us in a tizzy over global warming, and they're vicious about it. Dr. Heidi Cullen, the Weather Channel's climatologist, hosts a weekly program called "The Climate Code." Dr. Cullen advocates that the American Meteorological Society (AMS) strip their seal of approval from any TV weatherman expressing skepticism about the predictions of manmade global warming, according to a report by Marc Morano, communications director for the U.S. Senate Committee on Environment & Public Works.

Dr. Cullen has had a lot of help in demonizing skeptics of catastrophic manmade global warming. Scott Pelley, CBS News "60 Minutes" correspondent, compared skeptics of global warming to

"Holocaust deniers," and former Vice President Al Gore calls skeptics "global warming deniers." But it gets worse. Mr. Morano reports that on one of Dr. Cullen's shows, she featured columnist Dave Roberts, who, in his Sept. 19, 2006, online publication, said, "When we've finally gotten serious about global warming, when the impacts are really hitting us and we're in a full worldwide scramble to minimize the damage, we should have war crimes trials for these bastards—some sort of climate Nuremberg." (See the Morano report at: http://epw.senate.gov/fact.cfm?party=rep&id=264568.) He didn't say whether the death penalty should be administered to those found guilty of global warming denial.

The environmental extremists' true agenda has little or nothing to do with climate change. Their true agenda is to find a means to control our lives. The kind of repressive human control, not to mention government-sanctioned mass murder, seen under communism has lost any measure of intellectual respectability. So people who want that kind of control must come up with a new name, and that new name is environmentalism.

Last year, 60 prominent scientists signed a letter saying, "Observational evidence does not support today's computer climate models, so there is little reason to trust model predictions of the future. . . . Significant [scientific] advances have been made since the [Kyoto] protocol was created, many of which are taking us away from a concern about increasing greenhouse gases. If, back in the mid-1990s, we knew what we know today about climate, Kyoto would almost certainly not exist, because we would have concluded it was not necessary."

They added, "It was only 30 years ago that many of today's global-warming alarmists were telling us that the world was in the midst of a global-cooling catastrophe. But the science continued to evolve, and still does, even though so many choose to ignore it when it does not fit with predetermined political agendas." These scientists have probably won The Weather Channel's ire and might be headed toward a Nuremberg-type trial.

Do We Want Socialized Medicine?

Wednesday, February 14, 2007

Problems with our health care system are leading some to fall prey to proposals calling for a nationalized single-payer health care system like Canada's or Britain's. There are a few things that we might take into consideration before falling for these proposals.

London's *Observer* (3/3/02) carried a story saying that an "unpublished report shows some patients are now having to wait more than eight months for treatment, during which time many of their cancers become incurable." Another story said, "According to a World Health Organisation report to be published later this year, around 10,000 British people die unnecessarily from cancer each year—three times as many as are killed on our roads."

The *Observer* (12/16/01) also reported, "A recent academic study showed National Health Service delays in bowel cancer treatment were so great that, in one in five cases, cancer which was curable at the time of diagnosis had become incurable by the time of treatment."

The story is no better in Canada's national health care system. The Vancouver, British Columbia-based Fraser Institute has a yearly publication titled, "Waiting Your Turn." Its 2006 edition gives waiting times, by treatments, from a person's referral by a general practitioner to treatment by a specialist. The shortest waiting time was for oncology (4.9 weeks). The longest waiting time was for orthopedic surgery (40.3 weeks), followed by plastic surgery (35.4 weeks) and neurosurgery (31.7 weeks).

Canadians face significant waiting times for various diagnostics such as computed tomography (CT), magnetic resonance imaging (MRI) and ultrasound scans. The median wait for a CT scan across Canada was 4.3 weeks, but in Prince Edward Island, it's 9 weeks. A Canadian's median wait for an MRI was 10.3 weeks, but in Newfoundland, patients waited 28 weeks. Finally, the median wait for an ultrasound was 3.8 weeks across Canada, but in Manitoba and Prince Edward Island it was 8 weeks.

Despite the long waiting times Canadians suffer, sometimes resulting in death, under federal law, private clinics are not legally allowed to provide services covered by the Canada Health Act. Regardless of this prohibition, a few black-market clinics service patients who are willing to break the law to get treatment. In British Columbia, for example, Bill 82 provides that a physician can be fined up to $20,000 for accepting fees for surgery. According to a Canada News article, "Shortage of Doctors and Nurses Could Hurt Medicare Reforms" (3/5/03), about 10,000 doctors left Canada during the 1990s.

There's help for some Canadian patients. According to a Canadian Medical Association Journal article, "U.S. Hospitals Use Waiting-List Woes to Woo Canadians" (2/22/2000), "British Columbia patients fed up with sojourns on waiting lists as they await tests or treatment are being wooed by a hospital in Washington state that has begun offering package deals. A second U.S. hospital is also considering marketing its services." One of the attractions is that an MRI, which can take anywhere from 10 to 28 weeks in Canada, can be had in two days at Olympic Memorial Hospital in Port Angeles, Wash. Already, Cleveland is Canada's hip-replacement center.

Some of our politicians hold up the Canadian and British nationalized health care systems as models for us. You can bet that should we ever have such a system, they would exempt themselves from what the rest of us would have to endure.

There's a cure for our health care problems. That cure is not to demand more government but less government. I challenge anyone to identify a problem with health care in America that is not caused or aggravated by federal, state and local governments. And, I challenge anyone to show me people dying on the streets because they don't have health insurance.

Phony Science and Public Policy

Wednesday, April 11, 2007

The public has become increasingly aware that the science behind manmade global warming is a fraud. But maybe Americans like bogus science in pursuit of certain public policy objectives. Let's look at it.

Many Americans find tobacco smoke to be a nuisance. Some find the odor offensive, and others have allergies or asthma that can be aggravated by smoking in their presence. There's little question that tobacco smoke causes these kinds of nuisances, but how successful would anti-smokers have been in a court of law, or public opinion, in achieving the kind of success they've achieved based on tobacco smoke being a nuisance?

A serious public health threat had to be manufactured, and in 1993 the Environmental Protection Agency (EPA) stepped in to the rescue with their bogus environmental tobacco smoke (ETS) study that says secondhand tobacco smoke is a class A carcinogenic.

Why is it bogus? The EPA claimed that 3,000 Americans die annually from secondhand smoke, but there was a problem. They couldn't come up with that conclusion using the standard statistical 95 percent confidence interval. They lowered their study's confidence interval to 90 percent. That has the effect of doubling the margin of error and doubling the probability that mere chance explains those 3,000 deaths.

The Congressional Research Service (CRS) said, "Admittedly, it is unusual to return to a study after the fact, lower the required significance level, and declare its results to be supportive rather than unsupportive of the effect one's theory suggests should be present." The CRS was being kind. This kind of doctoring of research results would get a graduate student expelled from a university.

In 1998, the World Health Organization's International Agency for Research on Cancer released the largest ever and best formulated study on ETS. The research project ran for 10 years and in seven European countries. The study, not widely publicized, concluded that no statistically significant risk existed for nonsmokers who either lived or worked with smokers.

During the late '90s, at a Washington affair, I had the occasion to be in the presence of an FDA official. I asked him whether he would approve of pharmaceutical companies employing EPA's statistical techniques in their testing of drug effectiveness and safety. He answered no. I ask my fellow Americans who are nonsmokers: Do you support the use of fraudulent science in your efforts to eliminate tobacco smoke nuisance in bars, restaurants, workplaces and hotels?

You say, "Okay, Williams, the science is bogus, but how do we nonsmokers cope with the nuisance of tobacco smoke?" My answer is that it all depends on whether you prefer liberty-oriented solutions to problems or those that are more tyranny-oriented.

The liberty-oriented solution has to do with private property rights, whereby the owner of property makes the decision whether he will allow smoking or not. If one is a nonsmoker, he just doesn't do business with a bar or restaurant where smoking is permitted. A smoker could exercise the same right if a bar or restaurant didn't permit smoking. Publicly owned places such as libraries, airports and municipal buildings, where ownership is ill defined, presents more of a challenge.

The tyranny-oriented solution is where one group uses the political system to forcibly impose its preferences on others. You might be tempted to object to the term "tyranny," but suppose you owned a restaurant where you did not permit smoking and smokers used the political system to create a law forcing you to permit smoking. I'm sure you'd deem it tyranny.

The public policy debate on smoking has been settled through bogus science. My question is, how willing are we to allow bogus science to be used in the pursuit of other public policy agendas, such as restrictions on economic growth, in the name of fighting global warming?

FDA: Friend or Foe?

Wednesday, May 30, 2007

The U.S. Food and Drug Administration (FDA) is charged with ensuring that only safe and effective drugs are marketed. Such a task is highly complex and fraught with difficulties. Consumers, the ostensible beneficiaries, should examine and question the incentive structure that FDA officials face.

Some drugs are highly beneficial to certain patients but pose an unacceptable risk to others. Vioxx along with Celebrex are in a class of non-steroidal anti-inflammatory drugs (NSAID) known as COX-2 inhibitors. Salicylates, such as aspirin, are a subset of such drugs. COX-2 inhibitors are sometimes prescribed to adult patients for management of acute pain associated with osteoarthritis. Vioxx, since removed from the market, was very beneficial to patients who suffered from stomach bleeding and ulcers when they took other NSAIDs. For other adults, Vioxx presented an increased risk of a stroke or a life-threatening cardiovascular event.

So if you're an FDA official, what are your incentives in terms of whether to approve or disapprove the marketing of a drug that has a tremendous benefit to some patients and poses a health threat to others? Former FDA Commissioner Alexander Schmidt hinted at the answer when he said, "In all our FDA history, we are unable to find a single instance where a Congressional committee investigated the failure of FDA to approve a new drug. But the times when hearings have been held to criticize our approval of a new drug have been so frequent that we have not been able to count them. The message to FDA staff could not be clearer."

There's little or no cost to the FDA for not approving a drug that might be safe, effective and clinically superior to other drugs for some patients but pose a risk for others. My question to FDA officials is: Should a drug be disapproved whenever it poses a health risk to some people but a benefit to others? To do so would eliminate most drugs, including aspirin, because all drugs pose a health risk to some people.

According to the May 17th edition of the *Wall Street Journal*, in an editorial, "Our Lawless FDA," by Hoover Institution scholars Drs. David Henderson and Charles Hooper, the FDA recently rejected Arcoxia, a new COX-2 inhibitor from Merck. In explaining the FDA's disapproval, Robert Meyer, director of the agency's Office of Drug Evaluation, told reporters that "simply having another drug on the market" wasn't "sufficient reason to approve the product unless there was a unique role defined."

Henderson and Hooper argue that this position greatly exceeds the FDA's mandate to determine a drug's safety and effectiveness. Arcoxia has been tested on over 34,000 U.S. patients. Moreover, it has been approved for use in England, Germany and 61 other countries in Asia, Latin America and Europe. Meyer's explanation is nothing less than fascist arrogance.

According to the FDA's literature, its mandate is: "Once a new drug application is filed, an FDA review team—medical doctors, chemists, statisticians, microbiologists, pharmacologists, and other experts—evaluates whether the studies the sponsor submitted show that the drug is safe and effective for its proposed use." Nothing in the FDA mandate requires that a drug has to be better than what's currently available in order to win approval.

Henderson and Hooper argue that in the worst-case scenario where Arcoxia is no better than existing drugs, it would compete with those drugs. Two centuries of economic theory and evidence show that competition is good. A new drug that competes with existing drugs would moderate drug prices and cause competitors to stay on their toes.

While Henderson and Hooper don't say it, I smell a rat. Arcoxia is produced by Merck, which has several major competitors in the COX-2 inhibitor market. Some scientists on the FDA's advisory panel have paid affiliations with companies who'd benefit from less competition.

Health Care: Government vs. Private

Wednesday, July 25, 2007

Sometimes the advocates of socialized medicine claim that health care is too important to be left to the market. That's why some politicians are calling for us to adopt health care systems such as those in Canada, the United Kingdom and other European nations. But the suggestion that we'd be better served with more government control doesn't even pass a simple smell test.

Do we want the government employees who run the troubled Walter Reed Army Medical Center to be in charge of our entire health care system? Or, would you like the people who deliver our mail to also deliver health care services? How would you like the people who run the motor vehicles department, the government education system, foreign intelligence and other government agencies to also run our health care system? After all, they are not motivated by the quest for profits, and that might mean they're truly wonderful, selfless, caring people.

As for me, I'd choose profit-driven people to provide my health care services, people with motives like those who deliver goods to my supermarket, deliver my overnight mail, produce my computer and software programs, assemble my car and produce a host of other goods and services that I use.

There's absolutely no mystery why our greatest complaints are in the arena of government-delivered services and the fewest in market-delivered services. In the market, there are the ruthless forces of profit, loss and bankruptcy that make producers accountable to us. In the arena of government-delivered services, there's no such accountability. For example, government schools can go for decades delivering low-quality services, and what's the result? The people who manage it earn higher pay. It's nearly impossible to fire the incompetents. And, taxpayers, who support the service, are given higher tax bills.

Our health care system is hampered by government intervention, and the solution is not more government intervention but less. The tax treatment of health insurance, where premiums are deducted from employees' pre-tax income, explains why so many of us rely on our employers to select and pay for health insurance. Since there is a third-party payer, we have little incentive to shop around and wisely use health services.

There are "guaranteed issue" laws that require insurance companies to sell health insurance to any person seeking it. So why not wait until you're sick before purchasing insurance? Guaranteed issue laws make about as much sense as if you left your house uninsured until you had a fire, and then purchased insurance to cover the damage. Guaranteed issue laws raise insurance premiums for all. Then there are government price controls, such as the reimbursement schemes for Medicaid. As a result, an increasing number of doctors are unwilling to treat Medicaid patients.

Before we buy into single-payer health care systems like Canada's and the United Kingdom's, we might want to do a bit of research. The Vancouver, British Columbia-based Fraser Institute annually publishes "Waiting Your Turn." Its 2006 edition gives waiting times, by treatments, from a person's referral by a general practitioner to treatment by a specialist. The shortest waiting time was for oncology (4.9 weeks). The longest waiting time was for orthopedic surgery (40.3 weeks), followed by plastic surgery (35.4 weeks) and neurosurgery (31.7 weeks).

As reported in the June 28 National Center for Policy Analysis' "Daily Policy Digest," Britain's Department of Health recently acknowledged that one in eight patients waits more than a year for surgery. France's failed health care system resulted in the deaths of 13,000 people, mostly of dehydration, during the heat spell of 2003. Hospitals stopped answering the phones, and ambulance attendants told people to fend for themselves.

I don't think most Americans would like more socialized medicine in our country. By the way, I have absolutely no problem with people wanting socialism. My problem is when they want to drag me into it.

Deadly Environmentalists

Wednesday, August 15, 2007

Environmentalists, with the help of politicians and other government officials, have an agenda that has cost thousands of American lives.

In the wake of Hurricane Betsy, which struck New Orleans in 1965, the U.S. Army Corps of Engineers proposed building flood gates on Lake Pontchartrain, like those in the Netherlands that protect cities from North Sea storms. In 1977, the gates were about to be built, but the Environmental Defense Fund and Save Our Wetlands sought a court injunction to block the project.

According to John Berlau's recent book, "Eco-Freaks: Environmentalism is Hazardous to Your Health," U.S. Attorney Gerald Gallinghouse told the court that not building the gates could kill thousands of New Orleanians. Judge Charles Schwartz issued the injunction despite the evidence refuting claims of environmental damage.

We're told that DDT is harmful to humans and animals. Berlau, a research fellow at the Washington, D.C-based Competitive Enterprise Institute, says, "Not a single study linking DDT exposure to human toxicity has ever been replicated." In one long-term study, volunteers ate 32 ounces of DDT for a year and a half, and 16 years later, they suffered no increased risk of adverse health effects.

Despite evidence that, properly used, DDT is neither harmful to humans nor animals, environmental extremists fight for a continued ban. This has led to millions of illnesses and deaths from malaria, especially in Africa. After WWII, DDT saved millions upon millions of lives in India, Southeast Asia and South America. In some cases, malaria deaths fell to near zero. With bans on DDT, malaria deaths and illnesses have skyrocketed.

Environmental extremists see DDT in a different light. Alexander King, co-founder of the Club of Rome, said, "In Guyana, within almost two years, it had almost eliminated malaria, but at the same time, the birth rate had doubled. So my chief quarrel with DDT in hindsight is that it greatly added to the population problem." Jeff Hoffman, environmental attorney, wrote on grist.org, "Malaria was actually a natural population control, and DDT has caused a massive population explosion in some places where it has eradicated malaria. More fundamentally, why should humans get priority over other forms of life? . . . I don't see any respect for mosquitoes in these posts." Berlau's book cites many other examples of contempt for human life by environmentalists and how they've made politicians their useful idiots.

In 2001, thousands of Americans perished in the terrorist attack on the World Trade Center. In the early 1970s, when the World Trade Center complex was built, the asbestos scare had just begun. The builders planned to use AsbestoSpray, a flame retardant that adhered to steel. The New York Port of Authority caved in to the environmentalists' asbestos scare and denied its use. An inferior substitute was used as fireproofing.

After the attack, the National Institute of Standards and Technology (NIST) confirmed other experts' concerns about asbestos substitutes, concluding, "Even with the airplane impact and jet-fuel-ignited multi-floor fires, which were not normal building fires, the building would likely not have collapsed had it not been for the fireproofing."

Through restrictions on asbestos use, our naval vessels are more vulnerable to our enemies, a disaster waiting in the wings. The Columbia spaceship disaster was a result of the EPA's demand that NASA not use freon in its thermal insulating foam.

Congress mandates auto fuel mileage standards—Corporate Average Fuel Economy, or CAFE, standards—resulting in lighter, less crashworthy cars. In 2002, the National Academy of Sciences calculated that CAFE standards caused 2,000 additional traffic deaths each year. In 1999, a USA Today analysis of government and Insurance Institute data found that since the 1970s CAFE standards went into effect, 46,000 people died in crashes which they would have likely survived had they been riding in heavier cars.

None of this is news to politicians. It's just that environmental extremists have the ears of politicians, and potential victims don't.

Global Warming Hysteria

Wednesday, September 26, 2007

Despite increasing evidence that man-made CO_2 is not a significant greenhouse gas and contributor to climate change, politicians and others who wish to control our lives must maintain that it is.

According to the *Detroit Free Press*, Rep. John Dingell wants a 50-cents-a-gallon tax on gasoline. We've heard such calls before, but there's a new twist. Dingell also wants to eliminate the mortgage tax deduction on what he calls "McMansions," homes that are 3,000 square feet and larger. That's because larger homes use more energy.

One might wonder about Dingell's magnanimity in increasing taxes for only homes 3,000 feet or larger. The average U.S. home is around 2,300 square feet, compared with Europe's average of 1,000 square feet. So why doesn't Dingell call for disallowing mortgage deductions on houses more than 1,000 square feet? The reason is there would be too much political resistance, since more Americans own homes under 3,000 square feet than over 3,000. The full agenda is to start out with 3,000 square feet and later lower it in increments.

Our buying into global warming hysteria will allow politicians to do just about anything, upon which they can muster a majority vote, in the name of fighting climate change as a means to raise taxes.

In addition to excuses to raise taxes, congressmen are using climate change hysteria to funnel money into their districts. Rep. David L. Hobson, R-Ohio, secured $500,000 for a geothermal demonstration project. Rep. Adam B. Schiff, D-Calif., got $500,000 for a fuel-cell project by Superprotonic, a Pasadena company started by Caltech scientists. Money for similar boondoggles is being called for by members of both parties.

There are many ways to reduce CO_2 emissions, and being 71 years of age I know many of them. Al Gore might even consider me carbon neutral and possibly having carbon credits because my carbon offsets were made in advance. For example, for the first 15 years of my life, I didn't use energy-consuming refrigerators; we had an icebox.

For two decades I listened to radio instead of watching television and walked or used public transportation to most places. And for more than half my life I didn't use energy-consuming things such as computers, clothes dryers, air conditioning and microwave ovens. Of course, my standard of living was much lower.

The bottom line is, serious efforts to reduce CO_2 will lead to lower living standards through higher costs of living. And it will be all for naught because there is little or no relationship between man-made emissions and climate change.

There's an excellent booklet available from the National Center for Policy Analysis (ncpa.org) titled "A Global Warming Primer." Some of its highlights are:

"Over long periods of time, there is no close relationship between CO_2 levels and temperature."

"Humans contribute approximately 3.4 percent of annual CO_2 levels" compared to 96.6 percent by nature.

"There was an explosion of life forms 550 million years ago (Cambrian Period) when CO_2 levels were 18 times higher than today. During the Jurassic Period, when dinosaurs roamed the Earth, CO_2 levels were as much as nine times higher than today."

What about public school teachers frightening little children with tales of cute polar bears dying because of global warming? The primer says, "Polar bear numbers increased dramatically from around 5,000 in 1950 to as many as 25,000 today, higher than any time in the 20th century." The primer gives detailed sources for all of its findings, and it supplies us with information we can use to stop politicians and their environmental extremists from doing a rope-a-dope on us.

Silencing Dissent

Wednesday, August 8, 2007

Global warming has become a big-ticket item in the eyes of its supporters. At stake are research funds, jobs and the ability to control lives all over the globe. Most climatologists agree that over the last century, the Earth's average temperature has risen about one degree Celsius.

The controversy centers around the source of the temperature change—manmade or natural causes. Global warming alarmists hold the view that it's manmade emissions of CO_2 that's driving climate change, and they seek to suppress any dissent suggesting other causes.

According to the July 16 *Washington Times*, Michael T. Eckhart, president of the American Council on Renewable Energy (ACORE), sent a threatening missive to Marlo Lewis, senior fellow at the Washington, D.C.-based Competitive Enterprise Institute, which read: "Take this warning from me, Marlo. It is my intention to destroy your career as a liar. If you produce one more editorial against climate change, I will launch a campaign against your professional integrity. I will call you a liar and charlatan to the Harvard community of which you and I are members. I will call you out as a man who has been bought by Corporate America. Go ahead, guy. Take me on."

The Environmental Protection Agency, Department of Agriculture, Department of Commerce and the Department of Energy are all members of ACORE. Sen. James Inhofe, R-Okla., ranking member of the Environment and Public Works Committee, held hearings on the matter. Following the hearings, the senator sent letters to the agencies asking them to "reconsider their membership in ACORE."

Speaking at the American leg of Live Earth: The Concerts for a Climate in Crisis, Robert F. Kennedy Jr., the son of the late Robert F. Kennedy, said, "Get rid of all these rotten politicians that we have in Washington, who are nothing more than corporate toadies." Referring to skeptics of manmade global warming, he said, "This is treason. And we need to start treating them as traitors." Traitors are either shot or imprisoned. I wonder which Robert Kennedy has in mind for the skeptics.

University of Oregon's George Taylor holds the title of state climatologist. Oregon Gov. Ted Kulongoski wants to take that title from Taylor. The governor said Taylor's skepticism interferes with Oregon's stated goals to reduce greenhouse gases, the accepted cause of global warming in the eyes of a vast majority of scientists.

Earlier this year, the Weather Channel's Dr. Heidi Cullen called for the decertification of weathermen who were skeptical of manmade global warming. *Grist Magazine*'s staff writer David Roberts said that his solution for the "bastards" who were members of what he termed the global warming "denial industry" is, "When we've finally gotten serious about global warming, when the impacts are really hitting us and we're in a full worldwide scramble to minimize the damage, we should have war crimes trials for these bastards—some sort of climate Nuremberg."

"Global warming driven by greenhouse gas pollution (but ultimately by greed, racism and lying) is killing our Planet," says an article in *Media With Conscience*. It goes on to say, "Our Planet, the Earth— is under acute threat from Climate Criminals threatening the Third World with Climate Genocide and the Biosphere with Terracide (the killing of our Planet)." Sen. Inhofe maintains a website citing these and other many examples of attacks on skeptics of manmade global warming. (See http://epw.senate.gov/public/index.cfm?FuseAction= Minority.Blogs&ContentRecord_id=04373015-802a-23ad -4bf9-c3f02278f4cf.)

This kind of suppression of different ideas and dissent is simply the tip of a much larger iceberg that has many of its roots on today's college campuses. Suppression of ideas is far more dangerous to our civilization than manmade global warming—real or imagined. Given the horrible history of brutal attempts to silence people who have different ideas or dissent from the conventional wisdom, those of us in the academic and scientific communities ought to openly repudiate and condemn the efforts to silence global warming skeptics. This is particularly so in light of the mounting evidence that manmade CO_2

emissions have little or nothing to do with climate change. (See http://epw.senate.gov/public/index.cfm?FuseAction=Files.View&File Store_id=c5e16731-3c64-481c-9a36-d702baea2a42.)

Do We Want This?

Wednesday, June 22, 2005

America's socialists advocate that we adopt a universal healthcare system like our northern neighbor Canada. Before we buy into complete socialization of our healthcare system, we might check out the Canadian Supreme Court's June 9th ruling in Chaoulli v. Quebec (Attorney General). It turns out that in order to prop up government-delivered medical care, Quebec and other Canadian provinces have outlawed private health insurance. By a 4 to 3 decision, Canada's high court struck down Quebec's law that prohibits private medical insurance. With all of the leftist hype extolling the "virtues" of Canada's universal healthcare system, you might wonder why any sane Canadian would want to purchase private insurance.

Plaintiffs Jacques Chaoulli, a physician, and his patient, George Zeliotis, launched their legal challenge to the government's monopolized healthcare system after having had to wait a year for hip-replacement surgery. In finding for the plaintiffs, Canada's high court said, "The evidence in this case shows that delays in the public healthcare system are widespread, and that, in some serious cases, patients die as a result of waiting lists for public healthcare. The evidence also demonstrates that the prohibition against private health insurance and its consequence of denying people vital healthcare result in physical and psychological suffering that meets a threshold test of seriousness." Writing for the majority, Justice Marie Deschamps said, "Many patients on non-urgent waiting lists are in pain and cannot fully enjoy any real quality of life. The right to life and to personal inviolability is therefore affected by the waiting times."

The Vancouver, British Columbia-based Fraser Institute keeps track of Canadian waiting times for various medical procedures. According to the Fraser Institute's 14th annual edition of "Waiting Your Turn: Hospital Waiting Lists in Canada (2004)," total waiting time between referral from a general practitioner and treatment, averaged across all 12 specialties and 10 provinces surveyed, rose from 17.7

weeks in 2003 to 17.9 weeks in 2004. For example, depending on which Canadian province, an MRI requires a wait between 7 and 33 weeks.

Orthopaedic surgery might require a wait of 14 weeks for a referral from a general practitioner to the specialist and then another 24 weeks from the specialist to treatment. That statistic might help explain why Cleveland, Ohio, has become Canada's hip-replacement center.

As reported in a December 2003 story by Kerri Houston for the Frontiers of Freedom Institute titled "Access Denied: Canada's Healthcare System Turns Patients into Victims," in some instances, patients die on the waiting list because they become too sick to tolerate a procedure. Canada's Prime Minister Paul Martin responded to the court's decision saying, "We're not going to have a two-tier healthcare system in this country. What we want to do is strengthen the public healthcare system." That's the standard callous political response. He's telling Canadians to continue waiting, continue suffering and perhaps dying until the day comes when there's no more waiting. And though Canadian politicians can't give their citizens a date certain when there'll be no more waiting, they're determined to deny them alternatives to waiting for government-provided healthcare. I'd bet you the rent money that Prime Minister Martin and members of the Canadian Parliament don't have to wait months and years for a medical procedure.

I wonder just how many Americans would like to import Canada's healthcare system, which prohibits the purchase of private insurance and private healthcare services. In British Columbia, for example, Bill 82 provides that a physician can be fined up to $20,000 for accepting fees for surgery. In my book, it's medical Nazism for government to prohibit a person who wishes to purchase medical services from doing so. But let's not look down our noses at our northern neighbors, for we too are well along the road toward medical Nazism.

Destructive Western Policy

July 7, 2004

Ever since Rachel Carson's 1962 book "Silent Spring," environmental extremists have sought to ban all DDT use. Using phony studies from the Environmental Defense Fund and the Natural Resources Defense Council, the environmental activist-controlled Environmental Protection Agency banned DDT in 1972. The extremists convinced the nation that DDT was not only unsafe for humans but unsafe to birds and other creatures as well. Their arguments have since been scientifically refuted.

While DDT saved crops, forests and livestock, it also saved humans. In 1970, the U.S. National Academy of Sciences estimated that DDT saved more than 500 million lives during the time it was widely used. A scientific review board of the EPA showed that DDT is not harmful to the environment and showed it to be a beneficial substance that "should not be banned." According to the World Health Organization, worldwide malaria infects 300 million people. About 1 million die of malaria each year. Most of the victims are in Africa, and most are children.

In Sri Lanka, in 1948, there were 2.8 million malaria cases and 7,300 malaria deaths. With widespread DDT use, malaria cases fell to 17 and no deaths in 1963. After DDT use was discontinued, Sri Lankan malaria cases rose to 2.5 million in the years 1968 and 1969, and the disease remains a killer in Sri Lanka today. More than 100,000 people died during malaria epidemics in Swaziland and Madagascar in the mid-1980s, following the suspension of DDT house spraying. After South Africa stopped using DDT in 1996, the number of malaria cases in KwaZulu-Natal province skyrocketed from 8,000 to 42,000. By 2000, there had been an approximate 400 percent increase in malaria deaths. Now that DDT is being used again, the number of deaths from malaria in the region has dropped from 340 in 2000 to none at the last reporting in February 2003.

In South America, where malaria is endemic, malaria rates soared in countries that halted house spraying with DDT after 1993—Guyana, Bolivia, Paraguay, Peru, Brazil, Colombia and Venezuela. In Ecuador, DDT spraying was increased after 1993, and the malaria rate of infection was reduced by 60 percent. In a 2001 study published by the London-based Institute for Economic Affairs, "Malaria and the DDT Story," Richard Tren and Roger Bate say that "Malaria is a human tragedy," adding, "Over 1 million people, mostly children, die from the disease each year, and over 300 million fall sick."

The fact that DDT saves lives might account for part of the hostility toward it. Alexander King, founder of the Malthusian Club of Rome, wrote in a biographical essay in 1990: "My own doubts came when DDT was introduced. In Guyana, within two years, it had almost eliminated malaria. So my chief quarrel with DDT, in hindsight, is that it has greatly added to the population problem." Dr. Charles Wurster, one of the major opponents of DDT, is reported to have said, "People are the cause of all the problems. We have too many of them. We need to get rid of some of them, and this (referring to malaria deaths) is as good a way as any."

Spraying a house with small amounts of DDT costs $1.44 per year; alternatives are five to 10 times more, making them unaffordable in poor countries. Rich countries that used DDT themselves threaten reprisals against poor countries if they use DDT.

One really wonders about religious groups, the Congressional Black Caucus, government and non-government organizations, politicians and others who profess concern over the plight of poor people around the world while at the same time accepting or promoting DDT bans and the needless suffering and death that follow. Mosquito-borne malaria not only has devastating health effects but stifles economic growth as well.

Envirobamboozled

August 20, 2001

Time magazine: "Scientists no longer doubt that global warming is happening, and almost nobody questions the fact that humans are at least partly responsible." U.S. News & World Report chimed in, referring to the United Nation's Intergovernmental Panel on Climate Change (IPCC), "The most definitive—and scary—report yet, declaring that global warming is not only real but man-made."

According to a Consumers' Research article (July 2001) "Global Warming Science: Fact vs. Fiction," written by Messrs. LaRochelle and Spencer, the media has it all wrong. The news media leaped to erroneous conclusions from a summary of a yet-to-be-released 3,000-page report. A follow-up study on global warming was released June 2001 by the National Research Council (NRC) of the National Academy of Science.

MIT Professor Richard Lindzen, one of the NRC panelists and lead author of the IPCC report says, "Our primary conclusion was that despite some knowledge and some agreement, the science is by no means settled. We are quite confident (1) that global mean temperature is about 0.5 degrees Celsius higher than a century ago; (2) that atmospheric levels of carbon dioxide have risen over the past two centuries; and (3) that carbon dioxide is a greenhouse gas whose increase is likely to warm the earth. But—and I cannot stress this enough—we are not in a position to confidently attribute past climate change to carbon dioxide or to forecast what the climate will be in the future." Adding, "That is to say contrary to media impressions, agreement with the three basic statements tells us almost nothing relevant to policy discussions."

That conclusion shows just how much confidence we can have in what the media and environmental radicals tell us. You say, "Williams, are the environmentalist lying and deliberately frightening us?" That's part of their strategy. Consider what environmentalist activist Stephen Schneider said, "We have to offer up scary scenarios, make simplified dramatic statements, and make little mention of any doubts we may have. Each of us has to decide what the right balance is between being effective and being honest." (*Discover* 1989). Here's what former Senator Timothy Wirth (D. Colo.) said, "We've got to ride the global warming issue. Even if the theory of global warming is wrong, we'll be doing the right thing, in terms of economic policy and environmental policy" (Michael Fumento's *Science Under Siege*).

Dr. Fred Singer, president of The Science & Environmental Policy Project in Arlington, Virginia says there are four different independent data sets for measuring temperature. First are thermometers at weather stations around the world; they show warming over the past 30 years—but not in the U.S. The second are weather satellites. They show no warming. The third are weather balloons; they show no warming. The fourth are called proxy dates: tree rings, ice cores, lake sediments, etc. They show no warming.

Basing public policy on erroneous observations and predictions can be very costly in terms of human welfare and economic growth. Environmental activist predictions have been dead wrong. In *National Wildlife* (July 1975), Nigel Calder warned, "the threat of a new ice age must now stand alongside nuclear war as a likely source of wholesale death and misery for mankind." In the same issue, C. C. Wallen of the World Meteorological Organization warned, "The cooling since 1940 has been large enough and consistent enough that it will not soon be reversed." In 1968, Dr. Paul Erlich, author of *The Population Time Bomb* and environmentalists' guru, predicted that the earth would run out of food by 1977 and that the earth's 5 billion population would starve back to 2 billion people by 2025. Dr. Erlich also warned Britain's Institute of Biology in 1969, "If I were a gambler, I would take even money that England will not exist in the year 2000."

Why do we listen to these people?

Is This the America We Want?

June 11, 2003

Oreo cookies should be banned from sale to children in California. That's according to Stephen Joseph, who filed a lawsuit against Nabisco last month in California's Marin County Superior Court. Oreo cookies contain trans fat, an ingredient that makes the cookies crisp and their filling creamy. Joseph says that trans fat is so dangerous that our children should be protected from it.

Last year, Los Angeles Unified School District voted unanimously to ban the sale of soft drinks at all of the district's 677 schools. They said the new rule, scheduled to go into effect January 2004, will improve the health of its 736,000 students, of whom a recent survey of 900 of them found 40 percent to be obese.

New York lawyer Samuel Hirsch and George Washington University's Professor John F. Banzhaf brought lawsuits against fast food restaurants Burger King, McDonald's, Wendy's and Kentucky Fried Chicken. Hirsch and Banzhaf contend that these fast food restaurants are responsible for obesity; they ignore the fact that two-thirds of all meals are served at home.

The Washington-based Center for Science in the Public Interest (CSPI) also demands government control of what we eat. It calls for excise taxes on fatty foods, additional taxes on cars and television sets, and a doubling of the excise tax on beer. By making cars and televisions more expensive, it thinks it will force people to walk more and stop being couch potatoes.

CSPI's Michael Jacobson said, "We could envision taxes on butter, potato chips, whole milk, cheeses (and) meat." CSPI wants the tax revenues earmarked for government-sponsored exercise programs.

These tyrannical schemes also have government support. According to a *Consumer Freedom* article (www.consumerfreedom.com), former USDA spokesman John Webster said, "Right now, this anti-obesity campaign is in its infancy. . . . (W)e want to turn people around and give them assistance in eating nutritious foods."

The anti-obesity campaign might seem preposterous and amusing were it not for the successes of the anti-tobacco campaign premised on the idea that individuals are not responsible for their choices. It's a logical follow-up: Food producers, not people themselves, are responsible for overindulgence. Since we have socialized medicine, obesity adds to the nation's health-care costs through its contribution to obesity-related health problems such as diabetes, cancer and cardiovascular disease. According to the food Nazis, that means government has a stake in controlling what we eat.

Americans salute the results of the anti-tobacco campaign that brought successful multibillion-dollar suits against tobacco companies and levied steep tobacco taxes. In some jurisdictions, such as New York City, taxes have led to the tripling of cigarette prices, not to mention the creation of black markets. I'm wondering whether my fellow Americans would like the food Nazi campaign to produce the same outcome. In other words, how would we like taxes that create $10 hamburgers, $5 cans of beer and $12 for a pound of Oreo cookies?

Maybe as an alternative to taxes, there might be a call for laws similar to what's called the Dram Shop Act in some states, which prohibits the sale of alcohol to intoxicated persons. Applied to food, that law might ban the sale of hamburgers and fries to a fat person, or a mandate that scales be placed in front of cash registers where a customer is weighed prior to a sale.

Instead of hamburgers and fries, an overweight customer is offered a tasty salad instead. Instead of suing Nabisco to stop children from eating Oreos, we might have a law requiring proof of age prior to purchase. We could use endangering minors law to exact stiff penalties against parents who gave Oreos to their children.

The anti-obesity movement is simply another step down the road to serfdom and, what's worse, Americans are voluntarily assisting the nation's tyrants.

Weak-Kneed Corporate CEOs

February 16, 2005

On Jan. 20, 2005, J.P. Morgan Chase announced that it had completed research to determine whether it had any links to slavery. Its website (www2.bankone.com/presents/home/) announced: "Today, we are reporting that this research found that between 1831 and 1865 two of our predecessor banks—Citizens Bank and Canal Bank in Louisiana—accepted approximately 13,000 enslaved individuals as collateral on loans and took ownership of approximately 1,250 of them when the plantation owners defaulted on the loans."

J.P. Morgan Chase went on to "apologize to the American public, and particularly to African-Americans, for the role that Citizens Bank and Canal Bank played during that period." They added, "Since these events took place in Louisiana, we are establishing a $5 million college scholarship program for students living in Louisiana."

In January 2004, U.S. District Judge Charles Norgle dismissed a reparations lawsuit brought against companies such as J.P. Morgan Chase, Fleet Boston Financial and Brown & Williamson Tobacco that contended that either they or their corporate ancestors profited from insuring slave ships, using slaves or financing businesses built with slave labor. Judge Norgle said the statute of limitations had long past, the plaintiffs did not have standing, and they failed to establish a clear link to the companies they targeted. The court's decision comes close to a kiss of death for reparations through the judicial process but not through the mau-mau process.

Some corporations have chief executive officers who double as the corporation's chief appeasement officers. A CEO/CAO will do nearly anything to befriend anti-capitalist forces, and J.P. Morgan Chase is seen as a soft target. Maybe that's why the Rainforest Action Network, an eco-activist group, transported Fairfield County, Connecticut second-graders to New York City in an attempt to pressure J.P. Morgan Chase CEO William B. Harrison into agreeing to stop lending money to development projects that "cause global warming."

Corporate Social Responsibility Watch (csrwatch.com) keeps an eye on the leftist attack on American corporations and corporate cowardice in the face of these attacks. Last year, CSRW listed the "Top Ten Worst Moments in Free Enterprise for 2004."

Among those listed are Monsanto's CEO Hugh Grant, who caved in to pressure from Greenpeace and announced the company was shelving plans to develop genetically engineered wheat. Ford Motor Co. CEO William Ford Jr., in an effort to befriend environmentalists, publicly supported a 50-cent-per-gallon gas tax.

British Petroleum's CEO John Browne devised a $100 million-a-year public relations campaign that characterizes oil as a "necessary evil" and in the process deceitfully started changing its corporate identity from "British Petroleum" to "Beyond Petroleum."

Citigroup and Bank of America agreed to allow Rainforest Action Network to dictate their lending practices—such as not financing projects that don't meet with environmentalists' approval.

Also included among CSRW's top 10 are Whole Foods, Starbucks, Dunkin' Donuts, Kraft Foods and Procter & Gamble, which have been mau-maued into paying higher, so-called "fair trade" prices for coffee beans in the name of helping struggling farmers.

Do corporations have social responsibility? Yes. Nobel Laureate Professor Milton Friedman put it best in 1970 when he said that in a free society "there is one and only one social responsibility of business—to use its resources and engage in activities designed to increase its profits so long as it stays within the rules of the game, which is to say, engages in open and free competition without deception or fraud."

Only people, not businesses, have responsibilities. A CEO is an employee. He's an employee of shareholders and customers. When the corporate executive community fails to recognize that fact, and engages in activities unrelated to the pursuit of profits, lower national wealth, higher product prices, and lower return on investment are the result. Corporate executives caving in to anti-capitalists' attacks will not buy peace. Capitulation only whets anti-capitalist appetites for bigger, bolder and more widespread attacks and extortion.

Killing People

October 7, 2002

Activists in the environmentalist movement have a callous disregard for people. You say, "What do you mean, Williams? We can't think of a more caring people." First, I'm not talking about sensible people who're concerned about clean air and water. I'm talking about the movement leaders and the politicians they have under their thumbs. Let's look at it.

The New York Green Party said in its opposition to pesticide spraying to halt the spread of West Nile disease, "These diseases only kill the old and people whose health is already poor." In East Meadow and Hempstead, New York, local officials, following the advice of environmental activists, decided not to spray. Nassau County's Health Commissioner said, "We believe the risk of infection for residents remains quite low." Two county residents became infected with West Nile disease and died. Environment activist Lynn Landes says, "West Nile may be a nasty experience for a very few, fatal for an exceedingly rare number, but as diseases go it's no big deal." According to the most recent Centers for Disease Control statistics, 2,530 Americans have been infected with West Nile disease and 125 died, but to environmentalists that's "no big deal."

American deaths due to environmental activist callousness pale in comparison to other countries. How about a few statistics? In 1972, the activist-controlled Environmental Protection Agency banned DDT, a pesticide once considered a "miracle" for all of the lives it saved by killing the mosquitoes that carried malaria. The ban went into effect despite the evidence that with proper use it posed no health hazard to humans and only little substantial harm to animals. The EPA ban led to diminished DDT production making the pesticide less available to the world.

What were the effects? In what is now Sri Lanka there were 2,800,000 malaria cases and 7,300 malaria deaths in 1948; with the use of DDT there were only 17 cases and no deaths in 1964. After

DDT use was discontinued, Sri Lankan malaria cases rose to 500,000 in 1969. Worldwide malaria's devastating effects all but ended during the time that DDT use was widespread, roughly 1950–1970. DDT was seen as such a miracle that it earned Dr. Paul Muller the Nobel Prize in Medicine in 1948. In 1970, a committee of the National Academy of Sciences wrote, "To only a few chemicals does man owe as great a debt as to DDT. In a little more than two decades, DDT has prevented 500 million deaths due to malaria that otherwise would have been inevitable."

According to the World Health Organization, now about two and a half million people die of malaria each year. Most of the victims are in Africa and are children. According to American Council on Science and Health's president, Dr. Elizabeth Whelan, some sixty million or more lives have been needlessly lost since the ban on DDT took effect. Dr. Whelan says, "It's a real tragedy that DDT has been so demonized over the years by activist organizations such as Environmental Defense and the regulatory bodies that they have duped."

C.S. Lewis made an observation applicable to do-gooders everywhere, "Of all tyrannies a tyranny exercised for the good of its victims may be the most oppressive. It may be better to live under robber barons than under omnipotent moral busybodies. The robber baron's cruelty may sometimes sleep, his cupidity may at some point be satiated; but those who torment us for our own good will torment us without end for they do so with the approval of their own conscience."

They're Coming after You

February 25, 2002

Most Americans were pleased with the legislative attack on cigarette smokers, not to mention confiscatory tobacco taxes. We reveled in the EPA's dishonest study concluding that second hand smoke causes cancer. And, by the way, I'd like to hear whether the Food & Drug Administration would sanction pharmaceutical companies employing EPA's research methods to test drug safety, and if not, why not? The real reason for the attack on smokers is that many people are offended by the tobacco odor. Unfortunately, in their quest to eliminate tobacco fumes, Americans are willing to trade away constitutional principles and rule of law.

Tyrants are never satisfied. They've lined up new victims. Surgeon General David Satcher has provided them with ammunition by describing obesity as America's number one killer costing 300,000 lives annually. As a result of cardiovascular disease, diabetes and other obesity-related illnesses, it's costing us billions upon billions of health dollars. That means, according to John Banzhaf of George Washington University School of Law and other tyrants, America's food industry is to blame and is liable. New York University Professor Marion Nestle agrees saying that the food industry "can't behave like cigarette companies. . . . Yet there's a lot of people who benefit from people being fat and sick, and the whole setup is designed to make people eat more. So the response to the food industry should be very similar to what happened with the tobacco companies."

The Center for Science in the Public Interest (CSPI) is one of the Washington lobbies who want to control what we eat. These tyrants not only propose taxes on what they deem as non-nutritious foods, they've also proposed a 5 percent tax on new television sets and video equipment and a $65 tax on each new car or an extra penny per gallon of gas. You might ask why tax these items. CSPI Nazis see watching television and videos, riding instead of walking, as contributing to obesity. And, as they see it, just as tobacco companies were responsible for people smoking, television manufacturers are responsible for people being couch potatoes, automobile companies are responsible for people riding instead of walking, and the food industry is responsible for people eating too much.

Mothers Against Drunk Driving (MADD) have joined these tyrants. No reasonable person advocates drunk driving but MADD has another agenda. They wish to outlaw driving even after having one drink. They've successfully pushed Congress to lower the blood/alcohol level for a drunk driving arrest to .08 percent. But their true agenda was revealed by Steve Simon, Chairman, Minnesota State DUI Task Force when he said, "If .08 percent is good, .05 percent is better. That's where we're headed, it doesn't mean that we should get there all at once. But ultimately it should be .02 percent." That's the way Nazis work—incrementally. If they had demanded Congress to make the blood/alcohol .02, they wouldn't have gotten anything—not even .08 percent. I wouldn't be surprised if their ultimate agenda is alcohol prohibition.

The Center for Consumer Freedom (www.consumerfreedom .com) keeps up-to-date information on these and other tyrants. You might say, "What's the fuss, Williams? These people will never get away with controlling what we eat and drink!" Think again. In the '60s, when the anti-smoking zealots were simply asking for smoking and non-smoking sections on airplanes, no one would have ever anticipated today's tobacco taxes, laws and regulations.

Most evil done in the world is done in the name of promoting this or that good. By turning away from rule of law and constitutional government, Americans are following in the footsteps of the decent Germans who, during the 1920s and 30s, built the Trojan Horse that enabled Hitler to take over.

Government

Thomas Paine said, "Government, even in its best state, is but a necessary evil; in its worst state, an intolerable one." No other sentiment so expresses the concerns of the founders of our nation than a deep suspicion of government as seen by a few samples of their statements. John Adams said, "You have rights antecedent to all earthly governments; rights that cannot be repealed or restrained by human laws; rights derived from the Great Legislator of the Universe." Thomas Jefferson said, "The true theory of our Constitution is surely the wisest and best . . . [for] when all government . . . shall be drawn to Washington as the centre of all power, it will render powerless the checks provided of one government on another, and will become as . . . oppressive as the government from which we separated." James Jackson said, "We must confine ourselves to the powers described in the Constitution, and the moment we pass it, we take an arbitrary stride towards a despotic Government." James Madison, the acknowledged father of the Constitution, said, "The powers delegated by the proposed Constitution to the federal government are few and defined. Those which are to remain in the State governments are numerous and indefinite." And Thomas Jefferson warned, "The natural progress of things is for liberty to yield and government to gain ground."

This suspicion explains why the framers of our constitution sought to give us rules that limited the power of the federal government. The United States Constitution contains dozens of shall-not phrases against government, such as shall not abridge, infringe, deny, disparage and shall not be violated nor be denied. I have often commented that, after one dies and sees such a negative governing instrument at his next destination, he would surely know that he is in Hell because such distrust would be an affront to God.

It goes without saying that the three branches of our federal government are no longer bound by the Constitution as the framers envisioned; what is worse is the American acceptance of such rogue behavior. If it were ignorance on behalf of the American people and their representa-

tives, I would be optimistic because ignorance is curable through education, but I think it is design. Strong evidence of this is a measure that has been repeatedly introduced by Representative John Shadegg of Arizona called the Enumerated Powers Act that reads "Each Act of Congress shall contain a concise and definite statement of the constitutional authority relied upon for the enactment of each portion of that Act. The failure to comply with this section shall give rise to a point of order in either House of Congress. The availability of this point of order does not affect any other available relief." Simply put, if enacted, the Enumerated Powers Act would require Congress to specify the basis of authority in the U.S. Constitution for the enactment of laws and other congressional actions. Each time the Enumerated Powers Act has been introduced, it has received little or no support by members of Congress. That leads to the conclusion that members of Congress have no wish to be bound by their oath of office to uphold and defend the U.S. Constitution.

Many politicians, and others, who ignore the original meaning of our Constitution argue that it is a living document. Suggesting that the Constitution is a living document is equivalent to saying we do not have a Constitution. The Constitution represents our rules, and for rules to mean anything, they must be fixed. I have often asked how many people would like to play poker and have the rules be "living"? Perhaps, because of a "more modern" society or "evolving standards" that Hoyle could not possibly anticipate, maybe my two pair could beat your full house.

The framers recognized there might come a time to amend the Constitution, and they gave us Article V as a means for doing so, but today's Americans, compared to our ancestors, have little respect for the constitutional route to changing the Constitution. Early in the last century, some Americans thought it was a good idea to ban the manufacture and sale of alcohol. They found there was no constitutional authority for the same. They did not go to court asking the justices to twist the meaning of the Constitution to accomplish their goal. Regardless of the wisdom of their agenda, they respected the Constitution and sought passage of the Eighteenth Amendment.

Americans do not want their elected officials to uphold and defend the Constitution. Doing so would mean that one American could not live at the expense of another in the form of spending programs such as

Social Security, Medicare, aid to higher education, farm subsidies, food stamps, and other programs that make up close to two-thirds of a $3 trillion-plus federal budget for which there is absolutely no authority in the U.S. Constitution. What taxing and spending authority the Constitution grants Congress is mostly spelled out in Article I, Section 8 of the document.

The true tragedy, and foreboding for the future, is that any member of Congress who would take his oath of office seriously would not get elected to office. That is, any member of Congress who would campaign on the promise not to support farm or transportation subsidies, aid to higher education, and a host of other government programs would not be elected to office. So far as their economic interests are concerned, his constituents would be absolutely right in rejecting his candidacy. Why? Because if their representative does not bring home various handouts, it would not mean they will pay lower federal taxes; all that it would mean is that the handouts would go to residents of some other state or constituency. Once legalized theft begins, it pays all to participate. The columns that follow delve into various aspects of generalized constitutional contempt.

Competition or Monopoly

Wednesday, June 13, 2007

Are consumers better off with a competitive or monopolistic provision of goods and services? Let's apply that question to a few areas of our lives.

Prior to deregulation, when there was a monopoly and restricted entry in the provision of telephone services, were consumers better off or worse off than they are with today's ruthless competition to get our business? Anyone over 40 will recognize the differences. Competition has provided consumers with a vast array of choices, lower and lower prices and more courteous customer care than when government had its heavy hand on the provision of telephone services.

What about supermarkets? Would consumers be better off or worse off if one or two supermarkets were granted an exclusive monopoly in the provision of grocery services? The average well-stocked supermarket carries over 50,000 different items, has sales, prizes and pursues many strategies to win customers and retain their loyalty. Would they have the same incentives if they were granted a monopoly?

The government gives poor people food stamps. Would poor people be better off or worse off if, instead of being able to use their food stamps at any supermarket, they were forced to use them at a government store?

There's abundant evidence that suggests consumers are better off when providers of goods and services are driven by the profit motive where survival requires a constant effort to get and keep customers. Under what conditions can businesses survive, providing shoddy services, fewer choices, at higher and higher costs, without pleasing customers? If you said, "Where there's restricted competition and a government-sanctioned monopoly," go to the head of the class. There's no better example of this than in the case of government education.

ABC News anchor John Stossel produced a documentary aptly titled "Stupid in America: How We Cheat Our Kids" that gives a visual depiction of what's often no less than educational fraud. (The documentary can be viewed at www.youtube.com/watch?v=pfRUM mTs0ZA.) During the documentary, an international test is given to average high school students in Belgium and above-average New Jersey high school students. Belgian kids cleaned the New Jersey students' clocks and called them "stupid." It's not just in Belgium where high school students run circles around their American counterparts; it's the same for students in Poland, Czech Republic, South Korea and 17 other countries.

The documentary leaves no question about the poor education received by white students, but that received by many black students is truly disgusting and darn near criminal. Stossel interviewed an 18-year-old black student who struggled to read a first-grade book. ABC's "20/20" sent him to Sylvan Learning Center. Within 72 hours, his reading level was two grades higher.

"Stupid in America" included one story where a teacher sent sexually oriented e-mails to "Cutie 101," a 16-year-old student. Only after six years of litigation was the New York City Department of Education able to fire the teacher, during which time the teacher collected more than $300,000 in salary.

The solution to America's education problems is not more money, despite the claims of the education establishment. Instead, it's the introduction of competition that could be achieved through school choice. Most people agree there should be public financing of education, but there is absolutely no case to be made for public production of education. We agree there should be public financing of F-22 fighters, but that doesn't mean a case can be made for setting up a government F-22 factory.

A school choice system, in the form of school vouchers or tuition tax credits, would go a long way toward providing the competition necessary to introduce accountability and quality into American education. What's wrong with parents having the right, along with the means, to enroll their children in schools of their choice?

Stupid, Ignorant or Biased?

Wednesday, September 19, 2007

President Franklin D. Roosevelt's closest adviser and architect of the New Deal, Harry Hopkins, advised, "Tax and tax, spend and spend, elect and elect, because the people are too damn dumb to know the difference." Professor Bryan Caplan, my colleague at George Mason University, sheds some light on Hopkins' observation in his new book, "The Myth of the Rational Voter: Why Democracies Choose Bad Policies."

Caplan is far more generous than Hopkins. Instead, he says people harbor economic biases, several of which he discusses. There's the anti-market bias, the failure to believe that market forces determine prices. Many believe that prices are a function of a CEO's intentions and conspiracies. If a CEO wakes up feeling greedy, he'll raise prices. They also believe that profits are undeserving gifts. They fail to see that, at least in open markets, profits are incentives for firms to satisfy customers, find least-cost production methods and move resources from low-valued to high-valued uses.

Then there's the make-work bias, where many believe that labor is better to use than conserve. Thus, the destruction of jobs is seen as a danger. Technology, as well as outsourcing, throws some people out of work. Caplan reminds us that in 1800 it took nearly 95 of every 100 Americans, working on farms, to feed the nation. In 1900, it took 40. Today, it takes three. Workers no longer needed to farm became available to produce homes, cars, pharmaceuticals, computers and thousands of other goods. Caplan doesn't make the equation, but outsourcing, just as technological innovation, frees up labor to produce other things as well.

Next is the anti-foreign bias. Caplan explains that there are two methods for Americans to have cars. One is to get a bunch of workers into Detroit factories. Another is to grow a lot of wheat in Iowa. You harvest the wheat, load it on ships sailing westward on the Pacific Ocean, and a few months later the ships reappear loaded down with

Toyotas. We have cars as if we produced them. In other words, exchange is an alternative method of production.

Added to the anti-foreign bias is the balance-of-trade fallacy. Caplan says that nobody loses sleep over whether there's a trade balance between California and Nevada, or between him and iTunes. Trade balance fears arise only when another country is involved. The fallacy is not treating all purchases as a cost but only foreign purchases as a cost. There might be another bias as well. Caplan reports that, according to an opinion survey, 28 percent of Americans admitted they dislike Japan but only 8 percent dislike England and a scant 3 percent dislike Canada.

People have a pessimistic bias where they believe economic conditions are not as good as they really are and things are going from bad to worse. This is the message of doomsayers, but the reality is quite different. By any measure of well-being, Americans at the start of this century are far better off than Americans at the beginning of the last century. Perennial doom-and-gloom predictions about resource depletion, overpopulation and environmental quality are exaggerated and often the opposite of the truth. Preaching doom and gloom has been beneficial to the political class. They use it to gain more power and control.

Caplan is one of George Mason University Economics Department's up-and-coming young scholars. In fact, I'm proud to say, he was hired during my department chairmanship. "The Myth of the Rational Voter: Why Democracies Choose Bad Policies" is a highly readable and interesting political-economic discussion of why we choose bad policies. Those policies are harmful to the general public but beneficial to particular interest groups who gain from restrictions on peaceable, voluntary exchange. Maybe that's why our founders loathed a democracy and gave us a republic—which we've lost.

Congressional Constitutional Contempt

Wednesday, October 24, 2007

Here's the oath of office administered to members of the House and Senate: "I do solemnly swear (or affirm) that I will support and defend the Constitution of the United States against all enemies, foreign or domestic; that I will bear true faith and allegiance to the same; that I take this obligation freely, without any mental reservation or purpose of evasion; and that I will well and faithfully discharge the duties of the office on which I am about to enter. So help me God." A similar oath is sworn to by the president and federal judges.

In each new Congress since 1995, Rep. John Shadegg, R-Ariz., has introduced the Enumerated Powers Act (HR 1359). The Act, which has yet to be enacted into law, reads: "Each Act of Congress shall contain a concise and definite statement of the constitutional authority relied upon for the enactment of each portion of that Act. The failure to comply with this section shall give rise to a point of order in either House of Congress. The availability of this point of order does not affect any other available relief."

Simply put, if enacted, the Enumerated Powers Act would require Congress to specify the basis of authority in the U.S. Constitution for the enactment of laws and other congressional actions. HR 1359 has 28 co-sponsors in the House of Representatives.

When Shadegg introduced the Enumerated Powers Act, he explained that the Constitution gives the federal government great, but limited, powers. Its framers granted Congress, as the central mechanism for protecting liberty, specific rather than general powers. The Constitution gives Congress 18 specific enumerated powers, spelled out mostly in Article 1, Section 8. The framers reinforced that enumeration by the 10th Amendment, which reads: "The powers not delegated to the United States by the Constitution, nor prohibited by it to the States, are reserved for the States respectively, or to the people."

Just a few of the numerous statements by our founders demonstrate that their vision and the vision of Shadegg's Enumerated Powers Act are one and the same. James Madison, in explaining the Constitution in Federalist Paper No. 45, said, "The powers delegated by the proposed Constitution to the federal government are few and defined. Those which are to remain in the State governments are numerous and indefinite. The former will be exercised principally on external objects, as war, peace, negotiation, and foreign commerce."

Regarding the "general welfare" clause so often used as a justification for bigger government, Thomas Jefferson said, "Congress has not unlimited powers to provide for the general welfare, but only those specifically enumerated." James Madison said, "If Congress can do whatever in their discretion can be done by money, and will promote the general welfare, the government is no longer a limited one possessing enumerated powers, but an indefinite one subject to particular exceptions."

Congressmen, openly refusing to live up to their oath of office, exhibit their deep contempt for our Constitution. The question I've not been able to answer satisfactorily is whether that contempt simply mirrors a similar contempt held by most of the American people. I'm sure that if founders such as James Madison, John Adams or Thomas Jefferson were campaigning for the 2008 presidential elections, expressing their vision of the federal government's role, today's Americans would run them out of town on a rail. Does that hostility reflect constitutional ignorance whereby the average American thinks the Constitution authorizes Congress to do anything upon which they can get a majority vote or anything that's a good idea? Or, are Americans contemptuous of the constitutional limitations placed on the federal government?

I salute the bravery of Rep. Shadegg and the 28 co-sponsors of the Enumerated Powers Act. They have a monumental struggle. Congress is not alone in its constitutional contempt, but is joined by the White House and particularly the constitutionally derelict U.S. Supreme Court.

Bitter Partisan Politics

Wednesday, November 28, 2007

Some people complain about bitter partisan politics. I welcome it. The greater the number of decisions made in the political arena the greater the conflict. Let's look at it by way of a few examples:

I like the Lexus LS 460. I also like Dell computers. Many other people have a different set of preferences. Some might prefer a Cadillac and an HP computer while others prefer a Chrysler and IBM computer. With these strong preferences for particular cars and computers, we never see people arguing or fighting in an effort to impose their preferences for cars and computers on other people. There's car and computer peace. Why? You buy the car and computer that you want; I do likewise and we remain friends.

There's absolutely no reason for car and computer choices to remain peaceful. Suppose our car and computer choices were made in the political arena through representative democracy or through a plebiscite where majority ruled. We would decide collectively whether our cars would be Lexuses or Cadillacs or Chryslers. We also would decide collectively whether our computer would be a Dell or HP or IBM computer.

I guarantee you there would be nasty, bitter conflict between otherwise peaceful car and computer buyers. Each person would have reason to enter into conflict with those having different car and computer tastes because one person's win would necessarily be another person's loss. It would be what game theorists call a zero-sum game. How would you broker a peace with these parties in conflict? If you're not a tyrant, I'm betting you'd say, "Take the decision out of the political arena and let people buy whatever car and computer they wish."

Prayers in school, sex education and "intelligent design" are contentious school issues. I believe parents should have the right to decide whether their children will say a morning prayer in school, be taught "intelligent design" and not be given school-based sex education. I also believe other parents should have the right not to have their children exposed to prayers in school, "intelligent design" and receive sex education.

The reason why these issues produce conflict is because education is government-produced. That means there's either going to be prayers or no prayers, "intelligent design" or no "intelligent design" and sex education or no sex education. If one parent has his wishes met, it comes at the expense of another parent's wishes. The losing parent either must grin and bear it or send his child to a private school, pay its tuition and still pay property taxes for a school for which he has no use.

Just as in the car and computer examples, the solution is to take the production of education out of the political arena. The best way is to end all government involvement in education. Failing to get government completely out of education, we should recognize that because government finances something it doesn't follow that government must produce it. Government finances F-22 Raptor fighter jets, but there's no government factory producing them. The same could be done in education. We could finance education collectively through tuition tax credits or educational vouchers, but allow parents to choose, much like we did with the GI Bill. Government financed the education, but the veterans chose the school.

Government allocation of resources enhances the potential for human conflict, while market allocation reduces it. That also applies to contentious national issues such as Social Security and health care. You take care of your retirement and health care as you please, and I'll take care of mine as I please. If you prefer socialized retirement and health care, that's fine if you don't force others to participate. I'm afraid most Americans view such a liberty-oriented solution with hostility. They believe they have a right to enlist the brute forces of government to impose their preferences on others.

Attacking Lobbyists Wrong Battle

Wednesday, January 18, 2006

Jack Abramoff, the Washington lobbyist who's pled guilty to charges of conspiracy, fraud and tax evasion, has showered millions of dollars on the campaign coffers of both Republican and Democrat congressmen. Like a kid caught with his hands in the cookie jar, many congressmen seek to distance themselves by purging their coffers of Abramoff money. Senate Majority Leader Bill Frist, R-Tenn., in reaction to Abramoff's guilty plea, has pledged to "examine and act on any necessary changes to improve transparency and accountability for our body when it comes to lobbying."

Whatever actions Congress might take in the matter of lobbying are going to be just as disappointing in ending influence-peddling as their Bipartisan Campaign Reform Act of 2002, known as the McCain-Feingold bill. Before we allow ourselves to be bamboozled by our political leaders, we might do our own analysis to determine whether the problem is money in politics or something more fundamental.

Let's start this analysis with a question. Why do corporations, unions and other interest groups fork over millions of dollars to the campaign coffers of politicians? Is it because these groups are extraordinarily civic-minded Americans who have a deep interest in congressmen doing their jobs of upholding and defending the U.S. Constitution? Might it be that these groups and their Washington-based lobby arms, numbering in the thousands, just love participating in the political process? Anyone answering in the affirmative to either question probably also believes that storks deliver babies and there really is an Easter Bunny and Santa Claus.

A much better explanation for the millions going to the campaign coffers of Washington politicians lies in the awesome growth of government control over business, property, employment and other areas of our lives. Having such power, Washington politicians are in the position to grant favors. The greater their power to grant favors, the greater the value of being able to influence Congress, and there's no better influence than money.

The generic favor sought is to get Congress, under one ruse or another, to grant a privilege or right to one group of Americans that will be denied another group of Americans. A variant of this privilege is to get Congress to do something that would be criminal if done privately.

Here's just one among possibly thousands of examples. If Archer Daniels Midland (ADM) used goons and violence to stop people from buying sugar from Caribbean producers so that sugar prices would rise, making it easier for ADM to sell more of its corn syrup sweetener, they'd wind up in jail. If they line the coffers of congressmen, they can buy the same result without risking imprisonment. Congress simply does the dirty work for them by enacting sugar import quotas and tariffs. The two most powerful committees of Congress are the House Ways and Means and the Senate Finance committees. These committees are in charge of granting tax favors. Their members are besieged with campaign contributions. Why? A tweak here and a tweak there in the tax code can mean millions of dollars.

You ask what can be done? Campaign finance and lobby reform will only change the method of influence-peddling. If Congress did only what's specifically enumerated in our Constitution, influence-peddling would be a non-issue simply because the Constitution contains no authority for Congress to grant favors and special privileges. Nearly two decades ago, during dinner with the late Nobel Laureate Friedrich Hayek, I asked him if he had the power to write one law that would get government out of our lives, what would that law be? Professor Hayek replied he'd write a law that read: Whatever Congress does for one American it must do for all Americans. He elaborated: If Congress makes payments to one American for not raising pigs, every American not raising pigs should also receive payments. Obviously, were there to be such a law, there would be reduced capacity for privilege-granting by Congress and less influence-peddling.

Is There a Federal Deficit?

Wednesday, April 19, 2006

Let's push back the frontiers of ignorance about the federal deficit. To simplify things, I'll use round numbers that are fairly close to the actual numbers.

The nation's 2005 gross domestic product (GDP), what the American people produced, totaled $13 trillion. The federal government consumed $2.4 trillion, but it only received $2 trillion in tax revenues, leaving us with what's said to be a $.4 trillion budget deficit.

By the way, it's sheer constitutional ignorance to say that President Bush spends or lowers taxes. Article I, Sections 7 and 8, of the U.S. Constitution gives Congress authority to spend and tax. The president only has veto power that Congress can override.

Getting back to deficits, my question to you is this: Is there truly a deficit? The short answer is yes, but only in an accounting sense—not in any meaningful economic sense. Let's look at it. If Congress spends $2.4 trillion but only takes in $2 trillion in taxes, who makes up that $.4 trillion shortfall that we call the budget deficit? Neither the Tooth Fairy, Santa nor the Easter Bunny makes up the difference between what's spent in 2005 and what's taxed in 2005.

Some might be tempted to answer that it's future generations who will pay. That's untrue. If the federal government consumes $2.4 trillion of what Americans produced in 2005, it must find ways to force us to spend $2.4 trillion less privately in 2005. In other words, the federal government can't spend today what's going to be produced in the future.

One method to force us to spend less privately is through taxation, but that's not the only way. Another way is to enter the bond market. Government borrowing drives the interest rate to a level that it otherwise wouldn't be without government borrowing. That higher interest puts the squeeze on private investment in homes and businesses, thereby forcing us to spend less privately.

Another way to force us to spend less privately is to inflate the currency. Theoretically, Congress can consume what we produce without enacting a single tax law; they could simply print money. The rising prices, which would curtail our real spending, would act as a tax. Of course, an important side effect of doing so would be economic havoc.

Some Americans have called for a balanced budget amendment to the Constitution as a method to rein in a prolific Congress. A balanced budget is no panacea. For example, suppose Congress spent $6 trillion and taxed us $6 trillion. We'd have a balanced budget, but we'd be far freer with today's unbalanced budget. The fact of business is that the true measure of the impact of government on our lives is not the taxes we pay but the level of spending.

The founders of our nation would be horrified by today's level of American servitude to their government. From 1787 to the Roaring '20s, federal government spending, as a percentage of GDP, never exceeded 4 percent, except in wartime, compared to today's 20 percent.

The average taxpayer, depending on the state in which he lives, works from Jan. 1 to May 3 to pay federal, state and local taxes. That means someone else decides how four months' worth of the fruits of the average taxpayer's labor will be spent. The taxpayer is forcibly used to serve the purposes of others—whether it's farm or business handouts, food stamps or other government programs where the earnings of one American are taken and given to another.

This situation differs only in degree, but not in kind, from slavery. After all, a working description of slavery is the process where one person is forcibly used to serve the purposes of another. The difference is a slave has no rights to what he produces each year, instead of just four months.

Click It or Ticket

Wednesday, May 24, 2006

Virginia's secretary of transportation sent out a letter announcing the state's annual "Click It or Ticket" campaign May 22 through June 4. I responded to the secretary of transportation with my own letter that in part reads:

"Mr. Secretary: This is an example of the disgusting abuse of state power. Each of us owns himself, and it follows that we should have the liberty to take risks with our own lives but not that of others. That means it's a legitimate use of state power to mandate that cars have working brakes because if my car has poorly functioning brakes, I risk the lives of others and I have no right to do so. If I don't wear a seatbelt I risk my own life, which is well within my rights. As to your statement 'Lack of safety belt use is a growing public health issue that . . . also costs us all billions of dollars every year,' that's not a problem of liberty. It's a problem of socialism. No human should be coerced by the state to bear the medical expense, or any other expense, for his fellow man. In other words, the forcible use of one person to serve the purposes of another is morally offensive."

My letter went on to tell the secretary that I personally wear a seatbelt each time I drive; it's a good idea. However, because something is a good idea doesn't necessarily make a case for state compulsion. The justifications used for "Click It or Ticket" easily provide the template and soften us up for other forms of government control over our lives.

For example, my weekly exercise routine consists of three days' weight training and three days' aerobic training. I think it's a good idea. Like seatbelt use, regular exercise extends lives and reduces health care costs. Here's my question to government officials and others who sanction the "Click It or Ticket" campaign: Should the government mandate daily exercise for the same reasons they cite to support mandatory seatbelt use, namely, that to do so would save lives and save billions of health care dollars?

If we accept the notion that government ought to protect us from ourselves, we're on a steep slippery slope. Obesity is a major contributor to hypertension, coronary disease and diabetes, and leads not only to many premature deaths but billions of dollars in health care costs. Should government enforce, depending on a person's height, sex and age, a daily 1,400 to 2,000-calorie intake limit? There's absolutely no dietary reason to add salt to our meals. High salt consumption can lead to high blood pressure, which can then lead to stroke, heart attack, osteoporosis and asthma. Should government outlaw adding salt to meals? While you might think that these government mandates would never happen, be advised that there are busybody groups currently pushing for government mandates on how much and what we can eat.

Government officials, if given power to control us, soon become zealots. Last year, Maryland state troopers were equipped with night vision goggles, similar to those used by our servicemen in Iraq, to catch night riders not wearing seatbelts. Maryland state troopers boasted that they bagged 44 drivers traveling unbuckled under the cover of darkness.

Philosopher John Stuart Mill, in his treatise "On Liberty," said it best: "That the only purpose for which power can be rightfully exercised over any member of a civilized community, against his will, is to prevent harm to others. His own good, either physical or moral, is not a sufficient warrant. He cannot rightfully be compelled to do or forbear because it will be better for him to do so, because it will make him happier, because, in the opinions of others, to do so would be wise, or even right. These are good reasons for remonstrating with him, or reasoning with him, or persuading him, or entreating him, but not for compelling him, or visiting him with any evil, in case he do otherwise."

The Slippery Slope

Wednesday, June 14, 2006

Down through the years, I've attempted to warn my fellow Americans about the tyrannical precedent and template for further tyranny set by anti-tobacco zealots. The point of this column is not to rekindle the smoking debate. That train has left the station. Instead, let's examine the template.

In the early stages of the anti-tobacco campaign, there were calls for "reasonable" measures such as non-smoking sections on airplanes and health warnings on cigarette packs. In the 1970s, no one would have ever believed such measures would have evolved into today's level of attack on smokers, which includes confiscatory cigarette taxes and bans on outdoor smoking. The door was opened, and the zealots took over. Much of the attack was justified by an Environmental Protection Agency (EPA) secondhand smoke study that used statistical techniques, if used by an academic researcher, would lead to condemnation if not expulsion. Let's say that you support the attack on smokers. Are you ready for the next round of tyranny using tactics so successful for the anti-tobacco zealots?

According to a June 2 Associated Press report, "Those heaping portions at restaurants—and doggie bags for the leftovers—may be a thing of the past, if health officials get their way." The story pertains to a report, funded by the U.S. Food and Drug Administration (FDA) titled, "Keystone Forum on Away-From-Home Foods: Opportunities for Preventing Weight Gain and Obesity." The FDA says the report could help the American restaurant industry and consumers take important steps to successfully combat the nation's obesity problem. Among the report's recommendations for restaurants are: list calorie-content on menus, serve smaller portions, and add more fruits and vegetables and nuts. Both the Department of Health and Human Services and the FDA accept the findings of the report.

Right now, the FDA doesn't have the authority to require restaurants to label the number of calories, set portion sizes on menus or prohibit allowing customers from taking home a doggie bag. That's for right now, but recall that cigarette warning labels were the anti-tobacco zealots' first steps. There are zealots like the Washington-based Center for Science in the Public Interest who've for a long time attacked Chinese and Mexican restaurants for serving customers too much food. They also say, "Caffeine is the only drug that is widely added to the food supply." They've called for caffeine warning labels, and they don't stop there. The Center's director said, "We could envision taxes on butter, potato chips, whole milk, cheeses and meat." Visions of higher taxes are music to politicians' ears.

How many Americans would like to go to a restaurant and have the waiter tell you, based on calories, what you might have for dinner? How would you like the waiter to tell you, "According to government regulations, we cannot give you a doggie bag"? What about a Burger King cashier refusing to sell French fries to overweight people? You say, "Williams, that's preposterous! It would never come to that."

I'm betting that would have been the same response during the 1970s had someone said the day would come when cities, such as Calabasas, Calif., and Friendship Heights, Md., would write ordinances banning outdoor smoking. Tyrants always start out with small measures that appear reasonable. Revealing their complete agenda from the start would encounter too much resistance.

Diet decisions that people make are none of anybody else's business. Yes, there are untoward health outcomes from unwise dietary habits, and because of socialism, taxpayers have to pick up the bill. But if we allow untoward health outcomes from choices to be our guide for government intervention, then we're calling for government to intervene in virtually every aspect of our lives. Eight hours' sleep, regular exercise and moderate alcohol consumption are important for good health. Should government regulate those decisions?

The Pretense of Knowledge

Wednesday, July 12, 2006

One of the great contributions of Nobel Laureate economist Friedrich Hayek was to admonish us to recognize the insurmountable limits to human knowledge. Why? Not even the brightest minds, and surely not the U.S. Congress, can ever have the knowledge to shape an economic system entirely to our liking. To think we can represents the height of arrogance and a pretense of knowledge. The billions upon billions of interrelationships between an economic system's human and non-human elements defy human capacity to know.

Let's examine just a few pretenses of knowledge. Under Social Security law, Congress forces workers to set aside a portion of their earnings for retirement. Take a 25-year-old—let's call her "Mary"—who earns $40,000 a year. Her Social Security tax is about $2,500. Here's my question to you: Was having $2,500 forcibly taken out of Mary's pay for retirement her best possible use of that money? Mary might have saved and invested several years to open a small business. She might have put it toward private schooling or music lessons for her child, or any number of things that might have made her, and possibly our nation, wealthier in the future.

How about Congress' mandate for more fuel-efficient cars? According to a National Research Council of the National Academies of Sciences 2002 report, delivered by Dr. Leonard Evans to the Washington-based Competitive Enterprise Institute, Corporate Average Fuel Economy (CAFE) standards have contributed to between 1,300 and 2,600 traffic deaths a year. Congress' mandate for higher gasoline mileage leads to the production of lighter, smaller and less crash-worthy cars, resulting in unnecessary deaths. Through technological innovation and natural market forces, cars were already becoming more fuel efficient before CAFE standards were mandated. But more important, how does Congress know whether this loss of life is worth the amount of fuel saved? Do they even know or care about the tradeoff?

A major part of the knowledge problem that Congress faces, and, for that matter, any of us, is what's seen and what's unseen. In the case of Social Security, what's seen are the beneficiaries with a monthly check. What's not seen are the outcomes that might have been had people not been taxed for Social Security. According to the National Council for Capital Formation, Social Security lowers private saving and investment and, as a result, GDP is at least five percent lower than it otherwise would be. Moreover, had people been able to use the money for private retirement plans, they'd earn much more than the paltry sum Social Security pays out. The same principle applies to CAFE standards. What's seen are cars getting more miles per gallon. What's unseen, or the connection not made, are the thousands of Americans killed as a result of the less crash-worthy cars produced as a result of congressional mandates.

Another example of the seen/unseen problem is the Bush administration's 2002 steel tariffs. The tariffs' seen beneficiaries were steel industry executives, stockholders and the approximately 1,700 steelworker jobs saved. According to the Consuming Industries Trade Action Association, higher steel prices, resulting from the tariffs, caused thousands of job losses in the steel-using industries. Since companies that used steel had to pay higher prices, they became less competitive domestically and internationally.

Each of us is faced with the knowledge and the seen and unseen problems. I believe that most Americans would see themselves in a much better position of determining what's in our own best interests than politicians, who are mostly concerned with re-election. At least I hope that's the case.

Why We Love Government

Wednesday, November 29, 2006

Unlike today's Americans, the founders of our nation were suspicious, if not contemptuous, of government. Consider just a few of their words.

James Madison suggested that "All men having power ought to be distrusted to a certain degree."

Thomas Paine observed, "We still find the greedy hand of government thrusting itself into every corner and crevice of industry, and grasping at the spoil of the multitude. . . . It watches prosperity as its prey and permits none to escape without a tribute."

John Adams reminded, "You have rights antecedent to all earthly governments; rights that cannot be repealed or restrained by human laws; rights derived from the Great Legislator of the Universe."

Thomas Jefferson gave us several warnings that we've ignored: First, "The natural progress of things is for liberty to yield and government to gain ground." Second, "The greatest [calamity] which could befall [us would be] submission to a government of unlimited powers." And third, "Whensoever the General Government assumes undelegated powers, its acts are unauthoritative, void, and of no force."

In response to what Jefferson called an "elective despotism," he suggested that "The tree of Liberty must be refreshed from time to time with the blood of patriots and tyrants."

With sentiments like these, John Adams, Thomas Jefferson and James Madison became presidents. Could a person with similar sentiments win the presidency today? My guess is no. Today's Americans hold such liberty-oriented values in contempt, and any presidential aspirant holding them would have a zero chance of winning office.

Today's Americans hold a different vision of government. It's one that says Congress has the right to do just about anything upon which it can secure a majority vote. Most of what Congress does fits the description of forcing one American to serve the purposes of another

American. That description differs only in degree, but not in kind, from slavery.

At least two-thirds of the federal budget represents forcing one American to serve the purposes of another. Younger workers are forced to pay for the prescriptions of older Americans; people who are not farmers are forced to serve those who are; non-poor people are forced to serve poor people; and the general public is forced to serve corporations, college students and other special interests that have the ear of Congress.

The supreme tragedy that will lead to our undoing is that so far as personal economic self-interests are concerned, it is perfectly rational for every American to seek to live at the expense of another American. Why? Not doing so doesn't mean he'll pay lower federal taxes. All it means is that there will be more money for somebody else.

In other words, once Congress establishes that one person can live at the expense of another, it pays for everyone to try to do so. You say, "Williams, don't you believe in helping your fellow man?" Yes, I do. I believe that reaching into one's own pockets to help his fellow man is both laudable and praiseworthy. Reaching into another's pockets to help his fellow man is despicable and worthy of condemnation.

The bottom line: We love government because it enables us to accomplish things that if done privately would lead to arrest and imprisonment. For example, if I saw a person in need, and I took your money to help him, I'd be arrested and convicted of theft. If I get Congress to do the same thing, I am seen as compassionate.

This vision ought to bother the Christians among us, for when God gave Moses the commandment "Thou shalt not steal," I'm sure He didn't mean thou shalt not steal unless you got a majority vote in Congress.

The FairTax Book

Wednesday, December 13, 2006

Last year, talk-show host Neal Boortz and Congressman John Linder co-authored *The FairTax Book: Saying Goodbye to the Income Tax and the IRS*. It turned out to be a No. 1 *New York Times* Best Seller. In 2005, the Fair Tax bill was introduced in both the U.S. House of Representatives as H.R. 25 and the U.S. Senate as S.25. Rep. Linder plans to re-introduce the bill next year.

If enacted, the Fair Tax would eliminate: the federal individual income tax, alternative minimum tax, corporate and business taxes, capital gains tax, Social Security and Medicare taxes, and estate and gift taxes. These taxes would be replaced by a 23 percent sales tax on all goods and services sold at the retail level. The Fair Tax would be revenue-neutral in the sense that it would replace the revenue from current federal taxes; thus, it would change the way government is funded.

Our current tax code is an abomination, and we desperately need that change. The time Americans spend simply complying with our tax code comes to 5.8 billion hours of record-keeping, filing taxes, consulting, legal and accounting services. Breaking those hours down to a 40-hour work week, it translates into a workforce of 2.77 million people. That's more than the workforce of our auto, aircraft, computer and steel manufacturing industries combined.

The Fair Tax has much to recommend in its favor, such as being a more efficient form of taxation. It would go a long way toward protecting our privacy and preventing Congress from using the tax code to micromanage our lives. The Fair Tax is an excellent idea, but only under three conditions: first, the repeal of the Sixteenth Amendment that created the income tax; second, a provision fixing the tax at, say, 23 percent; and third, a constitutional amendment mandating that a tax increase requires a three-fourths vote of Congress. Notwithstanding any provisions within the Fair Tax, if the Sixteenth Amendment weren't repealed, down the road we'd find ourselves with a national sales tax and an income tax.

You say, "Williams, it sounds as if you don't trust Congress." I don't trust Congress any farther than I can toss an elephant. During the debate prior to ratification of the Sixteenth Amendment, congressmen said that only the rich would ever pay income taxes. In 1917, only one-half of one percent of income earners paid income taxes. Those earning $250,000 a year in today's dollars paid one percent, and those earning $6 million in today's dollars paid 7 percent. The lie that only the rich would ever pay income taxes was simply propaganda to dupe Americans into ratifying the Sixteenth Amendment.

Here's my prediction: The Fair Tax will never become law. The two most powerful congressional committees are the House Ways and Means and the Senate Finance committees. These committees write tax law, and as such they are able to confer tax privileges on some Americans at the expense of other Americans. The Fair Tax would reduce or eliminate this form of congressional privilege-granting power and, subsequently, campaign contributions from the beneficiaries would dwindle.

The method used to finance the federal government is very important, but I've always argued that government spending is the true measure of its impact on our lives. If there were a Fair Tax, what's to stop Congress from deficit spending or inflating the currency? Deficit spending and inflation are simply alternative forms, albeit less obvious, of taxation.

You say, "What's Williams' solution?" My solution is an amendment limiting federal spending to a fixed percentage, say, 10 percent of the gross domestic product. You say, "Why 10 percent?" If 10 percent is good enough for the Baptist Church, it certainly ought to be good enough for Congress.

Are We a Republic or a Democracy?

Wednesday, January 5, 2005

We often hear the claim that our nation is a democracy. That wasn't the vision of the founders. They saw democracy as another form of tyranny. If we've become a democracy, I guarantee you that the founders would be deeply disappointed by our betrayal of their vision. The founders intended, and laid out the ground rules, for our nation to be a republic.

The word democracy appears nowhere in the Declaration of Independence or the Constitution—two most fundamental documents of our nation. Instead of a democracy, the Constitution's Article IV, Section 4, guarantees "to every State in this Union a Republican Form of Government." Moreover, let's ask ourselves: Does our pledge of allegiance to the flag say to "the democracy for which it stands," or does it say to "the republic for which it stands"? Or do we sing "The Battle Hymn of the Democracy" or "The Battle Hymn of the Republic"?

So what's the difference between republican and democratic forms of government? John Adams captured the essence of the difference when he said, "You have rights antecedent to all earthly governments; rights that cannot be repealed or restrained by human laws; rights derived from the Great Legislator of the Universe." Nothing in our Constitution suggests that government is a grantor of rights. Instead, government is a protector of rights.

In recognition that it's Congress that poses the greatest threat to our liberties, the framers used negative phrases against Congress throughout the Constitution such as: shall not abridge, infringe, deny, disparage, and shall not be violated, nor be denied. In a republican form of government, there is rule of law. All citizens, including government officials, are accountable to the same laws. Government power is limited and decentralized through a system of checks and balances. Government intervenes in civil society to protect its citizens against force and fraud but does not intervene in the cases of peaceable, voluntary exchange.

Contrast the framers' vision of a republic with that of a democracy. In a democracy, the majority rules either directly or through its elected representatives. As in a monarchy, the law is whatever the government determines it to be. Laws do not represent reason. They represent power. The restraint is upon the individual instead of government. Unlike that envisioned under a republican form of government, rights are seen as privileges and permissions that are granted by government and can be rescinded by government.

How about a few quotations demonstrating the disdain our founders held for democracy? James Madison, Federalist Paper No. 10: In a pure democracy, "there is nothing to check the inducement to sacrifice the weaker party or the obnoxious individual." At the 1787 Constitutional Convention, Edmund Randolph said, " ... that in tracing these evils to their origin every man had found it in the turbulence and follies of democracy." John Adams said, "Remember, democracy never lasts long. It soon wastes, exhausts, and murders itself. There was never a democracy yet that did not commit suicide." Chief Justice John Marshall observed, "Between a balanced republic and a democracy, the difference is like that between order and chaos." In a word or two, the founders knew that a democracy would lead to the same kind of tyranny the colonies suffered under King George III. The framers gave us a Constitution that is replete with undemocratic mechanisms. One that has come in for recent criticism and calls for its elimination is the Electoral College. In their wisdom, the framers gave us the Electoral College so that in presidential elections large, heavily populated states couldn't democratically run roughshod over small, sparsely populated states.

Here's my question. Do Americans share the republican values laid out by our founders, and is it simply a matter of our being unschooled about the differences between a republic and a democracy? Or is it a matter of preference and we now want the kind of tyranny feared by the founders where Congress can do anything it can muster a majority vote to do? I fear it's the latter.

Not Yours to Give

Wednesday, February 9, 2005

Charity to man's fellow man is praiseworthy, and Americans are the most generous people on Earth. According to a quote by American philanthropist Daniel Rose in "An Exceptional Nation," an article in *Philanthropy* magazine (November/December 2004), "American private charitable contributions this year will exceed $200 billion, equal to about 10 percent of the total federal budget; that some 70 percent of U.S. households make charitable cash contributions; and that over half of all U.S. adults will volunteer an estimated 20 billion hours in charitable activities." Americans contribute six or seven times more than some of our European neighbors.

What about President Bush's $350 million commitment for earthquake and tsunami relief—is that just as praiseworthy? Let's look at it. Charity is reaching into one's own pockets to assist his fellow man in need. Reaching into someone else's pocket to assist one's fellow man hardly qualifies as charity. When done privately, we deem it theft, and the individual risks jail time.

What would some of our ancestors say about government "charity"? James Madison, the father of our Constitution, said, in a January 1794 speech in the House of Representatives, "The government of the United States is a definite government, confined to specified objects. It is not like state governments, whose powers are more general. Charity is no part of the legislative duty of the government."

A few years later, Virginia Rep. William Giles condemned a relief measure for fire victims, saying it was neither the purpose nor the right of Congress to "attend to what generosity and humanity require, but to what the Constitution and their duty require." Unlike President Bush, a few of our former presidents understood that charity is not a government function. Franklin Pierce, our 14th president, vetoed a bill to help the mentally ill, saying, "I cannot find any authority in the Constitution for public charity," adding that to approve such spending, "would be contrary to the letter and the spirit of the Constitution and subversive to the whole theory upon which the Union of these States is founded."

In 1887, President Grover Cleveland, our 22nd and 24th president, said, when he vetoed a bill to assist drought-inflicted counties in Texas, "I feel obliged to withhold my approval of the plan to indulge in benevolent and charitable sentiment through the appropriation of public funds. . . . I find no warrant for such an appropriation in the Constitution."

Tennessee Rep. Col. Davy Crockett, in a speech before the House of Representatives, said, in protest against a $10,000 appropriation for a widow of a distinguished naval officer, "We have the right, as individuals, to give away as much of our own money as we please in charity, but as members of Congress, we have no right to appropriate a dollar of the public money."

I'd like to ask President Bush and members of the 109th Congress whether they've discovered the constitutional authority for charitable expenditures undiscovered by James Madison, William Giles, Presidents Franklin Pierce and Grover Cleveland, and Davy Crockett. Major U.S. companies, such as American Express, Pfizer, Exxon Mobil and General Motors donated millions of dollars to tsunami relief efforts. Like those of the Bush administration and Congress, their actions aren't praiseworthy at all. The CEOs who authorized these "charitable" donations were reaching not into their own pockets but into the pockets of their shareholders.

I get the feeling that the train of constitutional principles has left the station and the recent tsunami episode is simply another symptom of American obliviousness to constitutional government. Today's politicians can't be held fully responsible for our abandonment of constitutional government. While they can be blamed for not being statesmen, the lion's share of the blame rests with 280 million Americans. Elected officials simply mirror public misunderstanding or contempt for constitutional principles. Tragically, adherence to the constitutional values of men like James Madison and Davy Crockett would spell political suicide in today's America.

Social Security Deceit

Wednesday, February 23, 2005

President Bush's call to allow Americans to take a portion of the money they pay as Social Security taxes to set up private retirement accounts has to be a good idea. Why? The more of what a person earns that's in his pocket and under his control, the better off he will be. At a later date, when the details of the president's plans are known, I'll address the various reform plans under debate. For now, let's look at some of the gross political deceit, lies and unkept promises that have become a part of Social Security.

Here's what a 1936 government Social Security pamphlet said: "After the first 3 years—that is to say, beginning in 1940—you will pay, and your employer will pay, 1.5 cents for each dollar you earn, up to $3,000 a year. . . . Beginning in 1943, you will pay 2 cents, and so will your employer, for every dollar you earn for the next 3 years. . . . And finally, beginning in 1949, twelve years from now, you and your employer will each pay 3 cents on each dollar you earn, up to $3,000 a year. . . . That is the most you will ever pay."

Had Congress lived up to those promises, where $3,000 was the maximum earnings subject to Social Security tax, controlling for inflation today's $50,000-a-year wage earner would pay about $700 in Social Security taxes, as opposed to the more than $3,000 that he pays today.

The next big lie is from the same Social Security pamphlet: "Beginning November 24, 1936, the United States government will set up a Social Security account for you. . . . The checks will come to you as a right." First, there's no Social Security account containing your money, but more importantly, the U.S. Supreme Court has ruled on two occasions that Americans have no legal right to Social Security payments.

In Helvering v. Davis (1937), the court held that Social Security was not an insurance program, saying, "The proceeds of both (employee and employer) taxes are to be paid into the Treasury like internal-revenue taxes generally, and are not earmarked in any way."

In a later decision, Flemming v. Nestor (1960), the court said, "To engraft upon Social Security system a concept of 'accrued property rights' would deprive it of the flexibility and boldness in adjustment to ever-changing conditions which it demands. . . ." That flexibility and boldness mean Congress can constitutionally cut benefits, raise retirement age, raise Social Security taxes and do anything it wishes, including eliminating payments.

If a private retirement company reneged on its promises, we could take it to court. If Congress reneges on its promises, there's no judicial course of action whatsoever.

Vital to any Ponzi scheme, like Social Security, is the ability to recruit as many suckers as possible. In 1999, a little noticed part of President Clinton's plan to "save" Social Security was to force 5 million previously exempted employees into Social Security. If they were forced into Social Security, it would have created billions in additional revenue. Guess what. Twelve senators, including five Democrats— Dianne Feinstein (D.-Calif.), Barbara Boxer (D.-Calif.), Christopher Dodd (D.-Conn.), Richard Durbin (D.-Ill.) and Edward Kennedy (D.-Mass.)—descended on the White House to demand that President Clinton not support forcing 5 million of their constituents into Social Security. They warned of the adverse impact on employees in terms of lower rates of return and lost flexibility.

Isn't that great? These are the same politicians who are now resisting President Bush's call to allow Americans to take a part of their Social Security taxes to put into private retirement accounts. If they'd go to bat for those 5 million workers to remain out of Social Security, to avoid the adverse impact of lower rates of return and lost flexibility, why would they fight to deny tens of millions of workers a right to use a portion of their taxes to do the same?

Stupid Airport Security

Wednesday, April 6, 2005

For most of my professional life, I've traveled frequently—sometimes boarding a commercial flight two, three or four times a month for lucrative speaking engagements. Over the past three years, the frequency has fallen to an average of once or twice a year. The reason is simple. I don't want to be arrested or detained for questioning some of the senseless airport security procedures. Don't get me wrong. I'm for security but against stupidity. Let's look at some of it starting off with a hypothetical question.

You're a detective. A woman reports a rape. How would you go about finding the perpetrator? Would you confine your search to males or would you include females as well?

You say, "Williams, that would be stupid to include females!" But not if Transportation Secretary Norman Mineta were your supervisor. You might be ordered to investigate females and males as possible suspects to avoid committing the politically incorrect sin of sex profiling.

With regard to airport security, Mineta said, "While the security procedures are not based on the race, ethnicity, religion or gender of passengers, we also want to assure that in practice, the system does not disproportionately select members of any particular minority group." That means Americans who fit no terrorist profile—mothers with children, blind and disabled people, elderly couples—are frisked, groped and hassled. What's even more stupid is that pilots and flight attendants face similar screening. Here's my question to you: If a pilot is intent on crashing a plane into a building, does he need to carry anything on board to do it?

On several occasions, having gone through screening without setting off any alarms, I've been pulled aside for additional screening. Imagine that you're there with a Transportation Security Administration (TSA) supervisor and I'm being subjected to additional screening. You offer him a bet whereby if Williams is discovered to be in possession of something that endangers security—a knife, gun or bomb—you'll pay him $5,000, and if I'm not, he'll pay you $100. Do you think he'll take your offer? I'm betting he wouldn't.

What about the TSA confiscation of "dangerous" personal items such as tweezers, hat pins, sewing scissors, knitting needles, etc.? I hope I'm not giving the TSA ideas, but I've watched a number of television shows featuring supermax prisons like California's Pelican Bay. Among the items prisoners fashion into lethal weapons are ball-point pens, belts, eyeglass temples, glass containers and toothbrushes, all of which the TSA permits on airplanes. So what's the TSA's reasoning for allowing ballpoint pens on planes but not tweezers?

Most hijackings and recent terrorist acts have been committed by young Muslim extremists. That's not to say that all or nearly all Muslims pose a threat to security. But if one is looking for potential terrorists, the larger proportion of resources should be spent screening Muslim passengers. Screening the blind and disabled, mothers and children, and senior citizens is not going to have much of a payoff unless the goal is not to have tweezers or a G.I. Joe doll holding a rifle on the plane.

If I were a terrorist, I'd appreciate the fact that the TSA treats every passenger as having an equal likelihood of being a security threat. Fewer resources would be available to screen me. When law-abiding people are the subject of profiling, it's unfair, and they are insulted—and rightfully so. The true source of the injustice they face are those responsible for making "Muslim" near synonymous with "terrorism."

Even if I don't fly commercial anymore, I care about the TSA's waste of resources. There are potential terrorist targets in many areas such as ports, railroads and infrastructure, but roughly 90 percent of TSA's funding is spent on airports operating under the assumption that every passenger and every bag have an equal likelihood of being a security threat. That's stupid.

Stupid Airport Security II

Wednesday, April 13, 2005

Hundreds of readers responded to last week's column about airport security. These were letters from Americans who fit no terrorist pro-file—airline pilots, mothers traveling with children, disabled people, elderly and other law-abiding Americans—and yet were frisked, groped and hassled. The Transportation Security Administration (TSA) behaves as if all passengers and all baggage pose an equal se-curity threat, and that's stupid, because not nearly all passengers and baggage pose a security threat. They've seized articles such as tweez-ers, toy soldiers, hat pins, sewing scissors and other items they deem as threatening to flight security.

I've solved my problem with the TSA. They have their procedures, and I have mine. Mine include minimizing my exposure to stupidity. Therefore, where I used to board a commercial flight three or four times a month, over the last three years, I've reduced it to once, maybe twice, a year.

Some of the letters reported more stupidity on behalf of the TSA than I imagined. I'll highlight some of them. One person wrote that he, his wife and son were stopped, questioned and searched at length by TSA and FBI officials. It turned out there was a terror alert for a person named Harry Smith (not the true name). The couple's 5-year-old son's name was also Harry Smith. How much brains do you think it requires for the FBI and TSA to immediately realize that their 5-year-old son was the wrong Harry Smith?

Another writer wrote about his 88-year-old, hunched over, arthritis-ridden father, barely able to walk, being searched, questioned and scanned and, as a result, brought to tears. Airline pilots going through security are searched and asked to empty their pockets, even though they wear photo identification tags and the TSA accepts the fact that they're indeed pilots. Here's my question: If a pilot wanted to fly a plane into a building, would he need a weapon to do so?

There's little threat of another 9-11 hijacking event. First, sky marshals are randomly assigned to flights. But more important than that is if a hijacking occurred, passengers, knowing they were being flown to their death, would subdue the hijackers. Giving them greater incentive to do so is the likelihood of an F-14 fighter jet flying up to shoot the plane down. The greater threat to airport security is the placement of a bomb onboard. The TSA practice of seizing harmless personal items from passengers is a waste of resources. Fortunately, the TSA now permits some items formerly prohibited, such as knitting needles, corkscrews and cigar cutters.

Let's apply a bit of economic analysis to the TSA. There's little cost borne by the TSA for harassing passengers. Screeners have an eight-hour-a-day job. So if you have to wait in long lines, be harassed and miss your plane, what's it to them, considering the docile passenger response? Many Americans accept the TSA policy, saying that it makes them feel safer. I'd ask those Americans how much safer they would feel seeing an 88-year-old arthritic man, barely able to walk, given the treatment. Asking the question whether every passenger is a security threat is similar to a munitions manufacturer asking whether every hand grenade is good. A munitions manufacturer wouldn't pull the pin on every hand grenade to see if it was a dud. He'd devise a test, otherwise he'd bear huge costs by assuming each hand grenade had the equal probability of being a dud. Similarly, the TSA should devise a test to determine which passenger poses the higher probability of being a security threat. A good start might be to establish passenger characteristics of previous terrorist attacks.

Stupid Airport Security III

Wednesday, April 20, 2005

Several airport security screeners have sent me polite letters criticizing some of my comments in my last two columns, prompting this question to you: In managing our personal security, should we guard against possible or probable threats? Consider the measures and the resource expenditures I might take to guard Mrs. Williams and me against all possible threats to our security.

Even though I live in Pennsylvania, well outside of tornado alley, I'd construct a tornado shelter because it's possible for a tornado to strike anywhere. I'd no longer get into my car and drive off without doing a thorough check of my car's hydraulic brake system for leakage. I'd build an iron-reinforced roof to guard against the possibility of a meteor. I'd also purchase a metal detector to do sweeps of my property to guard against the possibility someone might have buried a land mine. I'd hire a detective and forensic accountant. Even though Mrs. Williams and I have been married 45 years, it is possible that she might be stashing some of my money into a Swiss bank account.

Were I to take those measures, I'm sure the average person would label me as either paranoid or stupid. Why? It would take resources away from guarding against more probable threats to our security, such as burglary. While my focusing on all possible threats wouldn't be smart, it would make me a prime candidate to become a Transportation Security Administration (TSA) official. Their vision of airport security is to focus on the possible as well as the probable.

It is indeed possible for an 88-year-old man crippled with debilitating arthritis to be a terrorist. It's possible that one of our Marines returning from Iraq for stateside reassignment, carrying ID and official reassignment orders, is also a member of al Qaeda ready to take out an airplane. It's possible for a mother accompanied by her four children, or a 92-year-old woman, to be "mules" paid by terrorists to bring something on board to blow up the plane. It is also possible that a pilot plans to blow his plane up with a shoe bomb. That's reason for making him take his shoes off. It's possible that a blind person carrying a cigarette lighter will give it to a terrorist accomplice to light a shoe bomb in flight. There are other possible security threats. Women's stockings and underwear, as well as men's ties and belts, can be used as garrotes for strangulation. Soda straws can be used to blow poison darts.

While these are all possible threats, the question is, how probable are they? Resource expenditure on security threats just because they are possible means that those same resources cannot be spent on those far more probable. Moreover, if there were full implementation of the program to permit pilots to be armed, the more probable threats would become less so. In other words, arming pilots and some crew members would lessen a whole class of security threats.

The TSA's determined opposition to passenger profiling is in itself a threat to airport security. Take their additional screening. They have every incentive to be politically correct. But suppose the TSA had to pay $1,000 to each passenger they selected for additional screening who was found to be no security threat. You can bet they'd develop a screening method that made more sense, and it would include some sort of passenger profiling, including racial profiling. And, by the way, liberals shouldn't fret, because the U.S. Supreme Court has ruled in several affirmative action cases that provided there's a compelling state interest, race can be used in decision making.

It's my opinion that sensible TSA security measures would allow us to reallocate resources away from policing against possible but improbable threats to policing the far more probable source of threats—one being our border with Mexico.

Is It Permissible?

Wednesday, September 21, 2005

Last week, President Bush promised the nation that the federal government will pay for most of the costs of repairing hurricane-ravaged New Orleans, adding, "There is no way to imagine America without New Orleans, and this great city will rise again." There's no question that New Orleans and her sister Gulf Coast cities have been struck with a major disaster, but should our constitution become a part of the disaster? You say, "What do you mean, Williams?" Let's look at it.

In February 1887, President Grover Cleveland, upon vetoing a bill appropriating money to aid drought-stricken farmers in Texas, said, "I find no warrant for such an appropriation in the Constitution, and I do not believe that the power and the duty of the General Government ought to be extended to the relief of individual suffering which is in no manner properly related to the public service or benefit."

President Cleveland added, "The friendliness and charity of our countrymen can always be relied upon to relieve their fellow citizens in misfortune. This has been repeatedly and quite lately demonstrated. Federal aid in such cases encourages the expectation of paternal care on the part of the Government and weakens the sturdiness of our national character, while it prevents the indulgence among our people of that kindly sentiment and conduct which strengthens the bonds of a common brotherhood."

President Cleveland vetoed hundreds of congressional spending measures during his two-term presidency, often saying, "I can find no warrant for such an appropriation in the Constitution." But Cleveland wasn't the only president who failed to see charity as a function of the federal government. In 1854, after vetoing a popular appropriation to assist the mentally ill, President Franklin Pierce said, "I cannot find any authority in the Constitution for public charity." To approve such spending, argued Pierce, "would be contrary to the letter and the spirit of the Constitution and subversive to the whole theory upon which the Union of these States is founded."

In 1796, Rep. William Giles of Virginia condemned a relief measure for fire victims, saying that Congress didn't have a right to "attend to what generosity and humanity require, but to what the Constitution and their duty require." A couple of years earlier, James Madison, the father of our constitution, irate over a $15,000 congressional appropriation to assist some French refugees, said, "I cannot undertake to lay my finger on that article of the Constitution which granted a right to Congress of expending, on objects of benevolence, the money of their constituents."

Here's my question: Were the nation's founders, and some of their successors, callous and indifferent to human tragedy? Or, were they stupid and couldn't find the passages in the Constitution that authorized spending "on the objects of benevolence"?

Some people might say, "Aha! They forgot about the constitution's general welfare clause!" Here's what James Madison said: "With respect to the two words 'general welfare,' I have always regarded them as qualified by the detail of powers connected with them. To take them in a literal and unlimited sense would be a metamorphosis of the Constitution into a character which there is a host of proofs was not contemplated by its creators."

Thomas Jefferson explained, "Congress has not unlimited powers to provide for the general welfare, but only those specifically enumerated." In 1828, South Carolina Sen. William Drayton said, "If Congress can determine what constitutes the general welfare and can appropriate money for its advancement, where is the limitation to carrying into execution whatever can be effected by money?"

Don't get me wrong about this. I'm not being too critical of President Bush or any other politician. There's such a broad ignorance or contempt for constitutional principles among the American people that any politician who bore truth, faith and allegiance to the Constitution would commit political suicide.

Congressional Miracles

February 23, 2004

In Marcus Cook Connelly's spiritual play, "Green Pastures," God lamented to the Angel Gabriel, "Every time Ah passes a miracle, Ah has to pass fo' or five mo' to ketch up wid it," and adding "Even bein God ain't no bed of roses." That's something our congressmen should think about when they set out to create miracles.

George Will wrote an insightful article in the *Washington Post* (2/12/04) titled "Sweet and Sour Subsidies." He might have just as well titled it "Shooting Ourselves in the Foot." Chicago has been home to many of America's candy manufacturers but today they've fallen on hard times. In 1970, employment by Chicago's candy manufacturers totaled 15,000 and now it's 8,000 and falling. Brach used to employ about 2,300 people; now most of its jobs are in Mexico. Ferrara Pan Candy has also moved much of its production to Mexico. Yes, wages are lower in Mexico but wages aren't the only factor in candy manufacturers' flight from America. After all, Life Savers, which for 90 years manufactured in America, has moved to Canada where wages are comparable to ours.

One of the ignored stories in the clamor and demagoguery over job losses, not only in the candy industry but in others as well, is the devastating impact of congressionally created "miracles" on our industries. American sugar producers fight tooth and nail to keep foreign sugar imports out of our country. They've spent $722,000 in campaign contributions to both Democratic and Republican congressmen to enact sugar import tariffs and quotas.

As a result of their successful effort to get Congress to do their bidding, our domestic sugar prices are about three times higher than the world market price. While that's a miracle for the sugar industry and its employees, unfortunately, the miracle story doesn't end there. We all know that for every benefit there's a cost.

According to the Sugar Users' Association, an organization that represents companies who use sugar as an input, such as candy manufacturers, the protectionist miracle that Congress has created for the sugar industry has cost anywhere from 7,500 to 10,000 jobs in sugar-using industries due to higher sugar costs. Higher sugar costs make U.S. candy manufacturers less competitive in both domestic and world markets. Life Savers became more competitive simply by moving to Canada; they saved themselves a whopping $10 million dollars a year in sugar costs. You might ask, "How come sugar's cheaper in Canada? Are they a free trade country?" The answer is a big fat no. It's just that they don't have much, if any, of a sugar industry and hence there's little pressure on the Canadian Parliament to enact protectionist measures.

So what should Congress do? In the real world, when Congress enacts a miracle for one group of Americans, such as sugar producers, it creates a non-miracle for other Americans. Should Congress create a miracle for the sugar-using industry to offset the devastating effects of its miracle for sugar producers B like keeping imported candy out of the U.S? I don't know how that might work but I'm betting they'll run into the same problem God explained so aptly to the Angel Gabriel when He said, "Every time Ah passes a miracle, Ah has to pass fo' or five mo' to ketch up wid it." Surely, if Congress creates a miracle for candy manufacturers, that miracle is going to create a non-miracle for somebody else B at least those who eat candy or own candy retail stores.

Here's my suggestion for Congress. Just remember God's lament—"Even bein God ain't no bed of roses"—and get out of the miracle business.

Minimum Gasoline Prices

February 23, 2004

A couple of weeks ago heading down to George Mason University, I pulled into my favorite Wawa gasoline station just off the Bel Air, Maryland exit on I-95 South. At each of the twenty gasoline pumps there was a sign posted that Wawa would no longer dispense free coffee to its gasoline customers. Why? They were warned that dispensing free coffee puts them in violation of Maryland's gasoline minimum price law.

Here's my no-brainer question to you: do you suppose that Maryland enacted their gasoline minimum price law because irate customers complained to the state legislature that gasoline prices were too low? Even if you had just one ounce of brains you'd correctly answer no. Then the next question is just whose interest is served by, and just who lobbied for, Maryland's minimum gasoline price law? If you answered that it was probably Maryland's independent gas station owners, go to the head of the class.

Let's first establish a general economic principle. Whenever one sees statutory or quasi-statutory minimum prices, he is looking at a seller collusion against customers in general as well as particular sellers, those who are seen as charging too low a price. This economic principle applies whether you're talking about minimum wages, minimum dairy prices or minimum real estate sales commissions. Members of a seller's collusion call for statutory and quasi-statutory minimum prices so they can charge customers higher prices than they could otherwise in the absence of a statutory minimum.

You say, "Williams, that's preposterous; how can they sell legislators on the idea? After all buyers of gasoline are more numerous than sellers of gasoline." To answer that question you have to recognize a couple of other facts. First, legislators aren't known for being rocket scientists, and second, legislators love campaign contributions and satisfying the interests of lobbyists is more important to their political careers than serving the interests of consumers in general.

Lobbyists such as WMDA Service Station & Automotive Repair Association, the Gasoline Retailers Association and the Petroleum Marketers Association of America are able to sell legislators on the fairy tale that if high-marketing gasoline outlets such as Wawa, Sheetz, Wal-Mart and others are allowed to charge prices that are too low they'll drive all other gasoline stations out of business. Having done so, these high-marketing outlets could charge any price they pleased and make huge profits. In economics we call this strategy predatory pricing. It's an argument that has a ring of plausibility but there's little evidence anywhere anytime that a predatory pricing scheme produced results even remotely close to what would-be predators envisioned. Questioning this fairy tale and asking for evidence would never cross the mind of a legislator.

Another reason legislators can get away with establishing gasoline seller collusion has to do with another economic phenomenon called "narrow well-defined benefits and small widely dispersed costs." The beneficiaries of the gasoline sellers collusion are relatively few in number and well organized. The victims, mainly gasoline customers, are difficult to organize and the costs they bear are relatively small and widespread. In other words, how many gasoline consumers would be willing to spend their time and energy fighting to unseat a legislator whose actions imposed, say, a nickel a gallon additional cost upon them. It's cheaper just to pay the nickel a gallon more and forget about it but, that's not true about gasoline retailers. It is worth their time and energy to pressure legislators for minimum price laws and politicians know this.

Maryland is not the only state with statutory minimum gasoline prices. It's joined by 12 other states including New York, Michigan and Wisconsin. Wisconsin legislators have the gall to call its government-sponsored seller collusion the "Unfair Sales Act."

Dangers of No Tax Liability

March 28, 2004

In last week's column, I reported on the Washington, D.C.–based Tax Foundation's study that estimated that forty-four percent of income earners will legally have no 2004 federal income tax liability. Their study concluded, "When all of the dependents of these income-producing households are counted, there are roughly 122 million Americans—44 percent of the U.S. population—outside of the federal income tax system."

The Bush administration sees removing the income tax burden on Americans at the lower end of the earnings spectrum, families earning less than $50,000 a year, as desirable. When President Reagan successfully got Congress to remove 6 million Americans from the tax rolls, he described his tax reform initiative as one of the proudest achievements of his administration. At the time, I argued that doing so was nothing to be proud about and I extend that same criticism to President Bush.

You might ask, "Why?" In general, I've always held that a tax cut for anybody, at any time, for any reason is a good thing because it keeps more of our earnings in our pockets and out of Washington. But there's a problem. Removing so many Americans from federal income tax liability contributes to the political problem that we're witnessing this election: class warfare and the politics of envy.

When 122 million Americans are outside of the federal income tax system, it's like throwing chum to our political sharks. These Americans become a natural spending constituency for big government politicians. After all if you have no income tax liability, how much do you care about how much Congress spends and the level of taxation? Political calls for tax cuts fall upon deaf ears. Survey polls reveal this. According to The Harris Poll taken in June 2003, 51 percent of Democrats thought the tax cuts enacted by Congress were a bad thing while 16 percent of Republicans thought so. Among Democrats 67 percent thought the tax cuts were unfair while 32 percent of Republicans thought so. When asked whether the $350 billion tax cut package will help your family finances, 59 percent of those surveyed said no and 35 percent said yes. Tax cuts to many Americans means just one thing: they threaten the handouts they receive.

There might be a correction for the political problems caused by large numbers of Americans with zero income tax liability. It might be politically incorrect to even mention it. I do not own stock, and hence have no financial stake, in Ford Motor Company. Do you think I should have voting rights, or any say so, in the matters of the company? I'm guessing that your answer is no.

So here's my idea. Every American regardless of any other consideration should have one vote in any federal election. Then every American should get one additional vote for every $10,000 he pays in federal income tax. With such a system, there'd be a modicum of linkage between one's financial stake in our country and his decision-making capacity.

This is not a far out idea. The Founders worried about it. James Madison's concern about class warfare between the rich and the poor led him to favor the House of Representatives being elected by the people at large and the Senate elected by property owners. He said, "It is nevertheless certain, that there are various ways in which the rich may oppress the poor; in which property may oppress liberty; and that the world is filled with examples. It is necessary that the poor should have a defense against the danger. On the other hand, the danger to the holders of property cannot be disguised, if they be undefended against a majority without property."

National Sales Tax

November 8, 2004

Representative John Linder (R. Georgia) has authored H.R. 25 "To promote freedom, fairness, and economic opportunity by repealing the income tax and other taxes, abolishing the Internal Revenue Service, and enacting a national sales tax to be administered primarily by the States." Before we look at whether a national sales tax is a good idea, how about a little Economics 101 just to convince you that government spending, not government taxation, is the true measure of governmental impact on our lives?

Keeping the numbers small, suppose the annual value of what Americans produce, our (GDP), is $100. If government spends $40 of it, of necessity the government must force us to spend $40 less. There are several ways this can be done. Government could tax us $40. Government could borrow, thereby driving up interest rates, thus reducing private spending. Government could simply print money which would cause inflation and reduce our purchasing power. Finally, government could employ some combination of the three. The bottom line is that if government spends $40 of our GDP, we can't spend that same $40.

There's no question that tax reform is needed but tax reform is secondary to a much larger issue—federal spending. From 1787 to 1920, except during war, federal spending was a mere 3 percent of GDP compared to today's 20 percent. If the federal government takes only 3 percent of the GDP, just about any tax system is relatively non-oppressive. However, if government were to take 50, 60, or 70 percent of the GDP, you tell me what tax system would be non-oppressive.

There's no question that some forms of taxation are worse than others. In addition to its economic disincentive effects and intrusions on personal privacy, our income tax has huge compliance costs estimated to be between $250 and $500 billion. Abolition of the IRS, and the income tax code it enforces, replaced by a national sales, would create greater economic incentives, enhance personal privacy, and lower tax compliance cost by an estimated 90 percent. There'd also be greater faith and allegiance to our Founders' constitutional vision where Article I, Section 9 that says "No Capitation, or other direct, Tax shall be laid, unless in Proportion to the Census or Enumeration herein before directed to be taken." The Founders feared the abuse and the government power inherent in an income tax. Another benefit of a national sales tax is that our being taxed 23 to 30 percent with every purchase we become more aware of the cost of government. Income taxes and corporate taxes conceal that cost.

Before we accept a national sales tax, there are two minimal requirements. First, there must be a repeal of the 16th Amendment so Congress can't hit us with both an income and sales tax. Second, there must be a constitutional amendment fixing the national sales tax at a certain percentage that can only be increased by a three-fourths vote of the House of Representatives.

People have advocated a national sales tax or a flat income tax for years and I don't want to rain on their parade. But here's my prediction: Congress will never enact a sales tax or a flat tax. Why? The two most powerful congressional committees are the House Ways and Means Committee and the Senate Finance Committees. Both dispense tax favors to different Americans that come at the expense of other Americans. With a sales or flat tax, their Santa Claus roles, not to mention campaign contributions, would be diminished. On top of that they'd have restricted opportunities for social engineering through fiddling around with the tax code.

My personal preference is a constitutional amendment limiting federal spending to a fixed percentage, say 10 percent, of the GDP. You say, "Williams, why 10 percent?" My answer is that if 10 percent is good enough for the Baptist Church, it ought to be good enough for the U.S. Congress.

Income

Income lends itself to considerable demagoguery because people do not understand the sources of income or at least often behave as if they do not. It is okay to speak of the distribution of income if one is speaking of it in a statistical sense. But many times we hear people speaking of the distribution of income as if there were a dealer of dollars. Thus, the income distribution is unfair because the dollar dealer deals one person many dollars and deals others few. Thus, justice requires a redealing of the dollars—income redistribution of the ill-gotten gains of the few to the many. In the honest-to-God real world, for the most part, income is earned through one's capacity to serve his fellow man—in a word, one's productivity. That person might serve his fellow man as a carpenter who would repair a house or a plumber who might fix a toilet or a chemist who might produce a drug. For doing so, his fellow man gives him dollars that we might think of as "certificates of performance" that serve as proof that one has served his fellow man. The greater his capacity to serve his fellow man, and the greater the value his fellow man places on those services, the greater the number of the certificates of performance received. Those certificates of performance enable the carpenter, plumber, or chemist to make claims on what his fellow man produces, be it a car, a television, or groceries. This method of deciding who gets what would appear to be the height of morality—the requirement that one serve his fellow man in order to have a claim on what his fellow man produces. That moral standard contrasts with government allocation, where the government, through the tax code, takes what one's fellow man produces to give it to another.

Aside from this moral issue is the distortion of facts about income. Listening to some politicians and talking heads lamenting the plight of America's middle class and poor, you would have to conclude that things are going to hell in a handbasket. According to them, there's wage stagnation and the rich are getting richer and the poor becoming poorer. According to a U.S. Treasury study of income tax returns from 1996 and 2005, controlling for inflation, nearly 58 percent of the poorest in-

come group in 1996 had moved to a higher income group by 2005. Twenty-six percent of them achieved middle or upper-middle class income, and more than 5 percent made it into the highest income group. This finding of income mobility continues the findings of other studies since 1960.

What about claims of a disappearing middle class? Controlling for inflation, in 1967, 8 percent of households had an annual income of $75,000 and up; in 2003, more than 26 percent did. In 1967, 17 percent of households had a $50,000 to $75,000 income; in 2003, it was 18 percent. In 1967, 22 percent of households were in the $35,000 to $50,000 income group; by 2003, the number had fallen to 15 percent. During the same period, the $15,000 to $35,000 category fell from 31 percent to 25 percent, and the under $15,000 category fell from 21 percent to 16 percent. The conclusion is that if the middle class is disappearing, it's doing so by swelling the ranks of the upper classes. In fact, at least in terms of absolute values, we are going to have to change the definition of what is middle class and make it higher.

There is no evidence for the canard that the poor are getting poorer. The evidence shows that, while the rich are getting richer, the poor are getting richer too. The average poor person has what most Americans could not afford as recently as thirty or forty years ago. In 1971, only about 32 percent of all Americans enjoyed air-conditioning in their homes. By 2001, 76 percent of poor people had air-conditioning. In 1971, only 43 percent of Americans owned a color television; in 2001, 97 percent of poor people owned at least one. In 1971, 1 percent of American homes had a microwave oven; in 2001, 73 percent of poor people had one. Forty-six percent of poor households own their homes. Only about 6 percent of poor households are overcrowded. The average poor American has more living space than the average nonpoor individual living in Paris, London, Vienna, Athens, and other European cities. Nearly 75 percent of poor households own a car; 30 percent own two or more cars. Seventy-eight percent of the poor have a VCR or DVD player; 62 percent have cable or satellite TV reception; and 33 percent have an automatic dishwasher. There is little or no poverty in America in either the global or the intertemporal sense. But, given that fact, to avoid being poor, according to current definitions of poverty, is not rocket *science. Just graduate from high school, work at any kind of job, do not have children before marriage, and stay away from criminal activity. The columns that follow address these and other income issues.*

Should We Save Jobs?

Wednesday, January 26, 2005

Now that the elections are over, there's little political gain for demagoguery about jobs, but let's prepare ourselves for the next time. Losing a job means a financial crunch and readjustment regardless of the source of job loss. If it's not from an economic downturn, the loss might be a result of outsourcing, but much more likely, it's a result of technological innovation. Job destruction and job creation through natural market forces are enriching. Calling for Congress to save or create jobs is to court disaster.

Let's look at a bit of job-loss history. Anthony B. Bradley, a research fellow at the Grand Rapids, Mich.–based Acton Institute, has written an article on the subject, "Productivity and the Ice Man: Understanding Outsourcing." Citing the work of Forrester Research Inc., a technology research firm, Bradley says, "Of the 2.7 million jobs lost over the past three years, only 300,000 have resulted from outsourcing." Job losses and job gains have always been a part of our history.

Let's look at some of the history of job loss described in Bradley's article. We might also ponder whether measures should have been taken to save these jobs. In 1858, Lyman Blake patented a shoemaking machine that ultimately destroyed jobs hand-making shoes. In 1919, General Motors started selling Frigidaire. As Bradley says, "This 'electric ice box' wiped out a whole set of occupations, including icebox manufacturers, ice gatherers, and the manufacturers of the tools and equipment needed to handle large blocks of ice."

Auto manufacturers use thousands of robots for tasks that people used to do such as spot welding, painting, machine loading, parts transfer and assembly. Robots have replaced thousands of workers in electronic assembly and in mounting microchips on circuit boards, reports Bradley.

We could probably think of hundreds of jobs that either don't exist or exist in far fewer numbers than in the past—jobs such as elevator operator, TV repairman and coal deliveryman. "Creative destruction" is a discovery process where we find ways to produce goods and services more cheaply. That in turn makes us all richer.

That same principle applies when it's outsourcing serving as the engine for creative destruction. Daniel W. Drezner, assistant professor of political science at the University of Chicago, discusses outsourcing in "The Outsourcing Bogeyman" (*Foreign Affairs*, May/June 2004). Professor Drezner reports that for every dollar spent on outsourcing to India, the United States reaps between $1.12 and $1.14 in benefits. Why? U.S. firms save money and become more profitable, benefiting shareholders and increasing returns on investment. In the process, U.S. workers are reallocated to more competitive, mostly better-paying jobs.

Drezner also points out that large software companies such as Microsoft and Oracle have increased outsourcing and used the savings for investment and larger domestic payrolls. Nationally, 70,000 computer programmers lost their jobs between 1999 and 2003, but more than 115,000 computer software engineers found higher-paying jobs during that same period. By the way, when outsourcing doesn't work, companies backtrack, as have Dell and Lehman Brothers, which have moved some of their call centers back to the United States from India because of customer complaints.

The last election campaign featured great angst over the loss of manufacturing jobs. The number of U.S. manufacturing jobs has fallen, but it has little to do with outsourcing and a lot to do with technological innovation—and it's a worldwide phenomenon. During the seven years from 1995 through 2002, Drezner notes, U.S. manufacturing employment fell by 11 percent. Globally, manufacturing jobs fell by 11 percent. China lost 15 percent of its manufacturing jobs, and Brazil lost 20 percent. But guess what. Globally, manufacturing output rose by 30 percent during the same period. Technological progress is the primary cause for the decrease in manufacturing jobs.

What should a person do when innovation or international trade costs him his job? Do what the iceman did when Frigidaire cost him his job. Instead of calling on Congress to enact job protectionist measures, he did what was necessary to find another job.

The Temperamental Minimum Wage

Wednesday, May 9, 2007

The first fundamental law of demand postulates that the lower the price of something, the more will be demanded, and the higher the price, the less will be demanded. To my knowledge, there are no known exceptions to the law of demand. That was until last fall when 650 economists, including several Nobel Laureates, signed a letter calling for an increase in the minimum wage.

They said, "We believe that a modest increase in the minimum wage would improve the well-being of low-wage workers and would not have the adverse effects that critics have claimed." I'm not sure if these 650 economists meant increases in the minimum wage will have no effect on the employment of low-wage workers or if they meant its magnitude won't be large. If their argument is the former, I'm embarrassed for them.

Maybe these economists, like House Speaker Nancy Pelosi, see the law of demand as being somewhat temperamental—sometimes having an effect and sometimes not. This would be like a physicist suggesting that the velocity of light, in a vacuum, is temperamental— sometimes a constant and sometimes not. But they and Speaker Pelosi might have a point.

On Jan. 10, the House of Representatives voted to raise the minimum wage from $5.15 to $7.25 per hour. Their bill, for the first time, extended the federal minimum wage to the U.S. territory of the Northern Mariana Islands, but it exempted American Samoa, another U.S. Pacific Ocean territory. American Samoa would have been the only U.S. territory not subject to the federal minimum wage. If increases in the minimum wage, like my 650 fellow economists claim, are so helpful to low-wage workers, why deprive Samoan workers from the benefits? Are Speaker Pelosi and my fellow economists anti-Samoan?

StarKist Tuna, whose parent company is Del Monte, and Chicken of the Sea employ nearly 50 percent of the Samoan workforce. Samoan cannery workers earn about $3.50 an hour. I'll give you one guess what would happen if the minimum wage were raised to $7.25 an hour. Here's a hint: The average cannery wage in Thailand is 67 cents an hour, and in the Philippines, it's 66 cents. If you guessed that StarKist and Chicken of the Sea might move their operations to Thailand or the Philippines, go to the head of the class. Perhaps Speaker Pelosi agrees that mandating a higher wage would have an unemployment effect, but just in Samoa.

There's a better explanation for Speaker Pelosi's position that has nothing to do with the possible fickleness of the law of demand. StarKist, which owns one of the two Samoan packing plants, has been a big opponent of increases in the U.S. minimum wage. Del Monte, its parent company, is headquartered in Speaker Pelosi's San Francisco district. Chicken of the Sea is based in Southern California. It's not unreasonable to guess that Speaker Pelosi's position has to do with the interests of her well-heeled constituents. In any case, Samoans are off the hook for now because the proposed legislation enacting a higher minimum wage didn't pass Congress.

Many minimum wage supporters, like the Speaker, are hypocrites, but most supporters are decent people with an honest concern for the well-being of their fellow man. True compassion for our fellow man requires that we examine not the intentions behind public policy but the effects of that policy. There's no question that Congress can mandate the minimum wage at which a person is hired, but Congress hasn't found a way to mandate that a person have a level of productivity commensurate with the wage. Moreover, Congress hasn't chosen to mandate that an employer hire a person whose productivity is less than the minimum wage. This means higher minimum wages cause unemployment for the least-skilled workers.

Economists on the Loose

Wednesday, July 18, 2007

On July 11, *New York Times* reporter Patricia Cohen wrote an article titled, "In Economics Departments, a Growing Will to Debate Fundamental Assumptions." The article begins with, "For many economists, questioning free-market orthodoxy is akin to expressing a belief in intelligent design at a Darwin convention: Those who doubt the naturally beneficial workings of the market are considered deluded or crazy." Cohen then reports interviews with several prominent economists, one being Princeton professor Alan Blinder, former vice chairman of the Federal Reserve Bank.

Professor Blinder said, "What I've learned is anyone who says anything even obliquely that sounds hostile to free trade is treated as an apostate." Continuing his criticisms of mainstream economists, he adds that efforts to intervene in markets, such as mandatory minimum wages, industrial policy and price controls, are also viewed negatively.

First, let's establish a working definition of free markets; it's really simple. Free markets are simply millions upon millions of individual decision-makers, engaged in peaceable, voluntary exchange pursuing what they see in their best interests. People who denounce the free market and voluntary exchange, and are for control and coercion, believe they have more intelligence and superior wisdom to the masses. What's more, they believe they've been ordained to forcibly impose that wisdom on the rest of us. Of course, they have what they consider good reasons for doing so, but every tyrant that has ever existed has had what he believed were good reasons for restricting the liberty of others.

Tyrants are against the free market because it implies voluntary exchange. Tyrants do not trust that people acting voluntarily will do what the tyrant thinks they ought to do. Therefore, they want to replace the market with economic planning, or as Professor Blinder calls it—industrial policy.

Economic planning is nothing more than the forcible superseding of other people's plans by the powerful elite. For example, I might plan to purchase a car, a shirt or apples from a foreign producer because I see it in my best interest. The powerful elite might supersede my plan, through import tariffs and quotas, because they think I should make the purchases from a domestic producer.

My daughter might plan to work for the hardware guy down the street for $4 an hour. She agrees; he agrees; her mother says it's OK, and I say it's OK. The powerful elite say, "We're going to supersede that plan because it's not being transacted at the price we think it ought be—the minimum wage."

Cohen also interviewed Professor David Card, saying that he's done "groundbreaking research on the effect of the minimum wage." Literally hundreds of studies show that increases in the minimum wage cause unemployment for the least-skilled worker, a group dominated by teenagers, particularly black teenagers. But Professor Card's study asserts that increases in minimum wage actually increase employment. Besides the fact that reviews of his study show flawed statistical techniques, that assertion doesn't even pass the smell test. If it did, then whenever there's high unemployment, anywhere in the world, governments could eliminate it by mandating higher minimum wages.

Robert Reich, President Clinton's labor secretary, said that economists who question free market theories really "want to speak to the reality of our time." That's incredible. Reality doesn't depend on whether it's 1907 or 2007. Reich probably thinks the reality of the laws of demand depends on what year it is. I wonder whether he thinks the reality of the laws of gravity does as well.

The ideas expressed by economists interviewed by Cohen, while out of the mainstream of a large majority of economists, are solidly in the mainstream of mankind's traditional vision. Throughout history, the right to pursue one's goals in a peaceable, voluntary manner, without direction, control and coercion, has won a hostile reception. There's little older in history than the idea that some should give orders and others obey.

Are the Poor Getting Poorer?

Wednesday, October 31, 2007

People who want more government income redistribution programs often sell their agenda with the lament, "The poor are getting poorer and the rich are getting richer," but how about some evidence and you decide? I think the rich are getting richer, and so are the poor.

According to the most recent census, about 35 million Americans live in poverty. Heritage Foundation scholar Robert Rector, using several government reports, gives us some insights about these people in his paper: "Understanding Poverty and Economic Inequality in the United States" http://www.heritage.org/Research/Welfare/bg1796.cfm.

In 1971, only about 32 percent of all Americans enjoyed air conditioning in their homes. By 2001, 76 percent of poor people had air conditioning. In 1971, only 43 percent of Americans owned a color television; in 2001, 97 percent of poor people owned at least one. In 1971, 1 percent of American homes had a microwave oven; in 2001, 73 percent of poor people had one. Forty-six percent of poor households own their homes. Only about 6 percent of poor households are overcrowded. The average poor American has more living space than the average non-poor individual living in Paris, London, Vienna, Athens and other European cities.

Nearly three-quarters of poor households own a car; 30 percent own two or more cars. Seventy-eight percent of the poor have a VCR or DVD player; 62 percent have cable or satellite TV reception; and one-third have an automatic dishwasher.

For the most part, long-term poverty today is self-inflicted. To see this, let's examine some numbers from the Census Bureau's 2004 Current Population Survey. There's one segment of the black population that suffers only a 9.9 percent poverty rate, and only 13.7 percent of their under-5-year-olds are poor. There's another segment of the black population that suffers a 39.5 percent poverty rate, and 58.1 percent of its under-5-year-olds are poor.

Among whites, one population segment suffers a 6 percent poverty rate, and only 9.9 percent of its under-5-year-olds are poor. Another segment of the white population suffers a 26.4 percent poverty rate, and 52 percent of its under-5-year-olds are poor.

What do you think distinguishes the high and low poverty populations? The only statistical distinction between both the black and white populations is marriage. There is far less poverty in married-couple families, where presumably at least one of the spouses is employed. Fully 85 percent of black children living in poverty reside in a female-headed household.

Poverty is not static for people willing to work. A University of Michigan study shows that only 5 percent of those in the bottom fifth of the income distribution in 1975 remained there in 1991. What happened to them? They moved up to the top three-fifths of the income distribution—middle class or higher. Moreover, three out of 10 of the lowest income earners in 1975 moved all the way into the top fifth of income earners by 1991. Those who were poor in 1975 had an inflation-adjusted average income gain of $27,745 by 1991. Those workers who were in the top fifth of income earners in 1975 were better off in 1991 by an average of only $4,354. The bottom line is, the richer are getting richer and the poor are getting richer.

Poverty in the United States, in an absolute sense, has virtually disappeared. Today, there's nothing remotely resembling poverty of yesteryear. However, if poverty is defined in the relative sense, the lowest fifth of income-earners, "poverty" will always be with us. No matter how poverty is defined, if I were an unborn spirit, condemned to a life of poverty, but God allowed me to choose which nation I wanted to be poor in, I'd choose the United States. Our poor must be the envy of the world's poor.

Income Mobility

Wednesday, December 5, 2007

Listening to people like Lou Dobbs, John Edwards and Mike Huckabee lamenting the plight of America's middle class and poor, you'd have to conclude that things are going to hell in a hand basket. According to them, there's wage stagnation, while the rich are getting richer and the poor becoming poorer. There are a couple of updates that tell quite a different story.

The Nov. 13 *Wall Street Journal* editorial "Movin' On Up" reports on a recent U.S. Treasury study of income tax returns from 1996 and 2005. The study tracks what happened to tax filers 25 years of age and up during this 10-year period. Controlling for inflation, nearly 58 percent of the poorest income group in 1996 moved to a higher income group by 2005. Twenty-six percent of them achieved middle or upper-middle class income, and over 5 percent made it into the highest income group.

Over the decade, the inflation-adjusted median income of all tax filers rose by 24 percent. As such, it refutes Dobbs-Edwards-Huckabee claims about stagnant incomes. In fact, only one income group experienced a decline in real income. That was the richest one percent, who saw an income drop of nearly 26 percent over the 10-year period. The editors explain that these people might have been rich for a few years, had some capital gains, or could not stand up to the competition with new entrepreneurs and wealth creators.

The U.S. Treasury study confirms previous studies dating back to the 1960s, concluding, "The basic finding of this analysis is that relative income mobility is approximately the same in the last 10 years as it was in the previous decade." As such, it points to a uniquely American feature: Just because you know where a person ended up in life doesn't mean you can be sure about where he started. Most of today's higher income and wealthy did not start out that way.

What about claims of a disappearing middle class? Let's do some detective work. Controlling for inflation, in 1967, 8 percent of households had an annual income of $75,000 and up; in 2003, more than 26 percent did. In 1967, 17 percent of households had a $50,000 to $75,000 income; in 2003, it was 18 percent. In 1967, 22 percent of households were in the $35,000 to $50,000 income group; by 2003, it had fallen to 15 percent. During the same period, the $15,000 to $35,000 category fell from 31 percent to 25 percent, and the under $15,000 category fell from 21 percent to 16 percent. The only reasonable conclusion from this evidence is that if the middle class is disappearing, it's doing so by swelling the ranks of the upper classes.

What about the concentration of wealth? In 1918, John D. Rockefeller's fortune accounted for more than half of one percent of total private wealth. To compile the same half of one percent of the private wealth in the United States today, you'd have to combine the fortunes of Microsoft's Bill Gates ($53 billion) and Paul Allen ($16 billion), Oracle's Larry Ellison ($19 billion), and a third of Berkshire Hathaway's Warren Buffett's $46 billion. In 1920, America's richest one percent held about 40 percent of private wealth; by 1980, the private wealth held by the richest one percent fell to about 20 percent and has remained stable at that level since.

Demagogues duping Americans about stagnant and declining income give politicians justification to raise taxes and place regulatory obstacles in the path of risk-taking, productivity and hard work that will impede the enviable income mobility that has become a part of American tradition. Raising taxes on capital formation reduces the rate of capital formation. Raising taxes on income reduces incentives to work. Unfortunately, because so many Americans buy into the politics of envy, politicians have a leg up in enacting measures that cripple economic growth.

The Poverty Hype

Wednesday, January 4, 2006

Despite claims that the rich get richer and the poor get poorer, poverty is nowhere near the problem it was yesteryear—at least for those who want to work. Talk about the poor getting poorer tugs at the hearts of decent people and squares nicely with the agenda of big government advocates, but it doesn't square with the facts.

Dr. Michael Cox, economic adviser to the Federal Reserve Bank of Dallas, and Richard Alm, a business reporter for the *Dallas Morning News*, co-authored a 1999 book, *Myths of Rich and Poor: Why We're Better Off Than We Think*, that demonstrates the pure nonsense about the claim that the poor get poorer.

The authors analyzed University of Michigan Panel Study of Income Dynamics data that tracked more than 50,000 individual families since 1968. Cox and Alms found: Only five percent of families in the bottom income quintile (lowest 20 percent) in 1975 were still there in 1991. Three-quarters of these families had moved into the three highest income quintiles. During the same period, 70 percent of those in the second lowest income quintile moved to a higher quintile, with 25 percent of them moving to the top income quintile. When the Bureau of Census reports, for example, that the poverty rate in 1980 was 15 percent and a decade later still 15 percent, for the most part they are referring to different people.

Cox and Alm's findings were supported by a U.S. Treasury Department study that used an entirely different data base, income tax returns. The U.S. Treasury found that 85.8 percent of tax filers in the bottom income quintile in 1979 had moved on to a higher quintile by 1988—66 percent to second and third quintiles and 15 percent to the top quintile. Income mobility goes in the other direction as well. Of the people who were in the top one percent of income earners in 1979, over half, or 52.7 percent, were gone by 1988. Throughout history and probably in most places today, there are whole classes of people who remain permanently poor or permanently rich, but not in the United States. The percentages of Americans who are permanently poor or rich don't exceed single digits.

It doesn't take rocket science to figure out why people who are poor in one decade are not poor one or two decades later. First, they get older. Would anyone be surprised that 30, 40 or 50-year-olds earn a higher income than 20-year-olds? The 1995 Annual Report of the Federal Reserve Bank of Dallas found that "Average income tends to rise quickly in life as workers gain work experience and knowledge. Households headed by someone under age 25 average $15,197 a year in income. Average income more than doubles to $33,124 for 25- to 34-year-olds. For those 35 to 44, the figure jumps to $43,923. It takes time for learning, hard work and saving to bear fruit."

The Federal Reserve Bank of Dallas report listed a few no-brainer behaviors consistent with upward income mobility. Households in the top income bracket have 2.1 workers; those in the bottom have 0.6 workers. In the lowest income bracket, 84 percent worked part time; in the highest income bracket, 80 percent worked full time. That translates into: Get a full-time job. Only seven percent of top income earners live in a "nonfamily" household compared to 37 percent of the bottom income category. Translation: Get married. At the time of the study, the unemployment rate in McAllen, Texas, was 17.5 percent, while in Austin, Texas, it was 3.5 percent. Translation: If you can't find a job in one locality, move to where there are jobs.

The Federal Reserve Bank of Dallas report concludes, "Little on this list should come as a surprise. Taken as a whole, it's what most Americans have been told since they were kids—by society, by their parents, by their teachers."

Minimum Wage, Maximum Folly

Wednesday, April 26, 2006

About a fortnight ago, Mrs. Williams alerted me to an episode of Oprah Winfrey's show titled "Inside the Lives of People Living on Minimum Wage." After a few minutes of watching, I turned it off, not because of the heartrending tales but because most of what was being said was dead wrong. Let's look at it.

The show claims that 30 million Americans earn the minimum wage of $5 an hour. Actually, the federal minimum wage is $5.15 an hour, and 17 states mandate a higher minimum wage that approaches $7 an hour. At one point, Oprah did manage to clear up this aspect of the show's errors.

The U.S. Department of Labor reports: "According to Current Population Survey estimates for 2004, some 73.9 million American workers were paid at hourly rates, representing 59.8 percent of all wage and salary workers. Of those paid by the hour, 520,000 were reported as earning exactly $5.15" (http://www.bls.gov/cps/min wage2004.htm#2).

Workers earning the minimum wage or less tend to be young, single workers between the ages of 16 and 25. Only about two percent of workers over 25 years of age earn minimum wages.

According to the U.S. Bureau of Labor Statistics: Sixty-three percent of minimum wage workers receive raises within one year of employment, and only 15 percent still earn the minimum wage after three years. Furthermore, only 5.3 percent of minimum wage earners are from households below the official poverty line; forty percent of minimum wage earners live in households with incomes $60,000 and higher; and, over 82 percent of minimum wage earners do not have dependents.

The U.S. Department of Labor also reports that the "proportion of hourly-paid workers earning the prevailing Federal minimum wage or less has trended downward since 1979."

Another issue that's not often taken into consideration is there's a difference between what a worker takes home in pay and his total compensation. Employers must pay for legally required worker benefits that include Social Security, Medicare, unemployment insurance, workers' compensation, health and disability insurance benefits, and whatever paid leave benefits they offer, such as vacations, holidays and sick leave. It's tempting to think of higher minimum wages as an anti-poverty weapon, but such an idea doesn't even pass the smell test. After all, if higher minimum wages could cure poverty, we could easily end worldwide poverty simply by telling poor nations to legislate higher minimum wages.

Poor people are not poor because of low wages. For the most part, they're poor because of low productivity, and wages are connected to productivity. The effect of minimum wages is that of causing unemployment among low-skilled workers. If an employer must pay $5.15 an hour, plus mandated fringes that might bring the employment cost of a worker to $7 an hour, does it pay him to hire a person who is so unfortunate as to have skills that permit him to produce only $4 worth of value per hour? Most employers would view hiring such a person as a losing economic proposition.

Two important surveys of academic economists were reported in two issues of the *American Economic Review*, May 1979 and May 1992. In one survey, 90 percent, and in the other 80 percent, of economists agreed that increasing the minimum wage causes unemployment among youth and low-skilled workers.

Minimum wages can have a more insidious effect. In research for my book "South Africa's War Against Capitalism" (1989), I found that during South Africa's apartheid era, racist unions, who'd never admit blacks, were the major supporters of higher minimum wages for blacks.

Gert Beetge, secretary of South Africa's avowedly racist Building Worker's Union, in response to contractors hiring black workers, said, "There is no job reservation left in the building industry, and in the circumstances I support the rate-for-the-job [minimum wages] as the second best way of protecting our white artisans." Racists recognized the discriminatory effects of mandated minimum wages.

I'm trying to figure whether ineptitude explains the errors in Oprah's show or is a deliberate attempt to mislead.

Are CEOs Overpaid?

Wednesday, March 2, 2005

In the wake of the Enron and WorldCom corporate scandals, the purveyors of envy have found another opportunity to preach about what they consider the evils of high CEO salaries, retirements and bonuses. After all, according to them, evil must be afoot when a corporate executive earns more in a week that the average worker earns in an entire year. Let's look at it.

Dishonest Enron and WorldCom CEOs are rare among corporate executives. As such, all CEOs shouldn't be tarnished for the misdeeds of a few any more than we'd tarnish all newspaper reporters because a few among their ranks were liars like the *Boston Globe*'s Patricia Smith and Mike Barnicle, Jayson Blair of the *New York Times*, and the *Washington Post*'s Janet Cooke.

Is a CEO worth millions of dollars to a corporation? When Jack Welch became General Electric's CEO in 1981, the stock market judged the company to be worth about $14 billion. Through hiring and firing, buying and selling, Welch turned the company around before he retired in 2001. Today, GE is worth nearly $500 billion, making it one of the most valuable companies in the world. What's a CEO worth for providing the brains and leadership to turn a $14 billion corporation into one worth $500 billion? How about paying just a measly one-half of a percent of the increase in value? If that were the case, Welch's total compensation would have come to nearly $2.5 billion instead of the few hundred million that he actually received.

The Gillette Co. was in the early stages of corporate death in 2001 when Jim Kilts took over as CEO. The company's stock had lost almost half of its value in two years, and sales volume and market shares of its major brands had plummeted. Between the time Kilts took over at Gillette and this year's Jan. 28 announcement of Procter & Gamble's purchase of Gillette, Gillette's market value increased by $11.3 billion, a 34 percent improvement, and since the announcement, Gillette's value has risen by another $5.7 billion.

Kilts' salary and bonuses over the past four years, totaling about $17.5 million, haven't been especially large by CEO standards. Predictably, however, Kilts' pay and particularly the size of his compensation package from the merger—$153 million—have been the subject of media carping, particularly in Boston, where Gillette is headquartered. This figure is indeed large, but it, added to what Gillette has paid him since 2001, makes Kilts' total compensation a mere 1.5 percent of his contribution to Gillette's value.

Here are a couple of questions to you: If you were the owner of GE, and a CEO could turn your $14 billion corporation into a $500 billion one, how much would you be willing to pay that man in salary and bonuses? Or, in the case of Jim Kilts, turning Gillette from a corporation in steep decline into one Procter & Gamble was willing to buy for $57 billion, how much would you be willing to pay?

Then, you might ask yourself: If a corporate board of directors could buy a $300 computer that could do what a CEO could do, would it pay CEOs millions of dollars? By the same token, if an NFL owner could hire a computer to make the decisions that star quarterbacks make, why would he pay some of these guys yearly compensation packages worth more than $10 million?

There's another important issue. If one company has an effective CEO, it is not the only company that would like to have him on the payroll. In order to keep him, the company must pay him enough so that he can't be lured elsewhere. If you ask me, I know of only one class of workers who are overpaid and under worked—college professors.

How Not To Be Poor

Wednesday, May 11, 2005

Ministers Louis Farrakhan, Jesse Jackson, Al Sharpton, Washington, D.C.'s Mayor Anthony Williams and others recently met to discuss plans to celebrate the 10th anniversary of the October 1995 Million Man March. Whilst reading about the plans, I thought of an excellent topic for the event: how not to be poor.

Avoiding long-term poverty is not rocket science. First, graduate from high school. Second, get married before you have children, and stay married. Third, work at any kind of job, even one that starts out paying the minimum wage. And, finally, avoid engaging in criminal behavior. If you graduate from high school today with a B or C average, in most places in our country there's a low-cost or financially assisted post-high-school education program available to increase your skills.

Most jobs start with wages higher than the minimum wage, which is currently $5.15. A man and his wife, even earning the minimum wage, would earn $21,000 annually. According to the Bureau of Census, in 2003, the poverty threshold for one person was $9,393, for a two-person household it was $12,015, and for a family of four it was $18,810. Taking a minimum wage job is no great shakes, but it produces an income higher than the Bureau of Census' poverty threshold. Plus, having a job in the first place increases one's prospects for a better job.

The Children's Defense Fund and civil rights organizations frequently whine about the number of black children living in poverty. In 1999, the Bureau of the Census reported that 33.1 percent of black children lived in poverty compared with 13.5 percent of white children. It turns out that race per se has little to do with the difference. Instead, it's welfare and single parenthood. When black children are compared to white children living in identical circumstances, mainly in a two-parent household, both children will have the same probability of being poor.

How much does racial discrimination explain? So far as black poverty is concerned, I'd say little or nothing, which is not to say that every vestige of racial discrimination has been eliminated. But let's pose a few questions. Is it racial discrimination that stops black students from studying and completing high school? Is it racial discrimination that's responsible for the 68 percent illegitimacy rate among blacks?

The 1999 Bureau of Census report might raise another racial discrimination question. Among black households that included a married couple, over 50 percent were middle class earning above $50,000, and 26 percent earned more than $75,000. How in the world did these black families manage not to be poor? Did America's racists cut them some slack?

The civil rights struggle is over, and it has been won. At one time black Americans did not have the same constitutional protections as whites. Now, we do, because the civil rights struggle is over and won is not the same as saying that there are not major problems for a large segment of the black community. What it does say is that they're not civil rights problems, and to act as if they are leads to a serious misallocation of resources.

Rotten education is a severe handicap to upward mobility, but is it a civil rights problem? Let's look at it. Washington, D.C. public schools, as well as many other big city schools, are little more than educational cesspools. Per student spending in Washington, D.C., is just about the highest in the nation. D.C.'s mayors have been black, and so have a large percentage of the city council, school principals, teachers and superintendents. Suggesting that racial discrimination plays any part in Washington, D.C.'s educational calamity is near madness and diverts attention away from possible solutions.

Bill Cosby had the courage to speak out against individual irresponsibility. Surely those who profess to have the best interests of blacks at heart should be able to summon the courage to do so as well.

Dead-End Jobs

Wednesday, November 30, 2005

Certain jobs are derisively referred to as "burger flipper" or "dead-end" jobs. I'd like someone to define a dead-end job. For example, I started out as a professor of economics at California State University, Los Angeles and then at Temple University and for the past 25 years at George Mason University. It seems as though my employment might qualify as a dead-end job, for all I'll ever be is a professor of economics.

Those who demean so-called dead-end jobs probably aren't talking about my job. They're mockingly referring to jobs such as clerks at Wal-Mart, hotel workers, and food handlers and counter clerks at McDonald's. McJobs is the term applied to these positions. The term has even found its way into Merriam-Webster and the encyclopedia Wikipedia. Putting down so-called dead-end jobs is a destructive insult to honest work.

How dead-end is a McDonald's job? Jim Glassman, an American Enterprise Institute scholar, wrote an article in the Institute's June 2005 *On The Issues* bulletin titled "Even Workers with 'McJobs' Deserve Respect." He listed some well-known former McDonald's workers. Among them: Andy Card, White House chief of staff; Jeff Bezos, founder and CEO of Amazon.com; Jay Leno, "Tonight Show" host; Carl Lewis, Olympic gold medalist; Joe Kernan, former Indiana governor; and Robert Cornog, retired CEO of Snap-On Tools. According to Glassman, some 1,200 McDonald's restaurant owners began as crew members, and so did 20 of McDonald's 50 top worldwide managers. These people and millions of others hardly qualify as dead-enders.

The primary beneficiaries of so-called McJobs are people who enter the workforce with modest or absent work skills in areas such as: being able to show up for work on time, operating a machine, counting change, greeting customers with decorum and courtesy, cooperating with fellow workers and accepting orders from supervisors. Very often the people who need these job skills, which some of us might trivialize, are youngsters who grew up in dysfunctional homes and attended rotten schools. It's a bottom rung on the economic ladder that provides them an opportunity to move up. For many, the financial component of a low-pay, low-skill job is not nearly as important as what they learn on the job that can make them more valuable workers in the future.

Some demagogues charge that jobs at Wal-Mart and McDonald's only pay the minimum wage. That's plain wrong, as are many other things said about jobs that start at the minimum wage. According to the U.S. Bureau of Labor Statistics: Sixty-three percent of minimum wage workers receive raises within one year of employment, and only 15 percent still earn the minimum wage after three years. Moreover, only three percent of all hourly workers and two percent of wage and salary earners earn minimum wages. Most minimum wage earners are young—53 percent are between the ages of 16 and 24.

Furthermore, only 5.3 percent of minimum wage earners are from households below the official poverty line; 40 percent of minimum wage earners live in households with incomes of $60,000 and higher, and over 82 percent of minimum wage earners do not have dependents. My stepfather used to tell me that any honest work was better than begging and stealing. As a young person, I worked many jobs from shining shoes and picking blueberries to delivering packages and washing dishes. Today's tragedy for many a poor youngster is that the opportunities I had for learning the world of work and moving up the economic ladder have either been destroyed through legislation or demeaned by today's do-gooders.

Income Inequality

September 13, 2004

Last month the U.S. Bureau of Census reported its findings on income and poverty. Median real income remained constant between 2002 and 2003 at $43,000; the official poverty rate rose slightly from 12.1 percent to 12.5 percent for a total of 36 million Americans; poverty rates by race remained unchanged at 8 percent among whites, blacks 24 percent and Hispanics 22 percent. Dr. Daniel H. Weinberg, Bureau of Census Division Chief, added that income inequality remained unchanged with the lowest 20 percent of households ($18,000 and below) earning 3.5 percent of national income and the highest 20 percent ($86,900) about 50 percent.

The poverty report gives vice-presidential hopeful, Senator John Edwards, a little fodder for his "Two Americas" stump speech. That's the one where he says, "[There's] one America that does the work, another America that reaps the reward. One America that pays the taxes, another America that gets the tax breaks." This is demagoguery and unadulterated dishonesty that can only appeal to the misinformed and ignorant.

Let's look at who doesn't pay taxes. According to a study done by Scott Hodge, President of the Washington, D.C.-based Tax Foundation, and his colleagues, 41 percent of whites, 56 percent of blacks, 59 percent of American Indian and Aleut Eskimo and 40 percent Asian and Pacific Islanders will have no 2004 federal income tax liability. The Tax Foundation study concludes, "When all of the dependents of these income-producing households are counted, there are roughly 122 million Americans—44 percent of the U.S. population—are outside of the federal income tax system."

Who does pay federal income taxes? The top 20 percent of income-earners pay 80 percent and the top 50 percent pay 96.5 percent of total federal income taxes. Given these figures about who does and does not pay federal income taxes, what are we to make of John Edwards' stump speech? He's right in one sense. One group of Americans, those at the top, who work and pay virtually all federal income taxes and another group, those at the bottom, who work and pay little or no federal income taxes.

There's another issue about income inequality. If it's your vision that out there somewhere there's a pile of money to be divided among Americans, the reason the top fifth of Americans have much more than the bottom fifth is that they got to the pile of money first and took an unfair share. Justice, of course, would require that their ill-gotten gains be confiscated and redistributed to their rightful owners. But in a free society income is mostly determined by one's ability and willingness to produce goods and services that satisfy his fellow man. The top fifth of income earners (earnings greater than $84,000) are not only more productive, and have higher skills and education than the bottom fifth of income earners, they work more hours and have more people in their household working.

There's something else that's gets little attention. There's considerable income mobility in our country. According to IRS tax data, 85.8 percent of tax filers in the bottom fifth in 1979 had moved on to a higher quintile, and often to the top quintile, by 1988. Income mobility goes in the other direction as well. Of the people who were in the top one percent of income earners in 1979, over half, or 52.7 percent, were gone by 1988.

Here's my question to you. What are we to make of politicians, and other charlatans and quacks, who are knowingly dishonest and use the politics of envy to exploit American ignorance for political gain? It's immaterial whether you're for George Bush or for John Kerry winning the White House, but do you think politicians running on the politics of envy bodes well for the future of our country?

From Whence Income?

April 21, 2003

Here's part of a letter from a reader: "A hard-working, conscientious person can earn $10,000 a year in a fast-food restaurant. At the same time, movie stars and athletes, who make very little contribution to society, can earn in excess of $10,000,000 a year. A baseball player earns more with every swing of the bat than many people do in a year." The reader's inference is that there's something unfair about income differences of such magnitude. It also reflects ignorance about the sources of income in a free society; that's music to the ears of political demagogues with an insatiable taste for command and control.

I think some of the ignorance and much of the demagoguery stems from the usage of the phrase "income distribution." It might make some people think income is distributed; in other words there's a dealer of dollars. The reason that some people have few dollars while others have millions upon millions is that the dollar dealer is unjust. An alternative vision might be that there's a pile of money intended for all of us. The reason why some are rich and some are poor is that the greedy rich got to the pile first and took their unfair share. Clearly, in either case, justice would require a re-dealing, or redistribution, of the dollars where the government takes ill-gotten gains of the few and returns them to their rightful owners.

Most people, except a few congressmen, would view those explanations of the sources of income as nonsense. In a free society, for the most part, income is earned. It's earned by serving and pleasing one's fellow man. Why is it that Michael Jordan earns $33 million a year and I don't even earn one-half of one percent of that? I can play basketball but my problem is with my fellow man who'd plunk down $200 to see Jordan play and wouldn't pay a dollar to see me play. I'm also willing to sell my name as endorsements for sneakers and sport clothing but no one has approached me.

The bottom line explanation of Michael Jordan's income relative to mine lies in his capacity to please his fellow man. The person who takes exception to Jordan's salary or sees him, as my letter writer does, as making "little contribution to society," is really disagreeing with decisions made by millions upon millions of independent decision makers who decided to fork over their money to see Jordan play. The suggestion that Congress ought to take part of Jordan's earnings and give them to someone else is the same as arrogantly saying, "I know better who ought to receive those dollars."

Another part of the explanation for Jordan's high salary is simply a matter of supply and demand. If there were tens and tens of millions of people with Jordan's talents, you can rest assured he wouldn't be earning $33 million a year. And similarly you can bet that if people really valued hamburgers and there were only a few people with those skills, they'd be earning much more than they currently earn.

We might think of dollars as being "certificates of performance." The better I serve my fellow man, and the higher the value he places on that service, the more certificates of performance he gives me. The more certificates I earn the greater my claim on the goods my fellow man produces. That's the morality of the market. In order for one to have a claim on what his fellow man produces, he must first serve him. Contrast that moral standard to Congress's standing offer, "Vote for me and I'll take what your fellow man produces and give it to you."

The Morality of Markets

May 5, 2003

My recent column "From Whence Comes Income" sparked considerable favorable reader response, not to mention thoughtful reader correction of my grammar error in the title: "From Whence" is redundant. Quite a few readers were a bit confused about my assertion that market allocation of goods and services are infinitely more moral than the alternative.

The first principle of a free society is that each person owns himself. You are your private property and I am mine. Most Americans probably accept that first principle. Those who disagree are obliged to inform the rest of us just who owns us, at least here on earth. This vision of self-ownership is one of those "self-evident" truths to which the Founders referred to in the Declaration of Independence that "All Men are created equal, that they are endowed by their Creator with certain unalienable Rights, that among these are Life, Liberty, and the Pursuit of Happiness." Like John Locke and other philosophers who influenced them, the Founders saw these rights as preceding government and they said, "That to secure these Rights, Governments are instituted." The Framers of the Constitution recognized that while government was necessary to secure liberty it was also liberty's greatest threat. Having this deep suspicion of government, they loaded our Constitution with a host of anti-congressional phrases such as: "Congress shall make no law," "shall not be infringed," and "shall not be violated."

Once one accepts the principle of self-ownership, what's moral and immoral becomes self-evident. Murder is immoral because it violates private property. Rape and theft are also immoral; they also violate private property. Here's an important question: Would rape become morally acceptable if Congress passed a law legalizing it? You say, "What's wrong with you, Williams? Rape is immoral plain and simple no matter what Congress says or does!"

If you take that position, isn't it just as immoral when Congress legalizes the taking of one person's earnings to give to another? Surely if a private person took money from one person and gave it to another, we'd deem it theft and as such immoral. Does the same act become moral when Congress takes people's money to give to farmers, airline companies or an impoverished family? No, it's still theft, but with an important difference: it's legal and participants aren't jailed.

Market allocation of goods and services depends upon peaceable, voluntary exchange. Under such exchanges the essence of our proposition to our fellow man is: If you do something I like, I'll do something you like. When such a deal is struck, both parties are better off in their own estimation. Billions of these propositions are routinely made and carried out each day. For example, take my trip to the grocery store. My proposition to the grocer is essentially: "If you make me feel good by giving me that gallon of milk you own, I'll make you feel good by giving you three dollars that I own." If my proposition is accepted, the grocer is better off since he values the $3 more than the milk and I'm better off since I value the milk more than the $3.

Contrast the morality of market exchange with its alternative. I might go to my grocer with a pistol and propose: give me a gallon of milk or I'll shoot you. Or, I might lobby Congress to take his milk and give it to me. Either way I'm better off but the grocer is worse off.

Less there's misunderstanding there are legitimate and moral functions of government, namely that of preventing the initiation of force, fraud and intimidation and we're all duty-bound to cough up our share of the cost. All other matters in our lives should be left to civil society and its institutions.

The Politics of Envy

November 4, 2002

In his *New York Times Magazine* (10/20/02) article titled "For Richer: The Disappearing Middle Class," Princeton University economist Professor Paul Krugman wrote, "For the America I grew up in—the America of the 1950's and 1960's—was a middle-class society, both in reality and in feel. The vast income and wealth inequalities of the Gilded Age had disappeared. . . . Daily experiences confirmed the sense of a fairly equal society. The economic disparities you were conscious of were quite muted." Professor Krugman's vision of income inequality and the disappearing middle class is an excellent example of the classroom propaganda college professors use to exploit America's immature and inexperienced youth. Let's look at it.

A no-brainer is if the middle class has disappeared or is disappearing, means that America has become or is becoming a country where there's only the rich and the poor—like a Third World country. I'd like to see Krugman's evidence.

Krugman sees the 50s and 60s as a time of a "fairly equal society." Even if his observations were factually true, so what. Does it mean that the average person enjoyed a higher standard of living? The fact of business is that the 20th century has been the best ever for all Americans. Cato Institute scholars Stephen Moore and the late Julian Simon document this in *It's Getting Better All The Time*. Let's take a small sample of their evidence.

The average life expectancy in 1900 was 47 years. Today it is 77, and rising. The infant-mortality rate has dropped from 1 in 10 to 1 in 150. Americans who're considered poor have routine access to a quality of food, health care, consumer products, entertainment, communications and transportation that even the Vanderbilts, Carnegies and Rockefellers could have only dreamed of. Rich people have always had servants to spare them the drudgery of having to beat the dust out of rugs; the advent of vacuum cleaners spared the common man of that kind of drudgery. Henry Ford became very rich but the benefits reaped by the common man by being able to afford an auto trivialized whatever gains were reaped by Ford. Air conditioning and air travel, as late as the 50s, was something for the well-to-do; now half of poor people have air conditioning, travel by air and more than half own automobiles. In the 19th century, almost all teenagers toiled in factories or fields. Now, 9 in 10 attend high school. Today's Americans have three times more leisure time than their great-grandparents did. The price of food relative to wages has plummeted: In the early part of this century the average American had to work two hours to earn enough to purchase a chicken, compared with 20 minutes today.

College professors, politicians and others whose agenda calls for increased government control over our lives promote the lie that things are getting worse. If we buy into that lie, we'll kill the goose that lays the golden eggs. We might ask ourselves: why is it that so much of the progress of the past 100 years has originated in America? Moore and Simon provide a simple but compelling answer: "The unique American formula of individual liberty and free enterprise has cultivated risk taking, experimentation, innovation, and scientific exploration on a grand scale that has never occurred anywhere before."

Finally, let's keep in mind that inequality of income is a result and if we looked at the distribution of productivity, which economists haven't been able to do very well, we might not be surprised by inequality of income. In other words, how surprised would you be if I told you that I know how to play basketball, and I try hard, but nobody is willing to equalize incomes by paying me as much as Michael Jordan earns?

International

Almost every area in the international arena has become ripe for misunderstanding and wholesale demagoguery. Nowhere is this more apparent than in the area of international trade. Whenever there is trade, it occurs because both parties to the trade perceive that they will be better off than their next best alternative as a result. The people who rail against international trade the most are domestic competitors who lose sales because an American chooses to purchase from a foreign competitor. The push for restrictions on international trade in the forms of tariffs and quotas really seeks to deprive American consumers of the right to choose. To retain a bit of respectability, many trade restrictionists claim that they are for free trade and fair trade, but the assessment of whether a particular trade is fair or not is up to the parties conducting the trade.

Another part of the misunderstanding and demagoguery has to do with a trade imbalance that restrictionists argue is a result of our buying more from foreigners than they buy from us. But one party buying more from another party than that party buys from him typifies most trade relationships. For example, I purchase more from my grocer than he purchases from me. In turn he purchases more from his wholesaler than the wholesaler purchase from him. In reality, there is no trade imbalance, whether it is my making purchases from my grocer or my making purchases from Toyota of Japan.

Here is what happens. When I purchase $100 worth of goods from my grocer, my goods, or current account, rises by $100 and my capital account falls by $100. For the grocer, his goods account falls by $100 but his capital account rises by $100. It is the same when I purchase a car from Toyota. My capital account falls by say $70,000, but my goods account, in the form of a Lexus, rises by $70,000. Toyota's capital account rises by $70,000, but it might not use the money to by American goods but instead purchase $70,000 worth of U.S. stocks, bonds, or government debt instruments. Thus, although there is a deficit in what is *our current account, it is offset by a surplus of the same amount in our capital account.*

Third World poverty is another area in the international arena that requires a better understanding. The standard excuses for Third World poverty range from colonialism to lack of natural resources, but there is little evidence for such claims. Some of the world's richest countries were once colonies, such as the United States, Canada, Australia, and Hong Kong, and some of the world's poorest were never colonies, such as Ethiopia, Liberia, Tibet, Nepal, and Bhutan. South America and Africa are two of world's richest continents in terms of natural resources but are home to some of the world's most miserably poor people. Although Japan, the United Kingdom, and Hong Kong are natural-resource poor, they are home to some of the world's richest people.

There is little evidence that foreign aid is the key to economic development. Since World War II, the world's richest countries have poured trillions of dollars into foreign aid and many of the recipients are just as poor or poorer. What is minimally needed for economic development is rule of law, stable monetary systems, freer trade, and open markets—institutions that can only be developed domestically.

These international issues, as well as foreign policy issues, are highlighted in the columns that follow.

Goodies Cost

February 18, 2004

The first concept an economics student learns is that for every benefit there's also a cost or, as my longtime colleague and friend Nobel Laureate Milton Friedman has put it, "There's no free lunch." The person who receives the benefit might not pay or even be aware of the cost, but as sure as night follows day there is a cost paid by someone.

One of the effects of competition is that of revealing costs and least-cost methods of production. When the government gave AT&T a monopoly over much of the telecommunications industry and when the Civil Aeronautics Board sponsored the airline cartel, both telecommunication and air travel were far more expensive than they are today. The introduction of competition not only revealed that the services could be provided more cheaply but brought about massive innovation as well.

International trade is a form of competition and as such it also reveals costs and least-cost methods of production. American workers are the most productive workers in the world. According to the Bureau of Labor Statistics, in 2002 the United States led the world in worker productivity: U.S. workers averaged $71,600 in output each (in 1999 dollars). The next highest country was Belgium, where each worker averaged $64,100. But worker productivity can be sabotaged.

Suppose an American textile worker is paid $100 a day while his Indian counterpart earns $20, but if the American is ten times as productive as the Indian worker then the wage costs of using the American worker is lower. However, $100 in wages is not the only cost of hiring the American worker. There are numerous federal and state regulations that add to worker costs such as: OSHA requirements, EEOC mandates, Social Security and Medicare, Family Medical Leave and many other workplace regulations. Added to worker costs that businesses incur are: ADA, Clean Air Act, Endangered Species, and many other regulations. Then there are all sorts of frivolous and not-so-frivolous lawsuits brought against businesses. According to an Office of Advocacy of the U.S. Small Business Administration study, "The Impact of Regulatory Costs on Small Firms," federal regulatory costs on U.S. businesses were $451 billion in 2000. They cost small businesses (20 or fewer employees) about $7,000 per employee; medium businesses (20 to 499 employees) paid about $4,300; and large businesses (500 employees or more) paid about $4,400.

There're no two ways about it: there are benefits from all the costly federal, state, and local regulations imposed on American businesses. But we must also acknowledge that our federal, state and local regulatory agencies have no jurisdiction in India, China, Southeast Asia, Mexico and Latin America. That means for many products and services people who are far less productive, in a physical sense, than we are can beat us in the global marketplace.

We all can agree that there's no benefit that's worth any cost. If that weren't true, we'd do damn near anything that has a benefit, and that would include mandating a five mile per hour speed limit. Why? The benefits would be enormous in terms of the tens of thousands of highway fatalities and injuries avoided. We don't have a five mile per hour speed limit because we've decided that its benefit is not worth the enormous cost.

As said earlier competition reveals costs and least-cost methods of production. One need not take a position one way or another on the worthiness of the benefits of regulation to acknowledge that there are costs associated with them. But I think that intelligent decision making requires that we take their costs into account. It's not intelligent to stick our heads in the sand and deceive ourselves by pretending that others are to blame for our lack of competitiveness in some areas.

The Seen and Unseen

June 18, 2001

I buy more from my grocer than he buys from me. I buy more from my auto dealer than he buys from me. The trade imbalance doesn't stop there. My grocer and auto dealer both buy more from their wholesaler than the wholesaler buys from them. These are examples of trade deficits. What should President Bush and Congress do to eliminate these trade deficits to ensure a level playing field?

You say, "Williams, have you lost your marbles? There'll always be trade deficits like you describe. What's wrong with it?" You're absolutely right. But, what would you say if one seller, say Costco, had cheaper prices than another seller, say Food Giant? What action would you have President Bush and Congress take against Costco? How about taxing Costco's products so as to level the playing field between Costco and Food Giant? You say, "Williams, that's a trick! The only thing that taxing Costco will do is to enable Food Giant to charge customers higher prices, earn higher profits and pay employees higher wages. Consumers will be worse off." You're right again. Now let's apply your reasoning to a real world example.

Two weeks ago, some teachers, students, retirees and steelworkers gathered on Capitol Hill to press Congress and the Bush administration to use U.S. trade laws to address a problem described by Leo Gerard, President, United Steelworkers of America, as "Illegal foreign dumping of steel in the United States is devastating American families and communities." Leo Gerard claims that as a result of illegal dumping, more than 23,000 American steelworkers have lost their jobs since 1998 and 18 companies have been forced into bankruptcy. The Bush administration announced that actions will be initiated under Section 201 of U.S. trade laws.

Let's analyze this by substituting Timken Stahl, a German steel producer, for Costco, US Steel, an American company, for Food Giant and John Deere & Company, a manufacturer of heavy farm and construction equipment, for you and me as customers. Suppose

American steel companies and their unions are successful in getting Bush and congress to enact retaliatory measures against foreign steel producers for "illegal dumping." By the way, the real definition of dumping is when your competitor charges a price you think is too low.

To see the effect of trade restrictions, we need only to go back to the Reagan administration's "voluntary restraints" on steel imports. Professor Arthur T. Denzau of the Center for the Study of American Business found that the import restrictions saved nearly 17,000 jobs in the steel industry by enabling them to charge higher prices. Politicians love this; the beneficiaries are visible and seen. However, higher steel prices made American steel-using industries, such as John Deere, less competitive in domestic and international markets leading to a loss of 52,400 jobs, a net job loss of 35,400 jobs. These are the invisible and unseen victims of steel import restrictions. Politicians love invisible and unseen victims of their policies.

Maybe there's a case for helping those 23,000 American steelworkers who lost their jobs. But, let's recognize that costs of restrictions are always higher than the benefits going to the beneficiaries. Saving a $45,000 a year steelworker's job, in terms of higher prices in the rest of the economy, might cost as much as $125,000. It would be better if Congress enacted an Aid to Dependent Steelworkers bill where each unemployed steelworker is simply handed a $45,000 check each year. As a nation we'd surely come out ahead, but Congress would never do that. Why? The handout would be visible and it wouldn't politically fly.

The Anti–Free Trader's True Enemy

February 2, 2004

There's the "Free Trade but Fair Trade" crowd and the "Level Playing Field" crowd and the "America First" crowd all calling for tariffs and other international trade restrictions. Their supposed adversary is corporate America, seeking to boost profits by either importing goods made by cheaper foreign labor or relocating plants in foreign lands to directly take advantage of cheaper labor. They claim that this accounts for the loss of U.S. manufacturing jobs and other economic woes. Their argument has considerable emotional appeal but they've misidentified the true villain in the piece. Let's look at it.

Suppose U-Needa Shirt Company relocated its production facilities to India in order to take advantage of cheaper labor. This is America, the land of the free. There is absolutely nothing that prevents a group of Americans as investors and workers from setting up Made in America Shirt Company to sell shirts to the American people. This same opportunity exists for just about anything once manufactured in America but now made overseas. At this juncture, let's take a thinking pause and ask: is what Williams said in this paragraph true or false?

Let's proceed. You might ask, "How in the world can Made in America Shirt Company compete with U-Needa Shirt Company who has much lower labor costs?" That's a different question but it has nothing to do with the rights of American investors and workers to set up American-based manufacturing facilities. But let's answer the question anyway. American consumers are free to purchase from whomever they choose. Made in American Shirt Company would survive and prosper if American consumers chose to purchase shirts from it rather than U-Needa Shirt Company. Let's take another thinking break and ask: Is what Williams said in this paragraph true or false?

Here's where the crunch comes. It's probable that U-Needa Shirt Company, because of its lower costs, will be able to undercut prices charged by Made in America Shirt Company. Thus, we encounter that troubling consumer characteristic of preferring lower prices to higher prices. So what to do? Made in America Shirt Company might try to change American consumer preferences so that they're indifferent between high and low prices. I predict that's a strategy doomed to failure, except maybe for a few diehard customers. There're no two ways about it. The true enemy of Made in America Shirt Company and its workers is not U-Needa Shirt company but the American consumer and his preference for lower prices coupled with his freedom to purchase from whomever he pleases.

What to do? One strategy for Made in America Shirt Company and its workers is to get Washington to enact measures restricting consumer choices. But you have to be slick about it. You just can't ask President Bush and Congress to criminalize purchases from U-Needa Shirt Company. You must make a pretense of selflessness and speak of national defense concerns like "What if there were war and we had no shirts for our soldiers?" You must talk of being for free trade but fair trade and level playing fields.

There's another strategy. Suppose Made in America Shirt Company could cover all of its cost with a $20 shirt price while U-Needa Shirt could do so by charging $15? Made in America Shirt might ask Congress to enact an Aid to Dependent American Shirt Manufacturers law whereby it would receive a $5 per shirt handout; then it could meet U-Needa Shirt Company's price. That might not be politically viable because the handout is too visible. Congress might propose, "Rather than giving you a $5 per shirt handout, how about if we impose a $5 per shirt import tax on U-Needa Shirt Company's shirts? Then they'll have to charge $20. That way you get what you want—a level playing field; we get more tax dollars and nobody's the wiser."

Nonsense Ideas

Wednesday, February 21, 2007

There are some ideas and feelings that sound plausible but given just a wee bit of thought can be shown to border on lunacy. Let's examine a few.

Some U.S. companies have been accused of exploiting Third World workers with poor working conditions and low wages. Say that a U.S. company pays a Cambodian factory worker $3 a day. Do you think that worker had a higher-paying alternative but stupidly chose a lower-paying job instead? I'm betting the $3-a-day job was superior to his next best alternative.

Does offering a worker a wage higher than what he could earn elsewhere make him worse off or better off? If you answered better off, is the term exploitation an appropriate characterization for an act that makes another better off? If pressure at home forces a U.S. company to cease its Cambodian operations, would that worker be worse off or better off?

It might be a convenient expression to say that the U.S. trades with Japan, but is it literally true? Is it the U.S. Congress and President George Bush who trade with the National Diet of Japan, the Japanese legislature and Prime Minister Shinzo Abe? Or, is it U.S. and Japanese private parties, as individuals and corporations, who trade with one another?

Let's break it down further. Which comes closer to the truth: When I purchased my Lexus, did I deal with the U.S. Congress, the Japanese Diet, George Bush and Shinzo Abe, or did I deal with Toyota and its intermediaries? If we erroneously think of international trade as occurring between the U. S. and Japanese governments, then all Americans, as voters, have a say-so. But what is the basis of anyone having a say-so when one American engages in peaceable, voluntary exchange with another person, be they Japanese, Korean, British, Chinese or another American?

How many times have we heard: If it will save just one life, it's worth it? The "it" could be bike helmet laws, childproof medicine bottles, or formaldehyde and asbestos safety regulations. A good economist cringes hearing such statements because they only consider the benefits of an action while ignoring the cost. Looking at benefits only, just about anything is worth doing because there's usually a benefit. Let's look at it.

According to the National Highway Traffic Safety Administration, some 43,443 people were killed on the nation's highways in 2005. If Congress were to enact a 10 miles per hour national speed limit, we'd save thousands of lives each year. You say, "Williams, that would be stupid and impractical!" My response to you is: But look at all the lives that would be saved. What you really mean by stupid and impractical is that preventing thousands of highway fatalities is not worth the cost and inconvenience that would result from having to poke along at 10 miles per hour. Of course, calling a 10 miles per hour law stupid and impractical is a more socially acceptable way of saying those saved lives aren't worth it.

How about academics and researchers seeing grinding Third World poverty and chalking it up to a "vicious cycle of poverty"? This vision of poverty sees people as too poor to save. That means they can't create investment capital. Because they can't invest, they can't develop, and that keeps them poor. In other words, people are poor because they're poor.

According to the "vicious cycle of poverty" vision, the only escape is foreign aid. The only way this theory of Third World poverty would have any credibility is if every country were poor. There's no country that wasn't at some time poor, including our own. If poverty is so vicious, how did today's rich countries escape it?

Trade Deficits: Good or Bad?

Wednesday, January 17, 2007

Two recent articles ought to give pause to current political and jour-
nalistic ignorance, perhaps demagoguery, about our international
trade deficit. In a December *Wall Street Journal* article titled "Em-
brace the Deficit," Bear Stearns' chief economist David Malpass lays
additional waste to predictions of gloom and doom associated with
our trade deficit.

Since 2001, our economy has created 9.3 million new jobs, compared with 360,000 in Japan and 1.1 million in the euro zone (European Union countries that have adopted the euro), excluding Spain.
Japan and euro zone countries had trade surpluses, while we had large
and increasing trade deficits. Mr. Malpass says that both Spain and
the U.K., like the U.S., ran trade deficits, but they created 3.6 and
1.3 million new jobs, respectively. Moreover, wages rose in the U.S.,
Spain and the U.K.

Professor Don Boudreaux, chairman of George Mason University's Economics Department, wrote "If Trade Surpluses Are So
Great, the 1930s Should Have Been a Booming Decade"
(www.cafehayek.com). According to data he found at the National
Bureau of Economic Research's "Macrohistory Database" (http://
www.nber.org/databases/macrohistory/contents/index.html), it turns
out that the U.S. ran a trade surplus in nine of the 10 years of the
Great Depression, with 1936 being the lone exception.

During those 10 years, we had a significant trade surplus, with
exports totaling $26.05 billion and imports totaling only $21.13 billion. So what do trade surpluses during a depression and trade deficits
during an economic boom prove, considering we've had trade deficits
for most of our history? Professor Boudreaux says they prove absolutely nothing. Economies are far too complex to draw simplistic
causal connections between trade deficits and surpluses and economic welfare and growth.

Despite all the criticism from abroad and the doom-mongers at home, the world finds our economy attractive. Just as we've been chomping at the bit to buy foreign goods and services, foreigners have been chomping at the bit to invest trillions of dollars in the U.S. Mr. Malpass says our 10-year government bonds yield 4.6 percent per year compared with Japan's 1.6 percent; our government debt is 38 percent of GDP versus 86 percent in Japan; and while Europe's debt to GDP ratio is not as extreme as Japan's, it's not nearly as favorable as ours.

Here's a smell test. Pretend you're a man from Mars knowing absolutely nothing about Earth and you're looking for a nice place to land. You find out that there's one country, say, country A, where earthlings from other countries voluntarily invest and entrust trillions of dollars of their hard earnings. There are other countries where they're not nearly as willing to make the same investment. Which one of those countries would you deem the most prosperous and with the greatest growth prospects? You'd pick country A, which turns out to be the United States. As such, you'd be just like most of the world's population who, if free to do so, would invest and live in the U.S.

The late Professor Milton Friedman said, "Underlying most arguments against the free market is a lack of belief in freedom itself." Some people justify their calls for protectionism by claiming that they're for free trade but fair trade. That's nonsense. Think about it: When I purchased my Lexus from a Japanese producer, through an intermediary, I received what I wanted. The Japanese producer received what he wanted. In my book, that's a fair trade.

Of course, an American auto producer, from whom I didn't purchase my car, might whine that it was unfair. He would like Congress to impose import tariffs and quotas to make Japanese-produced cars less attractive and available in the hopes that I'd buy an American-produced car. In my book, that would be unfair.

World Poverty

Wednesday, February 7, 2007

If you're looking for a map of world poverty, check out the "2007 Index of Economic Freedom" jointly published by the Heritage Foundation and the *Wall Street Journal*. You might think that's a strangely titled source for a poverty map.

The 13th edition of the "Index of Economic Freedom" examines 10 economic characteristics of 157 countries. Among those characteristics are property rights, monetary stability, and freedom from government, trade restrictions, business regulations and government corruption. Using these measures of economic freedom, countries are ranked.

Hong Kong and Singapore, as they have for 13 years, rank as the world's two economically freest countries, with freedom scores of 89 and 86 percent free. Rounding out the top 10 freest economies are Australia (83), United States (82), New Zealand (82), United Kingdom (82), Ireland (81), Luxembourg (79), Switzerland (79) and Canada (79).

At the other end of the list are the least free countries. Ranking 157th, North Korea, with a freedom score of 3 percent, is the world's least free country. Ranking 156th is Cuba, 30 percent free, and in ascending order are: Libya (34) Zimbabwe (36), Burma (40), Turkmenistan (42), Congo (43), Iran (43), Angola (43), and Guinea-Bassau (45).

The "2007 Index of Economic Freedom" displays a color-coded map showing countries that are free, mostly free, moderately free, mostly unfree and repressed. Guess where one finds the world's most miserably poor people? If you guessed the mostly unfree and repressed countries, you guessed correctly.

Some people claim that some countries are rich because of abundant natural resources. That's nonsense! Africa and South America are probably the richest continents in natural resources, but are home to some of the world's poorest people. By contrast, countries like England, Japan and Hong Kong are poor in natural resources, but their people are among the world's wealthiest. Hong Kong even has to import its food and water. Some people use the history of colonialism as an excuse for poverty. That's also nonsense. The United States was a colony. So were Canada, Australia, New Zealand and Hong Kong, but they're rich countries.

The reason some countries are rich while others are poor is best explained by the amount of economic freedom its peoples enjoy and the extent of government control over economic matters. Don't make the mistake of equating economic freedom with democracy. After all, India, politically, is a democracy, but economically it is mostly unfree and poor, ranking 104th in economic freedom. There are countries on the economic freedom index that do not have much of a history of democracy, such as Chile, ranking 11th, and Taiwan, 26th, and yet these countries are far wealthier than some of their more democratic counterparts. Why? It's because their economic systems are free or mostly free, which is not guaranteed by a democratic political system.

The economic development lesson is clear: Have a system of economic freedom and grow rich. Extensive government control, weak property rights and government corruption almost guarantee poverty. A country's institutional infrastructure is critical to its economic growth and the well-being of its citizens. The most critical are protection of private property, enforcement of contracts and rule of law.

To help our fellow man around the world, we must convince him to create the institutional infrastructure for wealth creation. Foreign aid, International Monetary Fund bailouts and other handouts are not substitutes. They just make political survival possible for the elite whose self-serving policies keep a nation poor. Except for immediate disaster relief, foreign aid is probably the worst thing the West can do for poor countries. After all, how much foreign aid is necessary for a country to create the foundations for growth: rule of law, enforcement of contracts and private property rights protection?

Creating Effective Incentives

Wednesday, May 23, 2007

What should our response be if terrorists set off a nuclear explosion, or some other weapon of mass destruction, in one of our cities? I put this question to Professor Victor Hanson, senior research fellow at Stanford University's prestigious Hoover Institution, who spoke on the Iraq war at the Wynnewood Institute lecture series.

His answer to my question bore a slight resemblance to a classroom practice of mine. At the beginning of each semester, I tell my students that I'm getting old and a cell phone ringing during my lecture could be devastating to my train of thought. Therefore, the penalty for a student's cell phone going off in class is a five percent reduction in his total points for the semester and a five percent reduction in the total points of the students sitting on either side of him. Of course, the students are shocked. The penalty might not be fair, penalizing a person for the actions of another, but I've not had trouble with cell phones going off in class.

Professor Hanson's answer referenced his July 6, 2004, *National Review* article titled "Another 9/11? The Awful Response That We Dare Not Speak About." He argues that without the direct aid of countries like Iran, Syria and rogue elements within the Saudi Arabian, Jordanian and Pakistani governments, and millions of ordinary Arabs, who know who terrorists are and where they sleep and won't turn them in, a massive terrorist attack on the United States would be nearly impossible. That means terrorists have some kind of local support. If there is an attack on our country, with weapons of mass destruction, the first thing we can expect is for country officials to deny any responsibility. Hanson says that we should beforehand tell the leaders of Middle East countries that if there's an attack on the United States, we will hold them responsible if they're proven to have aided or sheltered the terrorists.

Holding the country responsible would mean that in response to an attack we'd totally destroy their military bases, power plants, communication facilities and, if necessary, totally destroy their major cities. You say, "Williams, that's unthinkable!" Yes, while unpleasant, it is thinkable. That's precisely how 50 years of peace were maintained between the Western powers and the former Soviet Union. The leaders of the USSR knew that any attack on the United States would provoke an immediate massive nuclear retaliation. As frightening as the policy of Mutually Assured Destruction was, in the absence of a better strategy, neither Americans nor Russians were incinerated.

Laying down such a gauntlet is nothing new; it simply requires courageous leadership. In the wake of the 1962 Cuban missile crisis, President John F. Kennedy credibly warned the leaders of the Soviet Union that: "It shall be the policy of this nation to regard any nuclear missile launched from Cuba against any nation in the Western Hemisphere as an attack by the Soviet Union on the United States, requiring a full retaliatory response upon the Soviet Union." There's little question that President Kennedy's "full retaliatory response" would have included nuclear weapons.

Unfortunately, today, there's neither the American leadership nor the American character to protect ourselves from people whose declared aim is to destroy us. It's not just Americans, but the West in general, who have lost the will to protect themselves from the barbarism of the Middle East. Keep in mind that the mighty Roman Empire fell to barbarians who ushered in the Dark Ages.

Rules of Engagement

Wednesday, May 2, 2007

The March 23 Iranian capture of 15 British Royal Navy sailors should raise a number of questions. The sailors were part of the crew of HMS Cornwall, a state-of-the-art frigate bristling with high-tech surveillance devices and advanced weaponry. The sailors, dispatched in small boats, were boarding and inspecting merchant vessels in Iraqi waters for contraband.

Why weren't the six Iranian patrol boats picked up by radar, and why weren't warning shots fired as they approached the British crafts? Was HMS Cornwall Commander Jeremy Woods incompetent, or was he ordered to stand by and do nothing?

Standard operating procedure for a Royal Navy boarding party is for the mother ship to be in a position of providing covering or warning fire. There is some speculation that, when the sailors were captured, Commodore Nick Lambert, Britain's senior officer in the area, was trying to work out rules of engagement with the Ministry of Defence in London. That strikes me as a hell of a time to be working out rules of engagement.

You say, "What should HMS Cornwall have done?" They should have fired warning shots, and if the Iranians persisted, they should have been blown out of the water. You might say, "That would have endangered the lives of the 15 British sailors!" That's one of the tragedies of war: People get killed.

Britain isn't alone in using questionable rules of engagement. U.S. troops have been in pitched battles with terrorists in Iraq and Afghanistan in which terrorists run into a mosque to seek safety. There have been reports that terrorists have used mosques as arms caches. However, U.S. Lt. Col. Christopher Garver unequivocally said that U.S. troops do not enter mosques for the "sole purpose of disrupting insurgent activities."

During the Italian campaign of WWII, U.S. forces found Germans using the historic Benedictine Monastery at Monte Cassino as an observation post. Our bombers turned the monastery into a heap of rubble. According to the laws of war, if combatants use protected property, such as places of worship and hospitals, as shields or camouflage, they are guilty of violations of the laws of war and are responsible for the protected property. Today's politically correct rules of engagement unnecessarily risk the lives of our fighting men and women and reduce their efficiency.

The capture of the 15 Royal Navy sailors raises another issue. Geneva Convention rules say, "No physical or moral coercion shall be exercised against protected persons, in particular to obtain information from them or from third parties," adding that prisoners of war "are entitled, in all circumstances, to respect for their persons . . . especially against all acts of violence or threats thereof, and against insults and public curiosity."

Iran's parading of prisoners before the media and coercing of confessions violate the Geneva Convention, which only requires prisoners to give their name, rank and serial number to a captor. How much of a world outrage was there to Iran's mistreatment of prisoners compared with the allegations of prisoner mistreatment by U.S. soldiers at Abu Ghraib? There was little or none.

The West's survival requires that we wake up and recognize the true character of the enemy we face. We are involved in a clash with a culture that has little regard for the Western values that hold the sanctity of human life dear. Terrorists specifically target civilian populations. It makes no difference to them whether their victims are babies, women or children. In fighting the war on terrorism, the West goes to considerable lengths, often risking the lives of our troops, to avoid civilian casualties. The West has the means, but not the will, to utterly destroy terrorists and countries that give them sanction. I hate to think of what the terrorists might do to give us the will.

The Pope Sanctions the OECD Thugs

Wednesday, August 29, 2007

London's *Times Online* recently reported that, according to Vatican sources, Pope Benedict XVI is working on his second encyclical, a doctrinal pronouncement that will condemn tax evasion as "socially unjust." (See www.timesonline.co.uk/tol/comment/faith/article223 7625.ece.) The pontiff will denounce the use of tax havens and off-shore banking by wealthy individuals because it reduces tax revenues for the benefit of society as a whole.

Pope Benedict could benefit from a bit of schooling. Tax avoid-ance is legal conduct whereby individuals arrange their affairs so as to reduce the amount of income that is taxable. Tax avoidance can run the gamut of legal acts, such as investing in tax-free bonds, having employer-paid health plans, making charitable gifts, quitting a job and banking in another country. Tax evasion refers to the conduct by in-dividuals to reduce their tax obligation by illegal means. Tax evasion consists of illegal acts such as falsely claiming dependents, income underreporting and padding expenses.

Pope Benedict's second encyclical puts him squarely in company with a group of thugs known as the Organization for Economic Co-operation & Development (OECD), an international bureaucracy headquartered in Paris and comprised of 30 industrial nations, mostly in Western Europe, the Pacific Rim and North America. One of its reports concluded that low-tax nations are bad for the world economy and identified 35 jurisdictions that are guilty of "harmful tax com-petition."

In the OECD's view, harmful tax competition is when a nation has taxes so low that saving and investment are lured away from high-taxed OECD countries. The blacklist of countries they've identified as tax havens, having strong financial privacy laws, low taxes or zero taxes on certain activities, includes Panama, the Bahamas, Liberia, Liechtenstein, the Marshall Islands and Monaco.

The OECD demands these nations, as well as offshore financial centers in the Caribbean and the Pacific, in effect surrender their fiscal sovereignty and act as deputy tax collectors for nations like France and Germany. This would be a dream for politicians and bad news for the world's taxpayers; fortunately the hard work of the Center for Freedom and Prosperity has stymied the OECD's proposed tax cartel.

Pope Benedict shares some of the OECD's goals in their attack on low-tax jurisdictions. To support its welfare state, European nations must have high taxes. Government spending exceeds 50 percent of the GDP in France, Sweden, Germany and Italy. If Europeans, as private citizens and businessmen, relocate, invest or save in other jurisdictions, it means less money is available to be taxed to support their welfare states. The pope expresses the same concern when he says that tax havens reduce tax revenues for the benefit of society as a whole. Survival of an ever-growing welfare state requires an assault on jurisdictional tax competition.

There's a more fundamental question that I'd put to the pope: Should the Roman Catholic Church support the welfare state? Or, put more plainly, should the Church support the use of the coercive powers of government to enable one person to live at the expense of another? Put even more plainly, should the Church support the government's taking the property of one person and giving it to another to whom it doesn't belong? When such an act is done privately, we call it theft.

The pope might say that the welfare state reflects the will of the people. Would that mean the Church interprets God's commandment to Moses "Thou shalt not steal" as not an absolute, but as "Thou shalt not steal unless you got a majority vote in parliament or congress"?

I share Pope Benedict's desire to assist our fellow man in need. But I believe that reaching into one's own pocket to do so is praiseworthy and laudable. Reaching into another's pocket to assist one's fellow man in need is despicable and worthy of condemnation.

How to Create Conflict

Wednesday, March 1, 2006

High up on my list of annoyances are references to the United States as a democracy and the suggestion that Iraq should become a democracy. The word "democracy" appears in neither of our founding documents—the Declaration of Independence nor the U.S. Constitution.

Our nation's founders had disdain for democracy and majority rule. James Madison, in Federalist Paper No. 10, said in a pure democracy "there is nothing to check the inducement to sacrifice the weaker party or the obnoxious individual." During the 1787 Constitutional Convention, Edmund Randolph said that "in tracing these evils to their origin every man had found it in the turbulence and follies of democracy."

John Adams said, "Remember, democracy never lasts long. It soon wastes, exhausts, and murders itself. There was never a democracy yet that did not commit suicide." Chief Justice John Marshall added, "Between a balanced republic and a democracy, the difference is like that between order and chaos." The founders knew that a democracy would lead to the same kind of tyranny suffered under King George III. Their vision for us was a republic.

But let's cut to Iraq and President Bush's call for it to become a democracy. I can't think of a worse place to have a democracy—majority rule. Iraq needs a republic like that envisioned by our founders—decentralized and limited government power. In a republican form of government, there is rule of law. All citizens, including government officials, are accountable to the same laws. Government intervenes in civil society to protect its citizens against force and fraud but does not intervene in the cases of peaceable, voluntary exchange.

Democracy, what the Bush administration calls for, is different. In a democracy, the majority rules either directly or through its elected representatives. The law is whatever the government determines it to be. Laws aren't necessarily based upon reason but power.

In other words, democracy is just another form of tyranny—tyranny of the majority.

In Iraq, Arabs are about 75 percent of the population, Kurds about 20 percent and Turkomen and Assyrian the balance. Religiously, Shia are about 60 percent of the population, Sunni 35 percent with Christian and other religions making up the balance. If a majority-rule democracy emerges, given the longstanding hate and distrust among ethnic/religious groups, it's a recipe for conflict. The reason is quite simple. Majority rule is a zero-sum game with winners and losers, with winners having the power to impose their wills on the minority. Conflict emerges when the minority resists.

The ideal political model for Iraq is Switzerland's cantonal system. Historically, Switzerland, unlike most European countries, was made up of several different major ethnic groups—Germans, French, Italians and Rhaeto-Romansch. Over the centuries, conflicts have arisen between these groups, who differ in language, religion (Catholic and Protestant) and culture. The resolution to the conflict was to allow the warring groups to govern themselves.

Switzerland has 26 cantons. The cantons are divided into about 3,000 communes. Switzerland's federal government controls only those interests common to all cantons—national defense, foreign policy, railways and the like. All other matters are controlled by the individual cantons and communes. The Swiss cantonal system enables people of different ethnicity, language, culture and religion to live at peace with one another. As such, Switzerland's political system is well suited to an ethnically and religiously divided country such as Iraq.

By the way, for President Bush and others who insist on calling our country a democracy, should we change our pledge of allegiance to say "to the democracy, for which it stands," and should we rename "The Battle Hymn of the Republic" to "The Battle Hymn of the Democracy"?

Disappearing Manufacturing Jobs

Wednesday, May 3, 2006

According to some pundits and political hustlers, free trade has led to a loss of "good manufacturing jobs." Let's look at it, but before doing so, let's first see whether we should work ourselves into a tizzy over other job losses.

In 1900, 41 percent of the U.S. labor force was employed in agriculture. Now, only two percent of today's labor force works in agricultural jobs. If declining employment is used as a gauge of an industry's health, agriculture is America's sickest industry.

Let's not stop with agriculture. In 1970, the telecommunications industry employed 421,000 workers in good-paying jobs as switchboard operators. Today, the telecommunications industry employs only 78,000 operators. That's a tremendous 80 percent job loss. What happened to all those agriculture and switchboard operator jobs? Were they exported to China and India by rapacious businessmen?

The easy and correct answer is that our agricultural sector has seen massive gains in productivity as a result of advances in farm machinery, innovation and technology. There have also been spectacular advances in telecommunications. In 1970, those 421,000 switchboard operators annually handled 9.8 billion long-distance calls. Now 100 billion long-distance calls a year require only 78,000 switchboard operators. What's more, the cost of making a long-distance call is a fraction of what it was in 1970.

Here's my question to you: Should Congress do something to restore all of those jobs lost in agriculture and telecommunications, and what might that something be?

The tremendous gains in productivity seen in agriculture, telecommunications and some other industries have benefited the manufacturing industry as well. According to David Huether, chief economist of the National Association of Manufacturers, U.S. manufacturers are producing and exporting more goods than ever before. While manufacturing output easily outpaces the larger U.S.

economy, manufacturing employment, at 14.2 million, is at its lowest level in more than 50 years.

How do we reconcile lower manufacturing employment with rising manufacturing output? In his April 3, 2006, *Business Week* article, "The Case of the Missing Jobs," Huether says, "Since 2001, with the aid of computers, telecommunications advances, and ever more efficient plant operations, U.S. manufacturing productivity, or the amount of goods or services a worker produces in an hour, has soared a dizzying 24 percent. That's 72 percent faster than the average productivity advance during America's four most recent recession-recovery cycles dating back to the 1970s. In short: We're making more stuff with fewer people." That means rapid economic growth doesn't translate into the kind of manufacturing job creation of earlier periods.

How about the claim that our manufacturing jobs are going to China? The fact of business is, since 2000, China has lost 4.5 million manufacturing jobs, compared with the loss of 3.1 million in the U.S.

Job loss is the trend among the top 10 manufacturing countries that produce 75 percent of the world's manufacturing output (the U.S., Japan, Germany, China, Britain, France, Italy, Korea, Canada and Mexico). Only Italy has managed not to lose factory jobs since 2000.

Economist Joseph Schumpeter referred to this process witnessed in market economies as "creative destruction," where technology and innovation destroy some jobs while creating others. While the process works hardships on some, any attempt to impede the process will make all of us worse off.

Imagine for a moment that technology hadn't destroyed most of the jobs of those 41 percent of Americans working in agriculture in 1900. Where in the world would we have gotten the manpower to make all those goods produced now that weren't even imagined in 1900? Jobs destroyed through the market forces of creative destruction make us all better off, and that applies also to job destruction that comes from peaceable, voluntary exchange with people in different cities, states and countries.

Foreign Aid to Africa

Wednesday, June 28, 2006

British Prime Minister Tony Blair, along with other G-8 leaders, have called for the doubling of foreign aid to African nations by 2010. The idea that foreign aid is a route out of poverty and political instability is not only bankrupted but a cruel and evil hoax as well.

Nearly every sub-Saharan African nation is poorer now than when they became independent during the '60s and '70s. Since that time, food production has fallen by roughly 20 percent. Since 1975, per capita GDP has fallen at a rate of half of one percent annually. Nigerian President Olusegun Obasanjo estimated, "Corrupt African leaders have stolen at least $140 billion from their people in the [four] decades since independence." The call for more aid by George Bush, Tony Blair and other G-8 leaders will produce nothing but more of the same.

Zimbabwe provides an excellent example of why foreign aid, as a way out of poverty, is a fool's errand. Salem University, Winston-Salem, N.C., professor Craig Richardson explores this further in "Learning from Failure: Property Rights, Land Reforms, and the Hidden Architecture of Capitalism," a paper written for the American Enterprise Institute's Development Policy Outlook Series (2006). Not that long ago, Zimbabwe was one of the more prosperous African countries. Professor Richardson writes, "Few countries have failed as spectacularly, or as tragically, as Zimbabwe has over the past half decade. Zimbabwe has transformed from one of Africa's rare success stories into one of its worst economic and humanitarian disasters." It has the world's highest rate of inflation, currently over 1,000 percent. To put this into perspective, in 1995, one U.S. dollar exchanged for eight Zimbabwe dollars; today, one U.S. dollar exchanges for 100,000 Zimbabwe dollars. Unemployment hovers around 80 percent. Its financial institutions are collapsing. The specter of mass starvation hangs over a country that once exported food.

What's the cause? President Robert Mugabe blames domestic

and foreign enemies, particularly England and the United States for trying to bring about his downfall. Of course, according to Mugabe, and some of the world's academic elite, there's that old standby excuse, the legacy of colonialism and multi-national firms exploiting the Third World. The drought is used to "explain" the precipitous drop in agricultural output. Then there's AIDS.

Let's look at drought and AIDS. Zimbabwe's next-door neighbor is Botswana. Botswana has the world's second-highest rate of AIDS infection, and if there's drought in Zimbabwe, there's likely a drought in Botswana, whose major geographic feature is the Kalahari Desert, which covers 70 percent of its land mass. However, Botswana has one of the world's highest per capita GDP growth rates. Moody's and Standard & Poor gives Botswana an "A" credit rating, the best credit risk on the continent, a risk competitive with countries in central Europe and East Asia.

Botswana compared to her other African neighbors prospers not because of foreign aid. There's rule of law, sanctity of contracts, and in 2004, Transparency International ranked Botswana as Africa's least corrupt country, ahead of many European and Asian countries. The World Forum rates Botswana as one of Africa's two most economically competitive nations and one of the best investment opportunities in the developing world.

Botswana shares a heritage with Zimbabwe, for it, too, was a British colony. What it doesn't share with Zimbabwe explains its success: the rule of law, minimal corruption and, most of all, respect for private property rights. No amount of western foreign aid can bring about the political and socioeconomic climate necessary for economic growth. Instead, foreign aid allows vicious dictators to remain in power. It enables them to buy the allegiance of cronies and the military equipment to oppress their own people, not to mention being able to set up "retirement" accounts in Swiss banks. The best thing westerners can do for Africa is to keep their money and their economic development "experts."

Will the West Defend Itself?

Wednesday, August 23, 2006

Does the United States have the power to eliminate terrorists and the states that support them? In terms of capacity, as opposed to will, the answer is a clear yes.

Think about it. Currently, the U.S. has an arsenal of 18 Ohio class submarines. Just one submarine is loaded with 24 Trident nuclear missiles. Each Trident missile has eight nuclear warheads capable of being independently targeted. That means the U.S. alone has the capacity to wipe out Iran, Syria or any other state that supports terrorist groups or engages in terrorism—without risking the life of a single soldier.

Terrorist supporters know we have this capacity, but because of worldwide public opinion, which often appears to be on their side, coupled with our weak will, we'll never use it. Today's Americans are vastly different from those of my generation who fought the life-and-death struggle of World War II. Any attempt to annihilate our Middle East enemies would create all sorts of hand wringing about the innocent lives lost, so-called collateral damage.

Such an argument would have fallen on deaf ears during World War II when we firebombed cities in Germany and Japan. The loss of lives through saturation bombing far exceeded those lost through the dropping of atomic bombs on Hiroshima and Nagasaki.

After the battle of Midway, and the long string of Japanese defeats in the Pacific, including Guam, Okinawa and the Philippines, had today's Americans been around, they'd be willing to negotiate with Japan for peace, pointing to the additional loss of lives if we continued the war. More than likely they would have made the same argument in 1945, when German defeat was imminent. Of course, had there been a peace agreement with Japan and Germany, all it would have achieved would have been to give them time to recoup their losses and resume their aggression at a later time, possibly equipped with nuclear weapons.

We might also note that the occupation of Germany and Japan didn't pose the occupation problems we face in Iraq. The reason is we completely demoralized our enemies, leaving them with neither the will nor the means to resist.

Our adversaries in the Middle East have advantages that the axis powers didn't have—the Western press and public opinion. We've seen widespread condemnation of alleged atrocities and prisoner mistreatment by the U.S., but how much media condemnation have you seen of beheadings and other gross atrocities by Islamists?

Terrorists must be pleased by statements of some members of Congress, such as those by Rep. John Dingell, D.-Mich., who recently said, "I don't take sides for or against Hezbollah." Hezbollah, backed by Iran, is responsible for the 1983 bombing of Beirut barracks killing 241 U.S. service members.

I'm not suggesting that we rush to use our nuclear capacity to crush states that support terrorism. I'm sure there are other less drastic military options. What I am suggesting is that I know of no instances where appeasement, such as the current Western modus operandi, has borne fruit.

What Europeans say about what should be done about terrorist states should fall on deaf ears. Their history of weakness and cowardice during the 1930s goes a long way toward accounting for the 60 million lives lost during World War II. During the mid-'30s, when Hitler started violating the arms limitations of the Versailles Treaty, France and Britain alone could have handily defeated him, but they pursued the appeasement route.

Anyone who thinks current Western appeasement efforts will get Iran to end its nuclear weapons program and end its desire to eliminate Israel is dumber than dumb. Appeasement will strengthen Iran's hand, and it looks as if the West, including the United States, is willing to be complicit in that strengthening.

Foreign Trade Angst

Wednesday, October 18, 2006

Patrick Buchanan's recent syndicated column titled "New Deal for U.S. Manufacturers" stokes the fires of misunderstanding and panic. Mr. Buchanan, my longtime friend, is right about a lot of things, but he's wrong about trade.

First, he laments, "Europeans, Japanese, Canadians and Chinese sell us so much more than they buy from us, because they have rigged the rules of world trade." But so what? I buy more from my grocer than he buys from me. It wouldn't make a difference if I lived 2 feet south of the U.S.-Canadian border and my grocer lived 2 feet north of it.

Like many, Buchanan worries about our foreign trade deficit, pointing out that it's reaching an annual rate of $816 billion, and that means "dependency on foreigners." Actually, the foreign dependency is a two-way street. I'll explain it, starting with the alleged trade deficit I run with my grocer.

When I purchase $100 worth of groceries, my goods account (groceries) rises by $100, but my capital account (money) falls by $100. That means there's really a balance in my trade account. By the same token, my grocer's goods account (groceries) falls by $100 but his capital account (money) rises by $100, also a balance in his trade account.

Mr. Buchanan writes, "Imports surged to $188 billion for the month [of July], as our dependency on foreigners for the vital necessities of our national life ever deepens." That means we imported $188 billion worth of goods. Do foreigners keep all those dollars they earned under a mattress? They are not that stupid. They use those dollars to import capital goods such as U.S. stocks, bonds and U.S. Treasury notes.

They might use some of it to build factories in the U.S. such as Honda, Novartis and Samsung. The dollar amount of those purchases is going to equalize the value of what we import. We sport a huge surplus in our capital account with foreigners. As such, they are dependent on us for a safe and profitable place to invest their earnings. That dependency contributes to our economic growth.

Then there's Buchanan's worry about U.S. manufacturing job loss. U.S. farming has a similar history. Farm employment peaked between 1840 and 1870. In 1900, 40 percent of American workers were employed in farming; today, it's less than two percent. Technological advances made that possible. U.S. manufacturing employment reached its peak in 1950 and has been in decline ever since.

This has more to do with technological innovation than outsourcing. It's a worldwide phenomenon. Since 2000, China has lost 4.5 million manufacturing jobs compared to the loss of 3.1 million in the U.S. Nine of the top 10 manufacturing countries, who produce 75 percent of the world's manufacturing output (the U.S., Japan, Germany, China, Britain, France, Italy, Korea, Canada, and Mexico), have lost manufacturing jobs, Italy being the exception. Because of technological progress, manufacturing output has risen while manufacturing employment has fallen.

I'm one of those whom Pat calls "robotic free-traders." That might be another label for those of us who support peaceable, voluntary exchange, and I plead guilty. Buchanan, like so many others, points to the government subsidies and tariff protections given to businesses in other countries, a practice from which we can't plead complete innocence. Protectionists call for "free trade but fair trade." They call for a "level playing field."

In effect, they're saying that if other governments rip off their citizens with business subsidies and import duties, forcing them to pay higher prices, our government should retaliate by using the same tools to rip off its citizens.

The next time I see Pat, I might ask him what he would do if we both were at sea in a rowboat and I shot a hole in my end of the boat. Would he retaliate by shooting a hole in his end?

Should We Trade at All?

Wednesday, October 25, 2006

There are only a handful of products that Americans import that cannot be produced at home and therefore create jobs for Americans. Let's look at a few of them.

We import cocoa from Ghana and coffee from African and Latin American countries. We import saffron from Spain and India and cinnamon from Sri Lanka. In fact, India produces 86 percent of the world tonnage of spices. There's absolutely no reason these products cannot be produced by Americans, and we could be cocoa, coffee and spices independent.

You say, "Williams, that's crazy! We don't have the climate and soil conditions to produce those products. Many spices, for example, require a moist tropical environment." No problem. We have the technology whereby we can simulate both the soil and weather conditions. We could build greenhouses in which to grow cinnamon trees and get our scientists to create the same soil conditions that exist in Sri Lanka. Greenhouses could also be built to simulate the climate conditions in Africa and Latin America to grow cocoa and coffee. In the case of cocoa, the greenhouses would have to be Superdome size to accommodate trees as high as 50 feet.

You say, "Williams, that's still crazy! Imagine the high costs and the higher product prices of your crazy scheme." I say, "Aha, you're getting the picture."

There are several nearly self-evident factors about our being cocoa, coffee and spices independent. Without a doubt, there would be job creation in our cocoa, coffee and spices industries, but consumers would pay a much higher price than they currently do. Therefore, nearly 300 million American consumers would be worse off, having to pay those higher prices or doing without, but those with the new jobs would be better off.

So let's be honest with ourselves. Why do we choose to import cocoa, coffee and spices rather than produce them ourselves? The answer is that it is cheaper to do so. That means we enjoy a higher standard of living than if we tried to produce them ourselves. If we can enjoy, say, coffee, at a cheaper price than producing it ourselves, we have more money left over to buy other goods. That principle not only applies to cocoa, coffee and spices. It's a general principle: If a good can be purchased more cheaply abroad, we enjoy a higher standard of living by trading than we would by producing it ourselves.

No one denies that international trade has unpleasant consequences for some workers. They have to find other jobs that might not pay as much, but should we protect those jobs through trade restrictions? The Washington-based Institute for International Economics has assembled data that might help with the answer. Tariffs and quotas on imported sugar saved 2,261 jobs during the 1990s. As a result of those restrictions, the average household pays $21 more per year for sugar. The total cost, nationally, sums to $826,000 for each job saved. Trade restrictions on luggage saved 226 jobs and cost consumers $1.2 million in higher prices for each job saved. Restrictions on apparel and textiles saved 168,786 jobs at a cost of nearly $200,000 for each job saved.

You might wonder how it is possible for, say, the sugar industry to rip off consumers. After all, consumers are far more numerous than sugar workers and sugar bosses. It's easy. A lot is at stake for those in the sugar industry, workers and bosses. They dedicate huge resources to pressure Congress into enacting trade restrictions. But how many of us consumers will devote the same resources to unseat a congressman who voted for sugar restrictions that forced us to pay $21 more for the sugar our family uses? It's the problem of visible beneficiaries of trade restrictions, sugar workers and bosses, gaining at the expense of invisible victims—sugar consumers. We might think of it as congressional price-gouging.

Should We Copy Europe?

Wednesday, November 22, 2006

Some Americans look to European countries such as France, Germany and its Scandinavian neighbors and suggest that we adopt some of their economic policies. I agree, we should look at Europe for the lessons they can teach us. Dr. Daniel Mitchell, research fellow at the Heritage Foundation, does just that in his paper titled "Fiscal Policy Lessons from Europe."

Government spending exceeds 50 percent of the GDP in France and Sweden and more than 45 percent in Germany and Italy, compared to U.S. federal, state and local spending of just under 36 percent. Government spending encourages people to rely on handouts rather than individual initiative, and the higher taxes to finance the handouts reduce incentives to work, save and invest. The European results shouldn't surprise anyone. U.S. per capita output in 2003 was $39,700, almost 40 percent higher than the average of $28,700 for European nations.

Over the last decade, the U.S. economy has grown twice as fast as European economies. In 2006, European unemployment averaged 8 percent while the U.S. average was 4.7 percent. What's more, the percentage of Americans without a job for more than 12 months was 12.7 percent while in Europe it was 42.6 percent. Since 1970, 57 million new jobs were created in the U.S., and just 4 million were created in Europe.

Dr. Mitchell cites a comparative study by Timbro, a Swedish think tank, showing that European countries rank with the poorest U.S. states in terms of living standards, roughly equal to Arkansas and Montana and only slightly ahead of West Virginia and Mississippi. Average living space in Europe is just under 1,000 square feet for the average household, while U.S. households enjoy an average of 1,875 square feet, and poor households 1,200 square feet. In terms of income levels, productivity, employment levels and R&D investment, according to Eurochambres (The Association of European Chambers of Commerce and Industry), it would take Europe about two decades to catch up with us, assuming we didn't grow further.

We don't have to rely on these statistics to make us not want to be like Europeans; just watch where the foot traffic and money flow. Some 400,000 European science and technology graduates live in the U.S. European migration to our country rose by 16 percent during the 1990s. In 1980, the Bureau of Economic Analysis put foreign direct investment in the U.S. at $127 billion. Today, it's more than $1.7 trillion. In 1980, there was $90 billion of foreign portfolio investment—government and private securities—in the U.S. Today, there's more than $4.6 trillion, much of it coming from Europeans who find our investment climate more attractive.

What's the European response to its self-made economic malaise? They don't repeal the laws that make for a poor investment climate. Instead, through the Paris-based Organisation for Economic Co-operation and Development (OECD), they attack low-tax jurisdictions. Why? To support its welfare state, European nations must have high taxes, but if Europeans, as private citizens and businessmen, relocate, invest and save in other jurisdictions, it means less money is available to be taxed.

Dr. Mitchell addresses this issue through his research at the Center for Freedom and Prosperity (www.freedomandprosperity.org). The OECD has a blacklist for countries they've identified as "tax havens." The blacklisted countries include Hong Kong, Macao, Malaysia (Labuan) and Singapore. Also targeted are Andorra, Brunei, Costa Rica, Dubai, Guatemala, Liberia, Liechtenstein, the Marshall Islands, Monaco, the Philippines and Uruguay. The blacklisted jurisdictions have strong financial privacy laws and low or zero rates of tax.

The OECD member countries want the so-called tax havens to change their laws to help them identify the earnings of their citizens. Most of all, OECD wants these countries to legislate higher taxes so as to reduce their appeal. A suggestion that we should be more like Europe is the same as one suggesting that we should be poorer.

Our Trade Deficit

Wednesday, May 25, 2005

I buy more from my grocer than he buys from me, and I bet it's the same with you and your grocer. That means we have a trade deficit with our grocers. Does our perpetual grocer trade deficit portend doom? If we heeded some pundits and politicians who are talking about our national trade deficit, we might think so. But do we have a trade deficit in the first place? Let's look at it.

Insofar as the grocer example, there are two accounts that I hold. One is my "goods" account, which consists of groceries. The other is my "capital" account, which consists of money. Let's look at what happens when I purchase groceries. Say I purchase $100 worth of groceries. The value of my goods account rises by $100. That rise is matched by an equal $100 decline in my capital account. Adding a plus $100 to a minus $100 yields a perfect trade balance. That transaction, from my grocer's point of view, results in his goods account falling by $100, but when he accepts my cash, his capital account rises by $100, again a trade balance.

The principle here differs not one iota if my grocer was located in another country as opposed to down the street. There'd still be a trade balance when both the goods account and the capital account are considered. Imbalances in goods accounts are all over the place. For example, my grocer buys more from his wholesaler than his wholesaler buys from him. The wholesaler buys more from the manufacturer than the manufacturer buys from him, but when we put capital accounts into the mix, in each case, trade is balanced.

International trade operates under the identical principle. When we as consumers purchase goods from China, and the Chinese don't purchase a like amount of goods from us, it is said that there's a trade deficit. But instead of purchasing goods, the Chinese might purchase corporate stocks, bonds or U.S. Treasury debt instruments. Just as in my grocer example, there is a balance of trade. The deficit in our nation's goods and services account, sometimes called current account, is matched by a surplus of equal magnitude in our capital account. A large portion of surpluses in our capital account consists of U.S. Treasury debt instruments held by foreigners. As of June 2004, China held nearly $200 billion, Japan over $1 trillion, and Europe combined held over $2 trillion.

Some politicians gripe about all the U.S. debt held by foreigners. Only a politician can have that kind of audacity. Guess who's creating the debt instruments that foreigners hold? If you said it's our profligate Congress, go to the head of the class. If foreigners didn't purchase so much of our debt, we'd be worse off in terms of higher inflation and interest rates. What about the possibility of foreigners dumping our debt? Foreigners aren't stupid. Dumping large amounts of Treasury bonds would drive down their value. Foreigners as well as we would take a hit.

The fact that foreigners are willing to exchange massive amounts of goods in exchange for slips of paper in the forms of currency, stocks and bonds should be a source of pride. It means America, with its wealth, rule of law and the sanctity of contracts, inspires foreigners to hold large amounts of their wealth in U.S. obligations. Their willingness to do so means something else: Trade increases competition. Ultimately it's competition, many producers competing for his dollar, that truly protects the consumer. Producers are protected, at the expense of consumers, by restrictions on competition. The quest to restrict competition is what lies at the heart of the trade deficit demagoguery. When's the last time you heard a consumer complaining about his buying more from a Chinese or Japanese producer than that producer buys from him?

Aid to Africa

Wednesday, July 13, 2005

British Prime Minister Tony Blair is pressuring the rich nations of the world to give more foreign aid to Africa—to the tune of $25 billion a year by 2010. The U.S. already gave $3.2 billion last year. In the wake of this pressure, we might ask ourselves whether it's foreign aid that Africa needs most for economic development.

A standard myth is there's a "vicious cycle of poverty" that makes economic development virtually impossible for the world's poor nations. This myth holds that poor countries are poor because income is so low that savings cannot be generated to provide the kind of capital accumulation necessary for economic growth. Thus, it is alleged, the only way out of perpetual poverty is foreign aid.

Let's examine the "vicious cycle of poverty" myth and whether foreign aid is a necessary ingredient for economic development. The U.S., Britain, France, Canada and most other countries were once poor. Andrew Bernstein of the Ayn Rand Institute wrote in an article titled "Capitalism Is the Cure for Africa's Problems" that pre-industrial Europe was vastly poorer than contemporary Africa.

A relatively well-off country, like France, experienced several famines between the 15th and 18th centuries as well as plagues and diseases that sometimes killed hundreds of thousands. In France, life expectancy was 20 years, in Ireland it was 19 years, and in early 18th-century London, more than 74 percent of the children died before reaching age 5.

Beginning in the late 18th century, there was a dramatic economic turnabout in Europe. How in the world did these once poor and backward countries break the "vicious cycle of poverty" and become wealthy, without what today's development experts say is absolutely necessary for economic growth—foreign aid handouts, World Bank and International Monetary Fund loans, and billions of dollars of debt forgiveness?

The answer is simple: Capitalism started taking root in Europe.

Capitalism is an economic system where there's peaceable, voluntary exchange. Government protects private property rights held in goods and services. There's rule of law and minimal government regulation and control of the economy.

Check out the Washington, D.C.-based Heritage Foundation's "Index of Economic Freedom." Heading its list of countries with the freest economic systems are: Hong Kong, Singapore, Luxembourg, Estonia, Ireland and New Zealand. Bringing up the rear as the countries with little or no economic liberty are: North Korea, Zimbabwe, Angola, Burundi and the Congo. It's not rocket science to conclude that economic liberty and the wealth of a nation and its peoples go together, not to mention greater human rights guarantees.

Some economic development "experts" attribute Africa's troubles to its history of colonialism. That's nonsense, because some of the world's richest countries are former colonies, such as the U.S., Canada, Hong Kong and Australia. In fact, many of Africa's sub-Saharan countries are poorer now than when they were colonies, and their people suffer greater human rights degradations, such as the mass genocide the continent has witnessed.

One unappreciated tragedy that attests to the wasted talents of its peoples is that Africans tend to do well all around the world except in Africa. This is seen by the large number of prosperous, professional and skilled African families throughout Europe and the United States. Back home, these same people would be hamstrung by their corrupt governments.

The worst thing that can be done is to give more foreign aid to African nations. Foreign aid goes from government to government. Foreign aid allows Africa's corrupt regimes to buy military equipment, pay off cronies and continue to oppress their people. It also provides resources for its leaders to set up "retirement" accounts in Swiss banks.

What Africa needs, foreign aid cannot deliver, and that's elimination of dictators and socialist regimes, establishment of political and economic freedom, rule of law and respect for individual rights. Until that happens, despite billions of dollars of foreign aid, Africa will remain a basket case.

Sweatshop Exploitation

January 26, 2004

Here's a question. Suppose you see people lining up for hours, and people willing to pay a month's salary in bribes, in order to get a $2 a day factory job, what might you conclude? Would you guess there are higher paying jobs around but the people are too lazy to look for them? Here's my guess: No matter how unattractive to us that $2 a day job is it might be that person's best known prospect.

New York Times reporter, Nicholas Kristof, recently wrote "Inviting All Democrats," *New York Times Online* (1/14/04), a story documenting the plight of Cambodia's poor. In Phnom Pen, hundreds of Cambodians traipse through trash dumps scavenging for plastic bags, metal cans, bits of food and whatever else they can find to sell. Kristof says, "Nhep Chanda averages 75 cents a day for her efforts. For her, the idea of being exploited in a garment factory—working only six days a week, inside, instead of in the broiling sun, for up to $2 a day— is a dream."

Many Democrat and Republican politicians, union leaders, and academic elite say that paying somebody $2 a day is exploitation. They've called for actions against American companies who exploit Third World workers through low pay, use of child labor and poor working conditions. But let's examine this with an eye toward asking whether exploitation is the right word to use. Let's start off with a personal question. Suppose you're earning $1,500 a month and I come along and offer you a job paying $3,000 a month with better working conditions. In no way do I coerce you into accepting my job offer. If you accept my job offer, then the only unambiguous conclusion is that you saw my offer as being superior to your next best alternative. When a person is offered an alternative, superior to his next best alternative, how much sense does it make to characterize it as exploitation?

If Nhep Chanda, who earns 75 cents a day toiling in nasty trash dumps, is offered a factory job at $2 a day, has she been made better off or worse off? Any reasonable person would conclude that she's better off. When one person makes another person an offer that makes that person better off, does it make sense to characterize it as exploitation? While we're at it, we might ask if anti-free trade demonstrations and other public pressures stop companies from having manufacturing facilities in places like Cambodia, paying $2 a day wages, will people like Nhep Chanda be worse off or better off? In other words, do we help people who have few miserable alternatives by destroying their best one?

Former presidential aspirant Congressman Dick Gephardt pledged that if he became president he'd press the World Trade Organization to establish an international minimum wage. Union leaders and their useful idiots in the anti-globalism movement have also called for minimum wages and better working conditions for workers of multi-national firms in Third World countries. Here's my question to you: Do you believe these people really care about the world's poor like Nhep Chanda? If you do, I have a fountain of youth I'd like to sell you.

There might be a few ministers, college students and other uninformed people who sincerely care about the Third World poor. But the thrust of the public relations campaign against the multi-nationals comes from the U.S. and European union movements and some businesses who see their jobs and profits threatened. They wish to raise the cost of overseas operations in order to forestall company relocation, or as Congressman Gephardt said he wants an international minimum wage high enough so that American workers are not competing with slave, sweat shop, and child labor around the world.

Self-Inflicted Poverty

June 21, 2004

Did you learn that the United States is rich because we have boun-tiful natural resources? That has to be nonsense. Africa and South America are probably the natural resources richest continents but are home to the world's most miserably poor people. On the other hand, Japan, Hong Kong, Taiwan and England are natural resources poor but its people are among the world's richest.

Maybe your college professor taught that the legacy of colonialism explains Third World poverty. That's nonsense as well. Canada was a colony. So was Australia, New Zealand and Hong Kong. In fact the richest country in the world, United States, was once a colony. By contrast, Ethiopia, Liberia, Tibet, Nepal, Sikkim and Bhutan were never colonies but they are home to the world's poorest people.

There's no complete explanation for why some countries are af-fluent while others are poor, but there are some leads. Rank countries along a continuum according to whether they were closer to being free market economies or whether they're closer to socialist or planned economies. Then rank countries by per capita income, we will find a general, not perfect, pattern whereby those having a larger free market sector its citizens enjoy a higher standard of living than those at the socialist end of the continuum. What is more important is that if we ranked countries according to how Freedom House or International Amnesty rates their human rights guarantees, we'd see that citizens of countries with market economies are not only richer but they tend to enjoy a greater measure of human rights protections. While there is no complete explanation for the correlation between free markets, higher wealth and human rights protections, you can bet the rent money that the correlation is not simply coincidental.

With but few exceptions, African countries are not free and most are basket cases. My colleague, John Blundell, director of the Lon-don-based Institute of Economic Affairs, highlights some of this in his article "Africa's Plight Will Not End With Aid," in *The Scotsman*

(6/14/04). Once a food exporting country, Zimbabwe stands on the brink of starvation. Last week President Robert Mugabe declared that he's going to nationalize all the farmland. You don't have to be a rocket scientist to figure that the consequence will be to exacerbate Zimbabwe's food problems. Sierra Leone, rich in minerals, especially diamonds, highly fertile land, the best port site in west Africa has declined into a condition of utter despair. It's a similar story in nearly all of south-of-Sahara Africa. Its people are generally worse off now than they were during colonialism both in terms of standard of living and human rights protections.

John Blundell says that the institutions westerners take for granted are entirely absent in most of Africa. Africans are not incompetent; they're just like us. Without the rule of law, private property rights, independent judiciary, limited government and an infrastructure for basic transportation, water, electricity and communication, we'd also be a diseased, broken and starving people.

What can the West do to help? The worst thing is more foreign aid. For the most part foreign aid is government to government and as such it provides the financial resources that allows Africa's corrupt regimes to buy military equipment, pay off cronies and continue to oppress their people. It also provides resources for the leaders to set up "retirement" accounts in Swiss banks. Even so-called humanitarian aid in the form of food is often diverted. Blundell reports that Mugabe's thugs rip labels off of wheat and corn shipments from the U.S. and Europe and re-label it as benevolence from the dictator. Most of what Africa needs the West cannot give and that's rule of law, private property rights, independent judiciary, and limited government. The one important way we can help is to lower our trade barriers.

The Appeasement Disease

August 23, 2004

President Bush's foreign policy critics at home and abroad share characteristics and visions that have previously led to worldwide chaos and untold loss of lives. These people believe that negotiation, appeasement and caving in to the demands of vicious totalitarian leaders can produce good-faith behavior. Their vision not only has a long record of failure but devastating consequences.

During the late 1930s, France and Britain hoped that allowing Hitler to annex Sudetenland from Czechoslovakia would satisfy his territorial ambitions. This was after a long string of German violations of the terms of the Versailles Treaty ending World War I. Appeasement didn't work. It was seen as weakness and it simply emboldened Hitler.

At the Yalta Conference, near the end of World War II, Winston Churchill and Franklin Roosevelt thought they could appease Josef Stalin by giving away Eastern Europe and making other concessions that ultimately marked the beginning of the nearly half-century Cold War and Soviet/China expansionism. War-weary westerners hoped that brutal tyrants would act in good faith.

Failing to stand up to Stalin resulted in unspeakable atrocities, enslavement and human suffering. Quite interestingly western leftist appeasers exempted communist leaders from the harsh criticism directed toward Hitler whose crimes made Hitler's slaughter of 21 million appear almost amateurish. According to Professor R. J. Rummel's research, in "Death by Government," from 1917 until its collapse the Soviet Union murdered or caused the death of 61 million people, mostly its own citizens. Since 1949, communist China's Mao Zedong regime was responsible for the death of 38 million of its own citizens.

History never exactly repeats itself but the vision of earlier appeasers was part of the West's vision of how to deal with Saddam Hussein. After devastating defeat in the first Gulf War, Iraq agreed to coalition peace terms. After documents were signed every effort was made by the Iraqis to frustrate implementation of the terms, particularly UN weapons inspections. Westerner appeasers, most notably Europeans, were quite willing to respond to Saddam Hussein's violation of peace terms in a fashion similar to their earlier counterpart's response to Adolf Hitler's violation of the peace terms of the Versailles Treaty. Had Britain or France launched a military attack on Germany in 1934–35 when Hitler started his arms buildup in violation of the Versailles Treaty, and before he fully developed his military capability, he would have been defeated and at least 50 million lives would have been spared.

What deters terrorists? We try to thwart them or kill them. What deters nations that might harbor or assist terrorist? We show them the kind of destruction we're prepared to rain down upon them. Whether we ultimately find nuclear, chemical or biological weapons in Iraq is one thing, but one clear message has been sent as a result of our actions in Iraq and Afghanistan. The world now knows, where it didn't know in the past, that we have the will to destroy a nation that supports terrorism. One measure of the benefit of that message is that Libya's Mohammar Qaddafi has decided to forgo his weapons program and Iran and North Korea might reconsider their agenda.

Some appeasers would like us to cut and run in the wake of terrorist threats just as Spain and the Philippines did. Others, especially our increasingly anti-Semitic European allies, would like us to be more "even-handed" in the Palestinian-Israel conflict. Even-handed might be translated as abandoning Israel. Such a move wouldn't bring any better results than when Britain's Prime Minister Neville Chamberlain sold the Czechoslovakians down the river to Hitler.

There's no evidence that today's fanatical terrorists and their nation state sympathizers have any taste for compromise and negotiation. They want western submission and they just might get that with presidential candidate John Kerry's promise that if elected he will wage "more sensitive war on terror."

Economic Stupidity

April 28, 2003

Imagine that you and I are in a row boat. I commit the stupid act of shooting a hole in my end of the boat. Would it be intelligent for you to respond by shooting a hole in your end of the boat? Or, imagine I were a politician and told you that the Russian, Chinese, Korean, Brazilian and German governments were ripping off their citizens by, on the one hand, taxing them to provide subsidies to their domestic steel industries, and on the other, erecting tariff barriers forcing them to pay higher prices for products made with or containing steel. Would you deem it responsible or intelligent of me to propose retaliatory tariff policy whereby Americans are ripped off until Russia, China, Korea, Brazilian and German governments stop ripping off their citizens?

Both of these scenarios are applicable to the Bush administration's 30 percent steel tariffs imposed last year. Those tariffs caused the domestic price for some steel products, such as hot-rolled steel, to rise as much as 40 percent. The clear beneficiaries of the Bush steel tariffs were steel industry executives, stockholders and the approximately 1,700 steelworker jobs that were saved. Tariff policy beneficiaries are always visible but its victims are mostly invisible. Politicians love this. The reason is simple. The beneficiaries know for whom to cast their ballots and the victims don't know whom to blame for their calamity.

According to a study by the Institute for International Economics, saving those 1,700 jobs in the steel industry cost American consumers $800,000 in the form of higher prices for each steelworker job saved. That's just the monetary side of the picture. According to a study commissioned by the Consuming Industries Trade Action Association, higher steel prices have caused at least 4,500 job losses in no fewer than 16 states—over 19,000 jobs in California, 16,000 in Texas and 10,000 in Ohio, Michigan and Illinois. In other words, industries that use steel are forced to pay higher prices and the products they produce become less competitive and they must lay off workers.

The average hourly wage of steelworkers ranges between $15 and $20 plus fringe benefits; so we might be talking about an annual wage package averaging $50,000 to $55,000. Here's my question to you: How much sense does it make for American consumers to have to pay $800,000 in higher prices to save a $50 to $55 thousand-dollar-a-year job? It'd make better economic sense for Congress to pass an Aid to Dependent Steelworkers Act whereby we'd tax ourselves so as to give each of those 1,700 steelworkers, whose jobs were saved, $100,000 year so they might take off and live in a nice beachfront condo in Florida or Bermuda. While less costly to Americans than President Bush's steel tariffs, it has no political future. The handout would make the protectionist policies apparent and hence repulsive to most Americans.

Article I, Section 8 of the U.S. Constitution says Congress has the authority "To regulate commerce with foreign nations, and among the several states, and with the Indian tribes." It wasn't the Framers' intent to give one group of Americans, such as those in the steel industry, the power to use Congress to tax other Americans.

When Congress creates a special advantage for some Americans, it must of necessity come at the expense of other Americans. Those Americans who're harmed, such as steel-using industries, descend on Congress asking for some kind of relief for themselves. It all reminds me of a passage from Marcus Connelly Cook's play *Green Pastures* wherein God laments to the Angel Gabriel, "Every time, Ah passes a miracle, Ah has to pass fo' or five mo' to ketch up wid it." I think Congress ought to get out of the miracle business.

Poverty Myths

November 4, 2002

A typical belief among the world's foreign aid agencies is there's a "vicious cycle of poverty" that makes economic development virtually impossible for the world's poor nations. This idea holds that poor countries are poor because income is so low that savings cannot be generated to provide the kind of capital accumulation necessary for economic growth. Thus, it is alleged, that the only way out of the poverty quagmire is foreign aid. As popular as the vicious cycle of poverty theory is among economic development "experts," it has to be one of mankind's most foolish ideas. "Explain yourself, Williams!" you say, "That's what my professors taught when I went to college and they're teaching the same thing to my kids." Let's look at it.

The vicious cycle of poverty theory can't even pass the straight-face test. After all how did countries such as United States, England, Canada, New Zealand, Switzerland and others break that cycle and become rich; were they simply "born" rich? That's a big fat no. So how in the world did these once poor and backward countries become wealthy without what today's development experts say is absolutely necessary for economic growth—foreign aid handouts, World Bank and International Monetary Fund (IMF) loans? Maybe part of the answer lies in the fact that there were no foreign aid handout programs and economic development experts around during their economic development.

According to a recently released report by Foundation policy analysts Paolo Pasicolan and Sara Fitzgerald, "The Millennium Challenge Account: Linking Aid with Economic Freedom," despite decades of economic aid most recipient nations are poorer now than they were before they first received development assistance. What foreign aid usually achieves is that of enabling Third World tyrants to retain power by having the resources to build grandiose projects that make little economic sense, pay off cronies and buy military equipment to suppress their people, not to mention setting up multi-million and even multi-billion dollar Swiss bank accounts.

Then there's the population myth that holds that countries are poor because they are overpopulated. That's nonsense. For example, the population density of China is 409 people per square mile; in Taiwan it's 1,478 per square mile and in Hong Kong, it's 247,500. Which people have higher incomes? If you said Hong Kong, you'd be dead right, but for people who see overpopulation as a cause of poverty, China should be the richest and Hong Kong the poorest. The late economist Lord Peter Bauer said, "Economic achievement and progress depend on people's conduct, not on their numbers."

The latest mythical explanation for Third World poverty is globalization and multinational corporation exploitation. Peaceable trade and contact with other nations have always raised the potential for higher living standards. In fact, Third World countries least touched by the West, whether the contact was in the form of imperialist conquest, trade, or multinational corporations, are among the poorest of the poor—countries like: Nepal, Tibet, Sikkim, Bhutan in Asia and Ethiopia and Liberia in Africa.

Poverty is mostly self-inflicted—indigenously created. What are some of the most commonly held characteristics of the non-poor world? In non-poor countries people tend to have greater personal liberty, their property rights are protected, contracts are enforced, there's rule of law and there's a market-oriented economic system rather than socialistic. A country need not be rich to create these wealth-enhancing institutions. That's much of the story of the U.S. In 1776 we were essentially a Third World nation but we established an institutional structure to become rich, an institutional structure that not only attracted investment but talented, hardworking immigrants as well. Contrast that to today's poor countries whose policies and institutional structure do just the opposite—repel investment and cause their most talented people to leave.

Do Peace Treaties Produce Peace?

April 22, 2002

Europe has been at peace for an unprecedented nearly six decades. Why? It surely is not because of peace treaties between enemy states and it's surely not because of disarmament. All that was tried before and failed. The best explanation for Europe's unprecedented period of peace is that it was an armed camp bristling with weapons. Both adversaries, NATO backed by the U.S. and the Warsaw Pact backed by the USSR, knew for sure that aggression would produce Armageddon. Another reason is that the previous aggressor, Germany, was utterly and completely defeated. Had the Nazis, seeing they were losing the war, successfully sued for peace and a cessation of the hostilities, there would not have been this unprecedented period of peace in Europe. The Nazis would have simply regrouped.

The world can be thankful that today's mindset wasn't around during the 1940s. When we laid waste through conventional and firebombing of Dresden and other German cities, and did the same thing to Tokyo and other Japanese cities, we didn't have to worry about the Red Cross and peace advocates going in afterwards taking pictures and then holding us up to ridicule for "collateral damage." If they did, the public would have turned a deaf ear. After all has there ever been war, at least during modern times, where non-combatants were not killed? Indeed, that is just one of the things that make war so horrible.

If we had captured Joseph Goebbels, Heinrich Himmler or Hideki Tojo during the war would anybody have cared much about their civil rights like some people are caring about the civil rights of Taliban captives in Guantanamo? I'm not making an argument for cruelty, but what civil rights are owed those hell bent on trying to destroy our civilization? During World War II, how many Americans would have demanded that a captured German spy or saboteur be supplied with a taxpayer-supplied legal team and jail amenities. Historically, spies and saboteurs have faced the hangman's noose or a firing squad.

This brings us to the Middle East crisis and the condemnation

Israel has received for its military retaliation for Palestinian terrorist attacks. During U.S. Secretary of State Powell's visit, world news cameras captured a haggard, bedraggled Chairman Arafat saying, "Is this acceptable? Is this acceptable?," referring to the Israel Defense Forces' quarantine and destruction of his headquarters. I was trying to imagine the response of Americans, back in the '40s, to one of our Axis adversaries asking the same question.

There's one weapon that international thugs have today that yesterday's international thugs didn't and that's "world opinion." Palestinian terrorists set off bombs to murder innocent Israeli civilians. When Israel retaliates, imposing high cost, Palestinians call up their only defensive weapon: world opinion. World opinion was also used by Saddam Hussein during the Gulf War by bringing the western media to see the destruction of a supposed baby milk factory by coalition forces.

How much should the western world care about the opinion of those who demonstrate open hostility to the values that we hold such as democratically elected officials, human rights, equality before the law? I say none whatsoever. At the same time neither am I of the mind that we should interfere with their choices except to say that their acts of aggression should be met with harsh retaliation. Were I prime minister of Israel, I'd trade peace for land on these terms: in exchange for each six months of peace, I'd completely turn over, say, five square miles of land and for just one terrorist attack, I'd send in the Israel Defense Forces to take it all back.

Congressional and Leftist Lies

Wednesday, November 14, 2007

An important component of the leftist class warfare agenda is to condemn President Bush's tax cuts for the rich. This claim is careless, ignorant or dishonest on at least two counts. First there's the constitutional issue. Article I, Section 8 reads, "The Congress shall have Power To lay and collect Taxes. . . ." That means the president has no taxing authority.

Presidents can propose or veto taxes and Congress can override vetoes. The bottom line is that all taxing authority rests with the U.S. Congress. The next time you hear someone condemn or praise Bush's tax cuts, ask them whether the Constitution has been amended to give the president taxing authority.

But what about those tax cuts for the rich? Are the rich now sharing a smaller burden of the federal income tax because their fair share of the burden has been shifted to the poor? The most recent Internal Revenue Service (IRS) statistics can give us some guidance. In 2005, the top 1 percent of income earners, those with an annual adjusted gross income of $365,000 and higher, paid 39 percent of all federal income taxes; in 1999, they paid 36 percent.

In 2005, the top 5 percent of income earners, those having an adjusted gross income of $145,000 and higher, paid 60 percent of all federal taxes; in 1999, it was 55 percent. The top 10 percent, earning income over $103,000, paid 70 percent. The top 25 percent, with income of over $62,000, paid 86 percent, and the top 50 percent, earning $31,000 and higher, paid 97 percent of all federal taxes.

What about any argument suggesting that the burden of taxes have been shifted to the poor? The bottom 50 percent, earning $30,000 or less, paid 3 percent of total federal income taxes. In 1999, they paid 4 percent. Congressmen know all of this, but they attempt to hoodwink the average American who doesn't.

The fact that there are so many American earners who have little or no financial stake in our country poses a serious political problem.

The Tax Foundation estimates that 41 percent of whites, 56 percent of blacks, 59 percent of American Indian and Aleut Eskimo and 40 percent Asian and Pacific Islanders had no 2004 federal income tax liability. The study concluded, "When all of the dependents of these income-producing households are counted, there are roughly 122 million Americans—44 percent of the U.S. population—who are outside of the federal income tax system." These people represent a natural constituency for big-spending politicians. In other words, if you have little or no financial stake in America, what do you care about the cost of massive federal spending programs?

Similarly, what do you care about tax cuts if you're paying little or no taxes? In fact, you might be openly hostile toward tax cuts out of fear that they might lead to reductions in handout programs from which you benefit. Survey polls have confirmed this. According to The Harris Poll taken in June 2003, 51 percent of Democrats thought the tax cuts enacted by Congress were a bad thing while 16 percent of Republicans thought so. Among Democrats, 67 percent thought the tax cuts were unfair while 32 percent of Republicans thought so. When asked whether the $350 billion tax cut package will help your family finances, 59 percent of those surveyed said no and 35 percent said yes.

Whether you're for or against President Bush matters little, but what do you think of politicians and their media dupes winning you over with lies about the rich not paying their fair share? And, by the way, $145,000 or even $345,000 a year hardly qualifies one as rich. It's not even yacht money.

Law and Society

John Adams warned that "the moment the idea is admitted into society that property is not as sacred as the laws of God, and that there is not a force of law and public justice to protect it, anarchy and tyranny commence. If 'Thou shalt not covet' and 'Thou shalt not steal' were not commandments of Heaven, they must be made inviolable precepts in every society before it can be civilized or made free." Private property rights are under siege in a way never contemplated by earlier Americans. The Fifth Amendment is clear saying, "Nor shall private property be taken for public use without just compensation." The U.S. Supreme Court made a mockery of the Fifth Amendment in its 2005 decision Kelo v. City of New London, where it held that private property could be taken under eminent domain laws and delivered to another private entity so long as it served a public **purpose**—in this case to generate higher tax revenue.

Other intrusions on private property rights are less appreciated. When the government dictates that there shall be no smoking in restaurants, bars, offices, and elsewhere, that too is an alienation of private property rights insomuch as one assumes that it is the owner of the property who has the right to determine how the property is used. Another ongoing attack on private property rights comes with the belief that people have a right to housing, food, or medical care, whether they can afford it or not. Because government has no resources of its own, it cannot give one American something that it does not first take from another American. Therefore, if one argues that a person has a right to housing, food, and medical care that he did not earn, it of necessity requires that some other American not have a right to something he did earn.

Law in the true sense consists of a set of general rules applicable to all persons, as opposed to laws that are simply orders by the legislature requiring particular people to do particular things. The rule of law is critical to the preservation of liberty. Unfortunately, most Americans neither understand nor appreciate this, and we are increasingly being ruled by arbitrary orders and privileges based on one's status. The fact of the *generalized disregard of the rule of law not only explains the ongoing threat to personal liberty but also helps explain government corruption, where people descend on Washington and state capitols demanding one privilege or another in exchange for political contributions.*

Other columns in this section include a look at societal changes, changes not for the better such as the tolerance for illegal immigration, attacks on Western values, and a generalized ignorance of, or contempt for, the U.S. Constitution.

Constitution Day

Wednesday, September 13, 2006

Each year since 2004, on Sept. 17, we commemorate the 1787 signing of the U.S. Constitution by 39 American statesmen. The legislation creating Constitution Day was fathered by Sen. Robert Byrd and requires federal agencies and federally funded schools, including universities, to have some kind of educational program on the Constitution.

I cannot think of a piece of legislation that makes greater mockery of the Constitution, or a more constitutionally odious person to father it—Sen. Byrd, a person who is known as, and proudly wears the label, "King of Pork." The only reason that Constitution Day hasn't become a laughingstock is because most Americans are totally ignorant of, or have contempt for, the letter and spirit of our Constitution.

Let's examine just a few statements by the framers to see just how much faith and allegiance today's Americans give to the U.S. Constitution. James Madison is the acknowledged father of the Constitution. In 1794, when Congress appropriated $15,000 for relief for French refugees who fled from insurrection in San Domingo (now Haiti) to Baltimore and Philadelphia, James Madison said disapprovingly, "I cannot undertake to lay my finger on that article of the Constitution which granted a right to Congress of expending, on objects of benevolence, the money of their constituents."

Today, at least two-thirds of a $2.5 trillion federal budget is spent on "objects of benevolence." That includes Medicare, Medicaid, Social Security, aid to higher education, farm and business subsidies, welfare, etc., ad nauseam.

James Madison's vision was later expressed by Rep. William Giles of Virginia, who condemned a relief measure for fire victims. Giles insisted that it was neither the purpose nor a right of Congress to "attend to what generosity and humanity require, but to what the Constitution and their duty require."

Some presidents had similar constitutional respect. In 1854, President Franklin Pierce vetoed a bill to help the mentally ill, saying, "I cannot find any authority in the Constitution for public charity," adding that to approve the measure "would be contrary to the letter and the spirit of the Constitution and subversive to the whole theory upon which the Union of these States is founded."

President Grover Cleveland vetoed many congressional appropriations, often saying there was no constitutional authority for such an appropriation. Vetoing a bill for relief charity, President Cleveland said, "I can find no warrant for such an appropriation in the Constitution, and I do not believe that the power and duty of the General Government ought to be extended to the relief of individual suffering which is in no manner properly related to the public service or benefit."

Constitutionally ignorant people might argue that the Constitution's "general welfare" clause justifies today's actions by Congress. Here's what James Madison said: "If Congress can do whatever in their discretion can be done by money, and will promote the General Welfare, the Government is no longer a limited one, possessing enumerated powers, but an indefinite one, subject to particular exceptions." Thomas Jefferson echoed, in a letter to Pennsylvania Rep. Albert Gallatin, "Congress has not unlimited powers to provide for the general welfare, but only those specifically enumerated."

James Madison explained the constitutional limits on federal power in Federalist Paper No. 45: "The powers delegated by the proposed Constitution to the federal government are few and defined . . . [to] be exercised principally on external objects, as war, peace, negotiation, and foreign commerce."

Here are my questions to you: Has our Constitution been amended to authorize federal spending on "objects of benevolence"? Or, is it plain and simple constitutional contempt by Congress, the president, the courts and, worst of all, the American people? Or, am I being overly pessimistic and it's simply a matter of constitutional ignorance?

Rules More Important Than Personalities

Wednesday, January 3, 2007

Not that many complimentary things are said about politicians. When a problem arises, people say, "Government ought to do something." They seem to have forgotten that it's the politicians who are running the government. Many think things can be changed by electing different politicians, but I ask: Given the incentives politicians face, why should we expect one politician to differ significantly from another? We should focus less on personalities and more on rules.

The kind of rules we should have are the kind that we'd make if our worst enemy were in charge. My mother created a mini-version of such a rule. Sometimes she would ask either me or my sister to evenly divide the last piece of cake or pie to share between us. More times than not, an argument ensued about the fairness of the division. Those arguments ended with Mom's rule: Whoever cuts the cake lets the other take the first piece. As if by magic or divine intervention, fairness emerged and arguments ended. No matter who did the cutting, there was an even division.

By creating and enforcing neutral rules, we minimize conflict. Consider one area of ruthless competition—sports. In Super Bowl XL, the Pittsburgh Steelers and the Seattle Seahawks had a lot on the line. Specifically, there's the $73,000 payment per man, contract enrichment and other benefits to the winners. Despite a bitterly fought contest and all that was at stake, the game ended peacefully and winners and losers were civil to one another.

How is it that players with conflicting interests and reasons for winning can play a game, agree with the outcome and walk away as good sports? It's a minor miracle of sorts. That "miracle" is that it is far easier to reach agreement about the game's rules than the game's outcome. The rules are known and durable, and the referee's only job is their evenhanded enforcement. Even football teams with losing records would find their long-run interests lie in known, durable and evenhandedly applied rules. They can more adequately devise a winning strategy because predictability is enhanced.

Suppose the game rules were flexible and referees played a role in determining the game's outcome. In other words, imagine the referees were more interested in what they saw as justice than enforcement of neutral rules. What might one predict about team behavior? Instead of trying to raise team productivity, owners would allocate resources to influence-peddling in the form of lobbying or bribing the referees.

In the case of last year's Super Bowl, the referees might have argued that since the Pittsburgh Steelers won four previous Super Bowl championships, justice demands that the game be rigged in favor of the Seattle Seahawks, who have never won a Super Bowl. It's easy to imagine all the conflict that would arise—team owners bringing lawsuits for what they see as biased referee decisions, and games ending in rancor and fights. There would be a reduction in the skill and fitness of all players and a lower overall quality of the sport. After all, if the outcome is determined by how well the team influences the referees, why spend resources recruiting and training superior players? It's better to use those resources for lobbying and bribes.

We have a set of rules that are known, neutral and intended to be durable. Those rules were created by our founders and embodied in the U.S. Constitution. Those rules have been weakened by a Congress of both parties that picks winners and losers in the game of life. The U.S. Supreme Court, which was intended to be a neutral referee, has forsaken that role and become a participant. All of this means we can expect a future of bitterly fought elections and enhanced conflict.

Property Rights

Wednesday, January 31, 2007

"Imprimis" is Hillsdale College's monthly publication that has over 1.25 million readers. It's Hillsdale's way of sharing the ideas of the many distinguished speakers invited to their campus. And, I might add, Hillsdale College is one of the few colleges where students get a true liberal arts education, absent the nonsense seen on many campuses.

The January edition of "Imprimis" contains an important speech by former New Jersey Superior Court Judge Andrew P. Napolitano titled "Property Rights After the Kelo Decision." For those who haven't kept up, the Kelo decision is the 2005 U.S. Supreme Court 5-4 decision that upheld the city of New London, Connecticut's condemnation of the property of one private party so that another private party could use it to build an office facility. Such a decision was a flagrant violation of the letter and spirit of the Fifth Amendment, which reads in part, "nor shall private property be taken for public use without just compensation." Public use, according to the Constitution's framers, means uses such as roads, bridges, and forts.

While most Americans appreciate the concept of yours and mine, Judge Napolitano's speech gives it greater focus. Formerly a law professor, Napolitano says, "When teaching law students the significance of private property, we tell them that each owner of such property has something called a 'bundle of rights.' The first of these is the right to use the property. The second is the right to alienate the property. The third and greatest is the right to exclude people from the property."

Can the government force one to sell his property? James Madison said yes, so long as it was for a public use and the owner was paid a fair market value. Thomas Jefferson was opposed to a person being forced to sell his property for a public use, arguing that the essence of private property is the right to exclude anyone, including government, from the property. But Madison's view prevailed, hence the Fifth Amendment provision.

In recent years, state and local governments have been running roughshod over private property rights in ways that would have horrified our founders. In the 1959 Courtesy Sandwich Shop case, a New York court held that if the tax collector collects more taxes by taking the private property of one party and transferring it to another, that's a public use permitted by the Constitution.

Recently, the city of Port Chester, N.Y., gave a private developer virtual power to condemn property within its designated redevelopment area. Bart Didden and Dominick Bologna, owners of property within the redevelopment area, approached the private developer for a permit to build a CVS pharmacy on their land. The developer told them to pay him $800,000 or give him a 50 percent interest in the CVS pharmacy or he'd have the local government condemn the land. Didden and Bologna refused, and the next day their land was condemned. The 2nd U.S. Circuit Court of Appeals upheld the local government's decision, which is nothing less than sanctioning extortion.

Napolitano concluded his speech pointing out something that few Americans appreciate. Natural rights do not come from government; they spring from our humanity. Or, as our founders put it, we are endowed by our "Creator with certain unalienable Rights, that among these are Life, Liberty and the Pursuit of Happiness," the latter meaning property. We establish governments to secure these rights.

Unfortunately, Americans have permitted governments at every level to become increasingly destructive of the ends they were created to serve. Under the color of law, government often does to us what thieves and crooks do, and like a nation of sheep we stand by and take it, and what's worse, sometimes we ask for it.

Democracy or Liberty

Wednesday, February 28, 2007

Does democracy really deserve the praise it receives? According to Webster's Dictionary, democracy is defined as "government by the people; especially: rule of the majority. " What's so great about majority rule? Let's look at majority rule, as a decision-making tool, and ask how many of our choices we would like settled by what a majority likes.

Would you want the kind of car that you own to be decided through a democratic process, or would you prefer purchasing any car you please? Ask that same question about decisions such as where you live, what clothes you purchase, what food you eat, what entertainment you enjoy and what wines you drink. I'm sure that if anyone suggested that these choices be subject to a democratic process, you'd deem it tyranny.

I'm not alone in seeing democracy as a variant of tyranny. James Madison, the father of our Constitution, said that in a pure democracy, "there is nothing to check the inducement to sacrifice the weaker party or the obnoxious individual." At the 1787 Constitutional Convention, Edmund Randolph said, ". . . that in tracing these evils to their origin every man had found it in the turbulence and follies of democracy." John Adams said, "Remember, democracy never lasts long. It soon wastes, exhausts, and murders itself. There was never a democracy yet that did not commit suicide." Chief Justice John Marshall observed, "Between a balanced republic and a democracy, the difference is like that between order and chaos."

Our founders intended for us to have a limited republican form of government where rights precede government and there is rule of law. Citizens, as well as government officials, are accountable to the same laws. Government intervenes in civil society only to protect its citizens against force and fraud but does not intervene in the cases of peaceable, voluntary exchange. By contrast, in a democracy, the majority rules either directly or through its elected representatives.

The law is whatever the government deems it to be. Rights may be granted or taken away.

Clearly, we need government, and that means there must be collective decision-making. Alert to the dangers of majority rule, the Constitution's framers inserted several anti-majority rules. In order to amend the Constitution, it requires a two-thirds vote of both Houses, or two-thirds of state legislatures, to propose an amendment, and requires three-fourths of state legislatures for ratification. Election of the president is not done by a majority popular vote but by the Electoral College.

Part of the reason for having two houses of Congress is that it places an obstacle to majority rule. Fifty-one senators can block the wishes of 435 representatives and 49 senators. The Constitution gives the president a veto to thwart the power of 535 members of Congress. It takes two-thirds of both houses of Congress to override the president's veto.

In Federalist Paper No. 10, James Madison wrote, "Measures are too often decided, not according to the rules of justice and the rights of the minor party, but by the superior force of an interested and overbearing majority." That's another way of saying that one of the primary dangers of majority rule is that it confers an aura of legitimacy and respectability on acts that would otherwise be deemed tyrannical. Liberty and democracy are not synonymous and could actually be opposites.

The Law versus Orders

Wednesday, June 20, 2007

Suppose a person is raped and we arrest the rapist. Should his status, whether he's a senator, professor or an ordinary man, play a role in the adjudication of the crime and subsequent punishment? I'm betting that the average person would answer that the law against rape is general and non-arbitrary and one's status should have nothing to do with the adjudication and punishment for the crime. That's precisely what is meant by "rule of law." Or, as English jurist A.V. Dicey put it, "Every man, whatever be his rank or condition, is subject to the ordinary law of the realm and amenable to the jurisdiction of the ordinary tribunals."

Law in the true sense consists of a set of general rules applicable to all persons, as opposed to laws that are simply orders by the legislature requiring particular people to do particular things. Rule of law is critical to the preservation of liberty. Unfortunately, most Americans neither understand nor appreciate this, and we are increasingly being ruled by arbitrary orders and privileges based upon one's status. Let's look at a few of them at the national level.

During the 1980s, many savings and loan banks made huge losses because of chicanery, stupidity and unwise investments. Congress bailed them out. In 1987, when the stock market crashed, many Americans incurred large losses because of unwise, perhaps stupid, investments. Equal treatment before the law would require that if Congress bails out one American who makes unwise or stupid investments, it should bail out any American who makes unwise or stupid investments. Instead, Congress gave particular people privileges because of their status.

A rule of law regime would require that we scrap the Internal Revenue Code in its current form. What justification is there for different tax treatment of one American because he has a higher income, minor children or receives his income from capital gains instead of wages? Equal treatment would require Congress to figure out the cost of the constitutionally authorized functions of the federal government, divide it by the adult population and send us each a bill for our share. You say, "What about the ability-to-pay principle of taxation to pay for the cost of government?" That's just a politics of envy concept that would be revealed as utter nonsense if applied to any other cost. Would you apply the ability-to-pay principle to, say, gasoline or food purchases where different prices are charged to different people depending on how many dependents they had, their income, or whether their income was derived from wages, dividends or capital gains?

The fact that Americans have become ruled by orders and special privileges helps explain all the money and graft that we see in Washington. We've moved away from a government with limited powers, as our Founders envisioned, to one with awesome powers. Therefore, it pays people to spend huge amounts of money to influence Congress in their favor, that is, get Congress to grant them privileges denied to other Americans.

Twenty-five years ago, during a dinner conversation with Nobel Laureate economist/philosopher Friedrich A. Hayek, I asked him if he could propose one law that would restore, promote and preserve liberty in our country, what would that law be? Hayek answered that the law he'd propose would read: Congress shall enact no law that does not apply equally to all Americans. Hayek's suggestion for full equality before the law was both simple and profound and would do untold wonders in fostering the liberties envisioned by our Founders. But I'm betting that most Americans would greet Hayek's proposal with contempt after they realized that it would mean Congress wouldn't be able enact orders and play favorites with different Americans.

Economics and Property Rights

Wednesday, September 5, 2007

Economic theory does not operate in a vacuum. Institutions, such as the property rights structure, determine how the theory manifests itself. Similarly, the law of gravity isn't repealed when a parachutist floats gently down to earth. The parachute simply affects how the law of gravity manifests itself.

Failure to recognize the effect of different property rights structures on outcomes leads to faulty analysis. Think about several questions. Which lake will yield larger, more mature fish—a publicly owned or a privately owned lake? Why is it that herds of cows flourished and buffalos did not? Who will care for a house better—a renter or owner?

The answer to each question has to do with the property rights structure. In a publicly owned lake, everyone has the right to the fish. In order to assert his right, the person has to catch the fish. This leads to overfishing because the person who tosses back an immature fish doesn't benefit himself. He benefits someone else who will keep the fish. It's a different story with a privately owned lake. The owner needn't catch a fish in order to assert his rights and can let the fish mature. It's the same principle with buffalo and other wildlife that's publicly owned. Through various rules and regulations, governments, though imperfectly, attempt to solve this property rights problem with licenses, fishing and hunting seasons and setting limits on catch and size.

Private property rights force the owner to take into account the effect of his current use of the property on its future value. A homeowner has a greater stake in what a house is worth 10 or 20 years from now than a renter. An owner would more likely make sacrifices and take the kind of care that lengthens the usable life of the house. But owners have methods to make renters share some of the interests of an owner through requiring security deposits against damage.

There's a completely ignored aspect of the effect of restrictions on private property rights and that's restrictions on profits. Pretend that you're an owner of a firm. There are two equally capable secretaries that you might hire. The pretty secretary demands $300 a week while the homely secretary is willing to work for $200. If you hired the homely secretary, your profits would be $100 greater. But what if there were a 50 percent profit tax? The profit tax reduces your rights to profit and reduces your cost of discriminating against the homely secretary. Instead of foregoing $100 without the profit tax, you'd forego only $50 by hiring the pretty secretary. The more the cost of doing something goes down, predictably, the more people will do of it. Wherever private property rights to profits are attenuated, we expect more choices to be made by noneconomic factors such as race and other physical attributes. T hat's especially the case in nonprofit entities like government and universities.

You say, "Hold it, Williams, government and universities have preferential hiring policies in favor of racial minorities; so you're wrong." No. When it was politically expedient, government and universities were the leaders in racial discrimination against racial minorities. Now that it's politically expedient to discriminate in favor of racial minorities, government and universities are in the forefront. For example, in 1936, there were only three black Ph.D. chemists employed by all of the white universities in the U.S., whereas 300 black chemists alone were employed by private industry. In government, blacks were only 1 percent of non-Postal Civil Service workers in 1930. By the way, where did blacks make their entry into white universities? If you said in sports, the moneymaking part of the university, go to the head of the class.

There are numerous issues and problems that are otherwise inexplicable unless we take into consideration the property rights structure.

Bogus Rights

Wednesday, February 8, 2006

Do people have a right to medical treatment whether or not they can pay? What about a right to food or decent housing? Would a U.S. Supreme Court justice hold that these are rights just like those enumerated in our Bill of Rights? In order to have any hope of coherently answering these questions, we have to decide what is a right. The way our Constitution's framers used the term, a right is something that exists simultaneously among people and imposes no obligation on another. For example, the right to free speech, or freedom to travel, is something we all simultaneously possess. My right to free speech or freedom to travel imposes no obligation upon another except that of non-interference. In other words, my exercising my right to speech or travel requires absolutely nothing from you and in no way diminishes any of your rights.

Contrast that vision of a right to so-called rights to medical care, food or decent housing, independent of whether a person can pay. Those are not rights in the sense that free speech and freedom of travel are rights. If it is said that a person has rights to medical care, food and housing, and has no means of paying, how does he enjoy them? There's no Santa Claus or Tooth Fairy who provides them. You say, "The Congress provides for those rights." Not quite. Congress does not have any resources of its very own. The only way Congress can give one American something is to first, through the use intimidation, threats and coercion, take it from another American. So-called rights to medical care, food and decent housing impose an obligation on some other American who, through the tax code, must be denied his right to his earnings. In other words, when Congress gives one American a right to something he didn't earn, it takes away the right of another American to something he did earn.

If this bogus concept of rights were applied to free speech rights and freedom to travel, my free speech rights would impose financial obligations on others to provide me with an auditorium and microphone. My right to travel freely would require that the government take the earnings of others to provide me with airplane tickets and hotel accommodations.

Philosopher John Locke's vision of natural law guided the founders of our nation. Our Declaration of Independence expresses that vision, declaring, "We hold these Truths to be self-evident, that all Men are created equal, that they are endowed by their Creator with certain unalienable Rights, that among these are Life, Liberty, and the Pursuit of Happiness." Government is necessary, but the only rights we can delegate to government are the ones we possess. For example, we all have a natural right to defend ourselves against predators. Since we possess that right, we can delegate authority to government to defend us. By contrast, we don't have a natural right to take the property of one person to give to another; therefore, we cannot legitimately delegate such authority to government.

Three-fifths to two-thirds of the federal budget consists of taking property from one American and giving it to another. Were a private person to do the same thing, we'd call it theft. When government does it, we euphemistically call it income redistribution, but that's exactly what thieves do—redistribute income. Income redistribution not only betrays the founders' vision, it's a sin in the eyes of God. I'm guessing that when God gave Moses the Eighth Commandment, "Thou shalt not steal," I'm sure he didn't mean "thou shalt not steal unless there was a majority vote in Congress."

The real tragedy for our nation is that any politician who holds the values of liberty that our founders held would be soundly defeated in today's political arena.

Results versus Process

Wednesday, October 11, 2006

Democrats plan to trumpet the income and wealth gap for political gain in this year's elections. According to the *Wall Street Journal* article "Democrats' Risky Strategy," Democratic candidates blame Republicans for economic inequality.

This strategy might sell because, in addition to envy, many people erroneously use income inequality as a measure of fairness. Income is a result. As such, results cannot establish whether there is fairness or justice.

Let's look at it. Suppose Tom, Dick and Harry play a weekly game of poker. Tom wins 75 percent of the time. Dick and Harry, respectively, win 15 percent and 10 percent of the time. Knowing only the poker game's result permits us to say absolutely nothing as to whether there has been poker justice. Tom's disproportionate winnings are consistent with his being either an astute player or a clever cheater.

To determine whether there has been poker justice, the game's process must be examined. Some process questions we might ask are: Were Hoyle's Rules obeyed, were the cards unmarked, were the cards dealt from the top of the deck, and did the players play voluntarily? If these questions yield affirmative answers, there was poker justice regardless of the game's result, with Tom winning 75 percent of the time.

Similarly, income is a result. In a free society, for the most part, income is a result of one's capacity to serve his fellow man and the value his fellow man places on that service. Say I mow your lawn and you pay me $30. That $30 might be seen as a certificate of performance. Why?

I go to the grocer and ask for 3 pounds of steak and a six-pack of beer that my fellow man produced. In effect, the grocer asks, "Williams, you're asking for something that your fellow man produced; what did you do for your fellow man?" I say, "I served my fellow man by mowing his lawn." The grocer says, "Prove it." That's when I give him my certificates of performance, the $30.

Google founders Sergey Brin and Larry Page are multi-billion-aires. Just as in the case of my mowing my fellow man's lawn, they became very wealthy by serving their fellow man. The difference is they served their fellow man far more effectively than I and hence received more "certificates of performance," enabling them to make greater claims on what their fellow man produces.

Their greater income is a result of their pleasing millions upon millions of their fellow man. They created wealth by producing a product that improves the lives of millions upon millions of people all around the globe. Should people like Messrs. Brin and Page, who have improved our lives, be held up to ridicule and scorn because they have a higher income than most of us? Should Congress use the tax code to confiscate part of their wealth in the name of fairness and income redistribution?

For the most part, income is a result of one's productivity and the value that people place on that productivity. Far more important than income inequality, there is productivity inequality. That suggests that if there's anything to be done about income inequality, we should focus on how to give people greater capacity in serving their fellow man, and we should make sure there's a climate of peaceable, voluntary exchange.

Think back to my poker example. If one is concerned about the game's result, which is more just—taking some of Tom's winnings and redistributing them to Dick and Harry, or teaching Dick and Harry how to play poker better?

The Law or Good Ideas?

Wednesday, March 30, 2005

Here's my question to you: Should we be governed by good ideas? You say, "Williams, what do you mean?"

Here's an example: I regularly bike for fun, cardiovascular fitness and, hopefully, for a longer, healthier life. In my opinion, that's a good idea. That being the case, would you deem it proper for Congress to enact legislation requiring Americans to bike regularly or perform some other cardiovascular fitness exercise?

What if Congress didn't act on this good idea? Would you deem it proper and acceptable if five out of nine U.S. Supreme Court justices, in the name of "evolving standards" and promoting the general welfare, decreed that we all participate in some fitness exercise?

Let's look at it. It's easy to dismiss my questions and example by saying they're stupid and far-fetched. A more enlightened response would be to quote from Thomas Jefferson: "Congress has not unlimited powers to provide for the general welfare, but only those specifically enumerated." In other words, Congress holds only those powers delegated or enumerated in the Constitution.

Your follow-up response might be another Thomas Jefferson quotation: "[T]hat whensoever the General Government assumes undelegated powers, its acts are unauthoritative, void, and of no force." That means if Congress or the courts were to mandate biking, we could ignore it.

Suppose biking advocates saw no hope in getting Congress to enact legislation mandating regular biking and saw the U.S. Supreme Court as a means to accomplish their ends. Tell me your preference. Would you prefer the justices to rule along the lines they did in the recent Roper v. Simmons case, finding the execution of teenagers unconstitutional because, as Justice Anthony Kennedy speaking for the 5-4 majority said, "It is proper that we acknowledge the overwhelming weight of international opinion against the juvenile death penalty"? Modified to fit my biking example, Justice Kennedy might say, "We acknowledge the overwhelming weight of international opinion that regular biking is a good idea."

Or, would you prefer the justices to say, "We're guided by the U.S. Constitution, and we find no constitutional authority to rule that Americans must regularly bike, despite your nonsense argument about the 'promoting the general welfare' clause; get out of our court"?

Whether "evolving standards," the "weight of international opinion" and good ideas should determine court decisions underlies much of the ongoing conflict over President Bush's federal court appointees. A federal court appointee who'd say his decisions are guided by the letter and spirit of our Constitution would be tagged by Democrat senators and a few Republican senators, such as Arlen Specter, as an extremist. They'd prefer justices who share former Chief Justice Charles E. Hughes' vision that, "We live under a Constitution, but the Constitution is what the judges say it is." Translated, that means we don't live under the Constitution; we live under tyrannical judges.

Many law professors, and others who hold contempt for our Constitution, preach that the Constitution is a living document. Saying that the Constitution is a living document is the same as saying we don't have a Constitution. For rules to mean anything, they must be fixed. How many people would like to play me poker and have the rules be "living"? Depending on "evolving standards," maybe my two pair could beat your flush.

The framers recognized there might come a time to amend the Constitution, and they gave us Article V as a means for doing so. Early in the last century, some Americans thought it was a good idea to ban the manufacture and sale of alcohol. They didn't go to court asking the justices to twist the Constitution to accomplish their goal. They respected the Constitution and sought passage of the 18th Amendment.

The founders were right about a lot of things, but they were dead wrong when they bought into Alexander Hamilton's Federalist Paper No. 78 prediction that the judiciary was the "least dangerous" branch of government.

Ignorance or Contempt

March 26, 2001

Congressmen, presidents and Supreme Court justices take an oath of office swearing to uphold and defend the U.S. Constitution. As if the Constitution itself isn't clear about what they must do, in Federalist Paper No. 45, James Madison, the acknowledged father of the Constitution described the document thusly: "The powers delegated by the proposed Constitution to the federal government are few and defined. Those which are to remain in the State governments are numerous and indefinite. The former will be exercised principally on external objects, as war, peace, negotiation, and foreign commerce. . . . The powers reserved to the several States will extend to all the objects which in the ordinary course of affairs, concern the lives and liberties, and properties of the people, and the internal order, improvement and prosperity of the State."

Both Madison's statement and the Constitution leave no doubt about the "few and defined" powers delegated to the federal government and the "numerous and indefinite" powers retained by the people and the states. I'd like to ask our 535 congressmen, our president and our nine Supreme Court justices which word or phrase in Madison's statement they find beyond comprehension, and which phrase in Article I, Section 8 of the Constitution, that outlines what Congress is permitted to do, they find beyond comprehension.

While congressmen, presidents and Supreme Court justices don't have much understanding, they aren't stupid, which isn't to say they're not ignorant about the Constitution and other matters. Let's explore the most charitable explanation for their day-to-day violations of both the letter and the spirit of our Constitution, namely that they're ignorant. But, I seriously doubt the suitability of ignorance as an explanation. Why? If ignorance were the explanation, I'd be optimistic. I'd simply send the president, congressmen and Supreme Court justices James Madison's Federalist Paper No. 45, explaining the Constitution. After that they'd mend their ways and eliminate most federal programs, state mandates and other gross constitutional violations.

You say, "Williams, if you think they'd do that, you've got to be crazy!" You're right; I would be crazy. The only other explanation for what presidents, congressmen and justices do is that they have contempt for the Constitution. But that's only a tiny part of the sad story. Imagine if James Madison or Thomas Jefferson were campaigning for the presidency in 2000. What would you think about their chances? They'd clearly lose if they expressed the constitutional values and respect they had when the document was written. They'd clearly be denounced by most Americans and possibly risk assassination.

Therefore, before we rush to lay the complete blame for constitutional contempt at the feet of politicians and judges, we might want to look at ourselves—we the American people. That is, politicians are doing what we elect them to office to do and if our Constitution stays in the way, it's the Constitution that must yield. The Constitution stands in the way of government programs such as: business bailouts, food stamps, Social Security, Medicare, Title I education programs and thousands of other federal acts.

You might ask, "Why should we pay any attention to a two hundred year document?" I'd say to escape Thomas Jefferson's prediction that, "The natural progress of things is for government to gain ground and for liberty to yield." After all if we ignore the constitutional protections found in Article I, Section 8 why not ignore other constitutional protections and make them just as meaningless?

If we continue our current path, future generations will curse us for squandering unprecedented liberty.

American Contempt for Rule of Law

June 1, 2001

What should be the characteristics of laws in a free society? Let's think about baseball rules (laws) as a means to approach this question. Some players, through no fault of their own, hit fewer home runs than others. In order to create baseball justice, how about a rule requiring pitchers to throw easier pitches to poorer home run hitters or simply rule what would be a double for anyone else a home run? Some pitchers aren't as good as others. How about allowing those pitchers to stand closer to the batter? Better yet, we could rule their first pitch a strike, regardless whether it is or not. In the interest of baseball justice, we might make special rules for some players and not others. That might level the playing field between old players and young players, black players and white players and fast runners and slow runners.

You say, "Williams, you can't be serious! Can you imagine all the chaos that would ensue: players lobbying umpires, umpires deciding who gets what favor, law suits, and not to mention fighting?" You're absolutely right. The reason baseball games end peaceably, and players and team owners satisfied with the process, whether they win or lose, is that baseball rules (law) are known in advance; they are applicable to all players; they're fixed and umpires don't make up rules as they go along. In other words, baseball rules meet the test of "abstractness." They envision no particular game outcome in terms of winners and losers. Baseball rules (laws) simply create a framework in which the game is played.

Laws or rules that govern a free society should have similar features; there should be "rule of law." Rule of law means: Laws are certain and known in advance. Laws envision no particular outcome except that of allowing people to peaceably pursue their own objectives. Finally, and most important, laws are equally applied to everyone, including government officials.

Sir Henry Maine, probably the greatest legal historian said, "The greatest movement of progressive societies has hitherto been a movement from status to contract." In non-progressive societies rule of law is absent. Laws are not general. They're applied according to a person's status or group membership. There's rule, not by legis, the Latin word for law, but by privileges, the Latin term for private law.

Let's look at our country and ask whether we live under rule of law. Just about every law that Congress enacts violates all of the requirements for rule of law. How do we determine violations of rule of law? It's easy. See if the law applies to particular Americans as opposed to all Americans. See if the law exempts public officials from its application. See if the law is known in advance. See if the law takes action against a person who has taken no aggressive action against another. If you conduct such a test, you will conclude that it is virtually impossible to find a single act of Congress that adheres to the principles of the rule of law. That's the very reason lobbyists descend upon Washington and cough up the big campaign bucks. They want Congress to use their law making power to grant them special privileges. But every indication I see, privilege granting is precisely what most Americans want, though they might disagree on who gets what privilege.

Most Americans have no inkling of what rule of law means. We think it means obedience to whatever laws Congress enacts and the President signs. That's a tragedy.

Liberty's Greatest Advocate

July 4, 2001

June 30th marked the 200th anniversary of the birth of Frederic Bastiat. If one were to list the top ten advocates of liberty, French philosopher-economist Frederic Bastiat would rank high on that list. He'd easily outrank any one of the Founders of our nation. I'm honored to have been invited by the New York-based Foundation for Economic Education (fee.org) to give the keynote address at a conference celebrating Bastiat's birthday that was held in Carcassonne, France, near where Bastiat spent most of his short life (1801–1850). You say, "Williams, who's this guy, Bastiat? We've never heard of him." Frederic Bastiat wrote several important works, among them Economic Sophisms and The Law. In all of his writings he attacked tyranny, economic ignorance and self-serving myths.

His observations about human nature and government are just as true today as during his time. Bastiat warned, "Now since man is naturally inclined to avoid pain—and since labor is pain in itself—it follows that men will resort to plunder whenever plunder is easier than work. History shows this quite clearly. And under these conditions, neither religion nor morality can stop it." What does Bastiat mean by plunder? Plunder is when people forcibly take the property of another. It's legalized plunder when people use government, such as our congress, to do the same thing. Or, as Bastiat put it, "The state is the great fiction by which everybody tries to live at the expense of everybody else."

Since people covet and try to take what belongs to others, Bastiat said, "It is evident, then, that the proper purpose of law [government] is to use the power of its collective force to stop this fatal tendency to plunder instead of to work. All the measures of the law should protect property and punish plunder."

Do our elected representatives protect property and punish plunder or do they punish property and protect plunder? It's a mixed story. Two-thirds to three-quarters of next year's $2 trillion federal budget represents legalized plunder, where Congress makes it possible for one American to live at the expense of another. Most expenditures made by Washington's behemoth agencies such as the Department of Agriculture, Department of Health and Human Services, Department of Education, Department of Housing and Urban Development, and the Social Security Administration represent earnings forcibly taken from one American and given to another American. This legalized plunder isn't limited to money handouts. There's plunder in the form of special privileges such as import tariffs and quotas, licenses and franchises, where government rigs the market in favor of certain sellers, particularly those making large campaign contributions.

Often legalized plunder is done in the name of the poor. Bastiat had a prediction about that, "When under the pretext of fraternity, the legal code imposes mutual sacrifices on the citizens, human nature is not thereby abrogated. Everyone will then direct his efforts toward contributing little to, and taking much from, the common fund of sacrifices. Now, is it the most unfortunate who gains from this struggle? Certainly not, but rather the most influential and calculating."

We Americans, at least the moral among us, are increasingly confronted with Bastiat's dilemma: "When law and morality contradict one another, the citizen has the cruel alternative of either losing his sense of morality or losing his respect for the law." Frederic Bastiat admired our country saying, and noting the exceptions of slavery and tariffs, ". . . look at the United States. There is no country in the world where the law is kept within its proper domain: the protection of every person's liberty and property." If Bastiat were alive today, I doubt whether he'd have that same level of admiration.

Corporate Courage

Wednesday, February 1, 2006

We all remember last year's despicable U.S. Supreme Court 5-4 Kelo v. City of New London, Conn., decision that held as constitutional that the rightful property of one American can be taken and transferred to another American so long as some public purpose is served. The Fifth Amendment to the U.S. Constitution states, "Nor shall private property be taken for public use, without just compensation." The key term is "public use," not "public purpose." That means that the powers of eminent domain can be used only to take property, with just compensation, to build public projects such as roads, forts or schools.

City of New London officials used the law of eminent domain to condemn the property of 15 homeowners and transfer it to private developers to build a luxury hotel, high-rent condominiums and office buildings. The city justified its actions by saying that taking the property away from the homeowners, and replacing it with a hotel, condos and office buildings, would generate jobs and more tax revenue. In a scathing dissent, Justice Sandra Day O'Connor said, "The specter of condemnation hangs over all property. Nothing is to prevent the state from replacing any Motel 6 with a Ritz-Carlton, any home with a shopping mall, or any farm with a factory." In other words, government officials can take your private property and transfer it to another private person, based on any flimsy claim that it will serve a better public purpose such as job creation and greater tax revenues.

This kind of government tyranny should be disavowed by every decent American. Stepping up to the plate is Branch Banking and Trust Company (BB&T), headquartered in Winston-Salem, N.C. BB&T is a full-service bank with 1,100 offices throughout the Southeast. On Jan. 25, BB&T announced that it will not lend to commercial developers that plan to build condominiums, shopping malls and other private projects on land taken from private citizens by government entities using eminent domain. On behalf of its board of directors, Chairman and Chief Executive Officer John Allison explained, "The idea that a citizen's property can be taken by the government solely for private use is extremely misguided, in fact, it's just plain wrong." Mr. Allison added, "One of the most basic rights of every citizen is to keep what they own. As an institution dedicated to helping our clients achieve economic success and financial security, we won't help any entity or company that would undermine that mission and threaten the hard-earned American dream of property ownership."

We all should applaud the directors and officers of Branch Banking and Trust Company for their courage. While boards of directors have a duty to maximize shareholder value, BB&T has shown that maximizing shareholder value is not solely a monetary phenomenon but has a moral component as well. As such they have chosen not to be accessories to last year's despicable U.S. Supreme Court decision.

Branch Banking and Trust Company directors have set the example for other financial institutions. It would make my day if the boards of directors of other financial institutions followed suit. If they don't, shareholders could supply them with a bit of backbone at annual meetings with a shareholder initiative that not lending to developers who have acquired private property through eminent domain law become corporate policy.

Congress has responded to the Kelo decision with the bipartisan Private Property Rights Protection Act of 2005 that "prohibits any state or political subdivision from exercising its power of eminent domain for economic development if that state or political subdivision receives federal economic development funds during the fiscal year." This measure demonstrates Congress' lack of courage. Why not start impeachment proceedings against justices who flagrantly violate their oath of office to uphold and defend the Constitution?

Confiscating Property

Wednesday, June 29, 2005

Last week's U.S. Supreme Court 5-4 ruling in Kelo v. New London helps explain the socialist attack on President Bush's nominees to the federal bench. First, let's look at the case.

The city government of New London, Conn., has run upon hard times, with residents leaving and its tax base eroding. Private developers offered to build a riverfront hotel, private offices and a health club in the Fort Trumbull neighborhood. But there was a bit of a problem. Owners of 15 homes in the stable middle-class Fort Trumbull neighborhood refused the city's offer to buy their homes, but no sweat. The city turned over its power of eminent domain—its ability to take private property for public use—to the New London Development Corporation, a private body, to take the entire neighborhood for private development. The city condemned the homeowners' properties. The homeowners sued and lost in the state court, and last week they lost in the U.S. Supreme Court.

The framers of our Constitution gave us the Fifth Amendment in order to protect us from government property confiscation. The Amendment reads in part: "[N]or shall private property be taken for public use, without just compensation." Which one of those 12 words is difficult to understand? The framers recognized there might be a need for government to acquire private property to build a road, bridge, dam or fort. That is a clear public use that requires just compensation, but is taking one person's private property to make it available for another's private use a public purpose? Justice John Paul Stevens says yes, arguing, "Promoting economic development is a traditional and long-accepted function of government."

Justice Sandra Day O'Connor dissented, saying, "Under the banner of economic development, all private property is now vulnerable to being taken and transferred to another private owner, so long as it might be given to an owner who will use it in a way that the legislature deems more beneficial to the public." She added that "the words 'for public use' do not realistically exclude any takings, and thus do not exert any constraint on the eminent domain power." In other words, state and local officials can now take your home for another private person to use so long as they can manufacture an argument that the latter use is more beneficial to the public.

Let's look at a few examples of how this might play out. You and your neighbor have two-acre lots. Your combined property tax is $10,000. A nursing home proprietor tells city officials that if they condemn your property and sell it to him to build a nursing home, the city would get $30,000 in property taxes. According to last week's U.S. Supreme Court ruling, this plan would be construed as beneficial to the public, and you'd have no recourse. Similarly, an environmental group might descend on public officials to condemn your land and transfer it to the group for a wildlife preserve. Again, a contrived public benefit for which you'd have no recourse.

The Court's decision helps explain the vicious attacks on any judicial nominees who might use framer-intent to interpret the U.S. Constitution. America's socialists want more control over our lives, property and our pocketbooks. They cannot always get their way in the legislature, and the courts represent their only chance. There is nothing complex about those 12 words the framers wrote to protect us from governmental property confiscation. You need a magician to reach the conclusion reached by the Court's majority. I think the socialist attack on judicial nominees who'd use framer-intent in their interpretation of the Constitution might also explain their attack on our Second Amendment "right of the people to keep and bear Arms." Why? Because when they come to take our property, they don't want to risk buckshot in their butts.

Attacking Western Values

December 13, 2004

School boards have recently banned songs and music containing references to Santa Claus, Jesus and other religious Christmas symbols. The New York City school system permits displays of Jewish menorahs and the Muslim star and crescent but not the Christian nativity scene. According to an Associated Press story (11/26/04), "A public school teacher is suing his district and principal for barring him from using excerpts from historical documents in his classroom because they contain references to God and Christianity." The historical documents in question are: the Declaration of Independence and "The Rights of the Colonists" by John Adams. Then there's Kandice Smith, an Alabama sixth grader who was threatened with discipline for exhibiting a cross necklace.

Eugene, Oregon's City Manager Jim Johnson banned Christmas trees and holiday decorations with religious themes from public spaces giving as his reason the need to "put a neutral face on a religious holiday in the workplace." A float proclaiming "Merry Christmas" was banned from Denver's Parade of Lights.

Under the pretense of the First Amendment's prohibitions against "establishment of religion" and the court's bogus "separation of church and state" interpretation of the same, we're witnessing a part of the ongoing attack on American values. The Constitution's "establishment of religion" clause was written to prevent the formation of anything similar to the official Church of England in the United States.

So why the attack on religion? Read the Declaration of Independence. You'll read phrases such as: "endowed by their Creator with certain unalienable Rights, "Laws of Nature and Nature's God," and "appealing to the Supreme Judge of the world." The vision held by the Framers is that our rights come not from government but from a "Creator" or "the laws of nature and of nature's God." That means the purpose and power of government is rightfully limited to protecting our natural God-given rights.

The idea that government doesn't grant rights is offensive to those who wish to control our lives. Therefore, to gain greater control, the idea of natural rights, God-given rights and Christian values must be suppressed. The idea that rights precede government was John Locke's natural law philosophy that had a significant influence on our nation's founders but they chose to refer to natural law as rights endowed by the Creator.

The attack on Christian ideas and Christian public displays is part and parcel of the leftist control agenda in another way. Certain components of the leftist agenda requires that our primary allegiance be with government. As such there must be an attack on allegiances to the teachings of the church and family. After all, for example, if you want popular acceptance of homosexual marriages, there must be a campaign against church teachings that condemn such practices.

Embolden by their successes in the courts and intimidation of public officials, there's no question there will be other leftist demands; there's no logical end point except complete Christian capitulation. There are Christian symbols and exhibits in many Washington, D.C. government buildings that will come down such as: Moses with the Ten Commandments inside the U.S. Supreme Court, George Washington praying in the Capitol Building, Abraham Lincoln's speech mentioning God carved inside the Lincoln Memorial. Religious programming on the radio and television will come under attack. After all there's Federal Communications Commission permission to use the "public airwaves."

If leftists say they have no such intention to go after television, radio and other public expressions of Christianity, what they really mean is that they haven't softened us up enough yet. I'm not quite sure of just how we respond to the ongoing attack on Christianity and American values but we'd better do something quickly.

Immigration vs. Gate-Crashing

Wednesday, April 12, 2006

My sentiments on immigration are inscribed at the foot of the Statue of Liberty: ". . . Give me your tired, your poor, Your huddled masses yearning to breathe free, The wretched refuse of your teeming shore, Send these, the homeless, tempest-tost to me, I lift my lamp beside the golden door."

These words of poet Emma Lazarus served as the welcome mat for tens of millions seeking liberty and opportunity in America—legally. Being a relatively land-rich and labor-scarce nation, immigration has always been good for our country. Plus, for most of our history, there was a guarantee that immigrants would come here to work. The alternative was starvation.

With today's welfare state, there's no such guarantee. People can come here, not work and not starve because the welfare state guarantees that they can live off the rest of us.

At the heart of today's immigration problem is its illegality. According to several estimates, there are 11 million people who are in our country illegally, mostly from Mexico. Many people, including my libertarian friends and associates, advance an argument that differs little from saying that people anywhere in the world have a right to live in the United States irrespective of our laws or preferences.

According to that vision, American people do not have a right to set either the number of people who enter our country or the conditions upon which they enter. Some of the arguments and terms used in the immigration debate defy reason. First, there's the refusal to call these people "illegal aliens." The politically preferred term is "undocumented workers," which is nothing less than verbal sleight-of-hand. After all, I, too, am an undocumented worker.

My colleague, Thomas Sowell, exposes some of this verbal sleight-of-hand in his recent column "Guests or Gate-Crashers?" He questions calling for "guest worker" status for people who, because they weren't invited, are not guests at all but gate-crashers. Sowell argues that the more substantive arguments for flaunting our immigration laws are just as phony.

How about the argument that "We can't catch all the illegals"? That's true, but should we apply that principle to other illegal acts? For example, we can't catch every rapist or burglar, but does it follow that we shouldn't try?

The base motives for much of the political response to illegal aliens are fear of losing the Hispanic vote and pressure by employers who want to maintain a source of cheap labor. Politicians are calling for "guest worker" programs, but they're really calling for amnesty. They are fearful of actually using that term because they know it's political suicide, but the "guest worker" proposal is essentially the same as amnesty.

The word amnesty comes from the Greek "amnestia," defined in part as: "the selective overlooking or ignoring of those events or acts that are not favorable or useful to one's purpose or position." That's what the proposed guest worker program essentially says: forget that you're here illegally.

In principle, the solution to people being in our country illegally is simple. No one in the country illegally should be eligible to receive any social services except emergency medical services. Efforts should be made to deport illegal aliens. Our borders should be made secure both against illegal entry of persons and potential threats to national security.

Finally, U.S. Citizenship and Immigration Services procedures for obtaining work permits and citizenship should be streamlined so that law-abiding people around the world can more easily contribute to and enjoy America's greatness.

The Greatest Generation

Wednesday, November 21, 2007

The "greatest generation" is a term sometimes used in reference to those Americans who were raised during the Great Depression, fought in World War II, worked in farms and factories and sacrificed for the war effort while maintaining the home front. Following the war, these Americans, many of whom were born between the turn of the century and 1930, went on to produce a level of wealth and prosperity heretofore unknown to mankind.

There's no question that this generation made an important contribution. Let's look at what else that generation contributed that might qualify them for the generation that laid the foundation for the greatest betrayal of our nation's core founding principle: limited federal government exercising only constitutionally enumerated powers.

When the greatest generation was born, federal spending as a percentage of gross domestic product (GDP) was 2.5 percent. As they are now dying off, federal spending is 20 percent of GDP and that doesn't include government meddling. If the grandparents of the greatest generation were asked to describe their contacts or relationship with the federal government, after a puzzled look, straining their recollection faculties, they might answer, "I used to chat with the mailman once in a while."

Today, there is little any American can do without some form of federal control, whether it's how much water we can use to flush a toilet, what kind of car we drive or how we prepare for retirement. Congress manages our lives in ways unimaginable to our ancestors through agencies created by the greatest generation, such as Health and Human Services, Housing and Urban Development, Social Security Administration and a host of alphabet agencies such as EPA, DOL, BLM, CDC and DOT.

There's little question that the greatest generation provided their offspring, the baby boomer generation, with goods and services that their parents could not afford to give them. But tragically, the greatest generation did not instill in their children what their parents instilled in them, the values and customs that make for a civilized society. In previous generations, people were held responsible for their behavior. Today, society at large pays for irresponsible behavior. Years ago, there was little tolerance for the kind of crude behavior and language that's accepted today. To see men sitting while a woman was standing on a public conveyance used to be unthinkable. Children addressing adults by their first name and their use of foul language in the presence of, and often to, teachers and other adults were unacceptable.

A society's first line of defense is not the law but customs, traditions and moral values. These behavioral norms, mostly transmitted by example, word-of-mouth and religious teachings, represent a body of wisdom distilled over the ages through experience and trial and error. They include important thou-shalt-nots such as shalt not murder, shalt not steal, shalt not lie and cheat, but they also include all those courtesies one might call ladylike and gentlemanly conduct. Policemen and laws can never replace these restraints on personal conduct. At best, the police and criminal justice system are the last desperate line of defense for a civilized society. This failure to fully transmit value norms to subsequent generations represents another failing of the greatest generation.

If there's an American generation that can justifiably be called the greatest generation, it's that generation responsible for the founding of our nation—men such as James Madison, Thomas Jefferson, John Adams, George Washington and millions of their fellow countrymen. This is the generation that threw off one form of oppression and laid the foundations for unprecedented human liberty. That is not a trivial achievement, for most often in mankind's history, one form of oppression has been replaced with another far worse, as we've seen in Russia, China and Africa.

Potpourri

A few of my columns do not fit the categories chosen. Many of them represent the economists' tendency to venture into areas not typically thought of as being in economics. Some of them are my pet peeves; some of them were articles published by the New York–based Foundation for Economic Education.

Illegal Immigration

Wednesday, July 11, 2007

President Bush and his pro-amnesty allies both in and out of Congress suffered a devastating defeat at the hands of the American people. Like any other public controversy, there are vested interests served on both sides of the amnesty issue, but I'd like to raise some ordinary non-rocket-science questions to the pro-amnesty crowd, many of whom are my libertarian friends.

Do people, anywhere in the world, have a right to enter the United States irrespective of our laws pertaining to immigration? Unless one wishes to obfuscate, there's a simple "yes" or "no" answer to that question. If a "yes" answer is given, then why should there be any immigration requirements, such as visas, passports and green cards, for anyone who wishes to visit or reside in our country? Why not abolish the U.S. Citizenship and Immigration Services?

If your answer is "no," one does not have a right to enter the U.S. irrespective of our laws, what does that make a person who does so? Most often we call a person whose behavior violates a law a criminal. If people commit criminal acts, should there be an effort to apprehend and punish them? In general, my answer is yes, with one important exception.

I was summoned for jury duty some years ago, and during voir dire, the attorney asked me whether I could obey the judge's instructions. I answered, "It all depends upon what those instructions are." Irritatingly, the judge asked me to explain myself. I explained that if I were on a jury back in the 1850s, and a person was on trial for violating the Fugitive Slave Act by assisting a runaway slave, I would vote for acquittal regardless of the judge's instructions. The reason is that slavery is unjust and any law supporting it is unjust. Needless to say, I was dismissed from jury duty. While our immigration laws are overly cumbersome and in urgent need of streamlining, they do not violate human rights and should be obeyed.

Many pro-amnesty supporters offer the canard that there are 12 to 20 million illegal immigrants in our country. We cannot keep every illegal immigrant out or expel the ones living here. That might be true, but it is also true that we can't prevent every rape and murder. Does that mean we shouldn't attempt to enforce the laws against rape and murder and try to prosecute the perpetrators?

In addition to greater efforts to secure our borders, there are several non-rocket-science steps we can take. People who are here illegally should be denied access to any social service such as Medicaid, public education and food assistance programs. An exception might be made for temporary emergency medical treatment. In some cities, such as Los Angeles, police are prohibited from asking people they stop about their immigration status. While state and local police shouldn't be turned into federal agents, they shouldn't knowingly conceal criminal acts.

The United States is a nation of immigrants from all over the world. The resulting ethnic mosaic goes a long way toward explaining our greatness as a nation. Immigration has always been a blessing for us, and it still is. But yesteryear's immigration and today's differ in several important respects. For the most part, yesteryear's immigrants came here legally. Because there was no welfare state, we were guaranteed that they'd work as opposed to living off the rest of us. Furthermore, they sought to assimilate and adopt our culture and become Americans. That's not so true today, where Hispanic activists seek to impose their language and culture on the rest of us. At some public schools, they've raised the Mexico flag atop the U.S. flag. They've announced that they seek to take back parts of the U.S. that were formerly Mexico.

Straight Thinking 101

Wednesday, June 27, 2007

Just about the most difficult lesson for first-year economics students, and sometimes graduate students, is that economic theory, and for that matter any scientific theory, is positive or non-normative. You might ask, "What's this business about positive and normative?" It's easy. Positive statements deal with what was, what is or what will be. Normative, or subjective, statements deal with what's good or bad, or what ought to be or should be. Confusing the two leads to considerable mischief.

The statement "Scientists cannot split the atom" is a positive statement. Why? If there's disagreement with the statement, there are facts to which we can appeal to settle the disagreement—just visit Stanford University's linear accelerator and watch atoms being split. The statement "Scientists shouldn't split the atom" is a normative statement. Why? There are no facts whatsoever to which we can appeal to settle any disagreement. One person's opinion on the matter is just as good as another's.

How about the statement "Gasoline prices are unreasonable"? If some think they're reasonable while others don't, the argument can go on forever without resolution because there are no facts to which we can appeal to settle the disagreement. However, there are facts that tend to back up the statement: Buyers of gasoline prefer lower prices while sellers prefer higher prices.

By the way, years ago, Mrs. Williams would arrive home complaining about unreasonable grocery prices. After airing her complaints, she'd ask me to unload her car full of groceries. Having completed the chore, I'd ask her whether she was unreasonable, suggesting that it was my opinion that only an unreasonable person would pay unreasonable prices. The conversation never went far in a pleasant direction.

Having explained the difference between positive and normative statements, I tell my students that in no way do I propose that they purge their vocabulary of normative statements. Normative statements are excellent tools for tricking others into doing what you want them to do. I simply caution that in the process of tricking others, there's no need to trick oneself into believing that one normative statement is better or more righteous than another.

A related term that doesn't make much economic sense is the term "need." The implication of an absolute, crying, dying or urgent need is that one cannot do without the need in question. Students sometimes say they absolutely need a car or a cell phone. At that point I ask them, how in the world was it that Gen. George Washington could defeat Britain, the mightiest nation on earth, without a cell phone or a car?

The problem with the term "need" is that it suggests there are no substitutes for the item in question. Thus, people will pay any price for it; however, the law of demand says that at some price, people will take less of something, including none of it. In response, a student might say, "Diabetics can't do without insulin" or "People can't do without food." I say, "Yes, they can; diabetics have been doing without insulin for thousands of years." In some poor African countries, people do without food. Of course, the results of doing without insulin or food are indeed unpleasant, but the fact that the results are unpleasant doesn't require us to deny that non-consumption is a substitute for consumption. Again, I tell my students not to purge their vocabulary of crying, dying and urgent needs; just don't trick yourself while you're tricking others.

You say, "Williams, it doesn't sound like economics is a very compassionate science." You're right, but neither is physics, chemistry or biology. However, if we wish to be compassionate with our fellow man, we must learn to engage in dispassionate analysis. In other words, thinking with our hearts, rather than our brains, is a surefire method to hurt those whom we wish to help.

Things to Think About

Wednesday, May 16, 2007

Last week, Japan pledged $100 million in grants to fight global climate change. The UN's Intergovernmental Panel on Climate Change (IPCC) is the world's major leader in the struggle against climate change. The World Conservation Union has recently recognized the work of women from all over the world fighting against climate change. We might want to ask whether it's too late to worry about fighting climate change. Let's look at it.

About 65 million years ago, the Earth experienced one of the most rapid and extreme global climate changes recorded in geologic history. The period has been named the "Paleocene-Eocene Thermal Maximum." The ocean was 18 to 27 degrees hotter than it is today. Antarctica, which is today's coldest place on Earth, was home to temperate forests, beech trees and ferns. The Earth had no permanent polar ice caps.

In the past 65 million years, the Earth's temperature has increased and decreased with no help from mankind. My questions to the anti-climate change warriors are: Can mankind really stop climate change, and what is the "correct" Earth temperature?

Now let's turn to gun control laws. What do Virginia Tech's 32 murders, Columbine High School's 13 murders, Jonesboro Westside Middle School's five murders, Germany's Gutenberg High School's 16 murders, the murder of 14 legislators in Zug, Switzerland, and the murder of eight city council members in a Paris suburb all have in common? Answer: All the murders were committed in "gun-free zones." So a reasonable question is: Does legislation creating gun-free zones prevent murder and mayhem?

In 1970, Israel adopted a policy to arm teachers and parents serving as school aids with semi-automatic weapons. Attacks by gunmen at Israeli schools have ceased. At Appalachian Law School in Virginia, a gunman who had already murdered three people was stopped from further carnage by two armed students. Gun possession stopping crime is not atypical, though it goes unreported by the media. According to various research estimates, from 764,000 to as many as 2.5 million crimes are prevented by armed, law-abiding people either warning a criminal that they're armed, brandishing their weapon or shooting a criminal. In the interest of truth in packaging, I think we should rename "gun-free zones" to "defenseless zones."

Now let's consider income tax laws. This tax filing year found 20 million Americans having to pay the Alternative Minimum Tax (AMT). That's up from fewer than 4 million last year. The AMT was legislated in 1969 to make sure that the rich paid their share of taxes by eliminating several legal tax avoidance means. Now a person earning $75,000, hardly rich, can be slapped with the AMT.

During the legislative debate on the 16th Amendment, congressmen argued that only the rich would ever be liable for income taxes. For that reason, getting the rich, the income tax had widespread American support. In 1917, only one-half of 1 percent of income earners paid income taxes—of that .5 percent, those earning $250,000 a year in today's dollars paid 1 percent, and those earning $6 million in today's dollars paid 7 percent. Today, most income earners are liable for federal income taxes.

One is tempted to argue that people are stupid to fall for congressional get-the-rich scams. As a good social scientist, I know that stupidity is a poor explanation for human behavior because people are not stupid in the long run. It might be historical ignorance from one generation to another, where one generation has no knowledge of the promises Congress made to the previous generation. That enables Congress to see each generation as new suckers for their get-the-rich scams.

Historical Tidbits

Karl Marx is the hero of some labor union leaders and civil rights organizations, including those who organized the recent protest against proposed immigration legislation. It's easy to be a Marxist if you haven't read his writings. Most people agree that Marx's predictions about capitalism turned out to be dead wrong.

What most people don't know is that Marx was an out and out racist and anti-Semite. He didn't think much of Mexicans. Concerning the annexation of California after the Mexican-American War, Marx wrote: "Without violence nothing is ever accomplished in history." Then he asks, "Is it a misfortune that magnificent California was seized from the lazy Mexicans who did not know what to do with it?" Friedrich Engels, Marx's co-author of the "Manifesto of the Communist Party," added, "In America we have witnessed the conquest of Mexico and have rejoiced at it. It is to the interest of its own development that Mexico will be placed under the tutelage of the United States." Much of Marx's ideas can be found in a book written by former communist Nathaniel Weyl, titled *Karl Marx, Racist* (1979).

In a July 1862 letter to Engels, in reference to his socialist political competitor, Ferdinand Lassalle, Marx wrote, ". . . it is now completely clear to me that he, as is proved by his cranial formation and his hair, descends from the Negroes from Egypt, assuming that his mother or grandmother had not interbred with a nigger. Now this union of Judaism and Germanism with a basic Negro substance must produce a peculiar product. The obtrusiveness of the fellow is also nigger-like."

Engels shared much of Marx's racial philosophy. In 1887, Paul Lafargue, who was Marx's son-in-law, was a candidate for a council seat in a Paris district that contained a zoo. Engels claimed that Paul had "one eighth or one twelfth nigger blood." In an April 1887 letter to Paul's wife, Engels wrote, "Being in his quality as a nigger, a degree nearer to the rest of the animal kingdom than the rest of us, he is undoubtedly the most appropriate representative of that district."

Though few claim him as their own, such as leftists claim Karl Marx, Thomas Carlyle is another unappreciated historical figure. Carlyle is best known for giving economics the derogatory name "dismal science," an inversion of the phrase "gay science," which at the time (1849) referred to life-enhancing knowledge. Most people have incorrectly learned that the term "dismal science" had its origins in reference to Thomas Malthus' gloomy predictions that the global population would grow faster than food supplies, condemning mankind to perpetual poverty and starvation. My George Mason University colleague, Professor Davy Levy, and his co-author, Sandra Peart, tell the true story in their 2001 book, *The Secret History of the Dismal Science: Economics, Religion and Race in the 19th Century.*

Carlyle first used the term "dismal science" in his 1849 pamphlet entitled "An Occasional Discourse on the Nigger Question." He attacked the ideas of Adam Smith, John Stuart Mill and other free market, limited government economists for their belief in the fundamental equality of man and their anti-slavery positions. The fact that economics assumes that people are all the same and are equally deserving of liberty was offensive to Carlyle and led him to call economics the dismal science. Carlyle argued that blacks were subhuman, "two-legged cattle," who needed the tutelage of whites wielding the "beneficent whip" if they were to contribute to the good of society. Carlyle was by no means alone in denouncing economics for its anti-slavery and pro-equality position.

No less a historical figure and a Christmastime favorite, Charles Dickens, author of *A Christmas Carol*, shared Carlyle's positions on pro-slavery and blacks as subhuman.

Marx, Engels, Carlyle and Dickens all share one belief prevalent throughout mankind's history down to today: the belief that some people are endowed with superior intelligence and wisdom and they've been ordained to forcibly impose that wisdom on the masses.

Running Out of Oil?

Wednesday, July 19, 2006

"Proven" oil reserves, oil that's economically and technologically re-coverable, are estimated to be more than 1.1 trillion barrels. That's enough oil, at current usage rates, to fuel the world's economy for 38 years, according to Leonardo Maugeri, vice president for the Italian energy company ENI. Mr. Maugeri provides a wealth of information about energy in "Two Cheers for Expensive Oil," published by *Foreign Affairs* (March/April 2006) and reprinted on the same date in *Current*.

There are an additional 2 trillion barrels of "recoverable" reserves. Mr. Maugeri says these oil reserves will probably meet the "proven" standard in a few years as technological improvement and increased sub-soil knowledge come online. Estimates of recoverable oil don't include the huge deposits of "unconventional" oil such as Canadian tar sands and U.S. shale oil, plus there are vast areas of our planet yet to be fully explored. For decades, alarmists have claimed we're running out of oil. In 1919, the U.S. Geological Survey predicted that world oil production would peak in nine years. During the 1970s, the Club of Rome report, "The Limits to Growth," said that, assuming no rise in consumption, all known oil reserves would be entirely con-sumed in just 31 years.

There are several factors that explain today's high prices. There has been a huge surge in demand for oil as a result of rapid economic growth in China and India, as well as in the United States. Another factor is the under-exploration. Mr. Maugeri says Saudi Arabia has 260 billion barrels of proven reserves, accounting for 25 percent of the world's total, but only one-third of the oil known to lie below its surface. Russia's reserves are three times its proven reserves of 50 billion barrels. While high prices are beginning to stimulate invest-ments in oil exploration, they've lagged for several decades out of fear of oil gluts and low prices. It's going to be 2010 before today's in-vestments yield fruit.

A substantial increase in oil production alone cannot ease today's high prices because of weak refining capacity. Not a single refinery has been built in the United States for 30 years. Improvements to existing refineries failed to keep up with growing demand and tougher environmental regulations. We're the world's only industrialized country with a net deficit in refining capacity that comes to 20 percent of domestic demand. That makes us highly vulnerable to disasters like last year's hurricanes. Exacerbating weak refining capacity are regulations whereby gasoline produced for one state may not be sold in another. There are 18 mandated different types of gasoline sold in the United States.

The long-term outlook for oil is good. There's an increase in oil-drilling technology and exploration. Oil as a source of energy has been in decline. In 1980, oil was 45 percent of energy consumption; today, it's 34 percent, yielding ground to natural gas, coal and nuclear energy. Recently, the House of Representatives passed "The Deep Ocean Energy Resources Act of 2006," which now awaits a Senate vote. Offshore oil exploration has been banned since 1982, despite Department of the Interior estimates that suggest the presence of 19 billion barrels of oil and 84 trillion cubic feet of natural gas. The House of Representatives also passed the "Refinery Permit Process Schedule Act of 2006." Should these measures become law, our energy capacity will be enhanced significantly.

America stands alone in the world as the only nation that has placed a substantial amount of its domestic oil and natural gas potential off-limits. That reflects the awesome control that radical environmentalists have over Congress. With high fuel prices, Americans might be ready to put an end to that control.

Passing of a Giant

Wednesday, December 6, 2006

Nobel Laureate and Professor Milton Friedman, at age 94, succumbed to heart failure on Nov. 16. While the man is gone, those of us who hold personal liberty as society's highest end will always remember his steadfast support of the principles of personal liberty.

Professor Friedman, above all, was an economist's economist. During his professional life, his research on statistical techniques, consumption behavior and monetary theory became part and parcel of today's accepted wisdom among economists. His research on monetary theory and the role of money in an economy has provided central banks worldwide with the knowledge, whether they use it or not, for monetary stability.

Professor Friedman will surely be remembered for these intellectual contributions, but what he'll be remembered for the most is his steadfast support for personal liberty. In 1947, he joined with Friedrich Hayek and 40 other free-market academics, mostly economists of international distinction, to form the Mont Pelerin Society. The Society's founding purpose was to reduce the academic isolation among liberty-oriented scholars at a time when socialism was seen as the wave of the future.

The Mont Pelerin Society now boasts more than 500 members worldwide, eight of whom have been Nobel Laureates. I'm proud to be a member.

Friedman's first big step into public policy issues, as an indefatigable defender of personal liberty, came in his 1962 book *Capitalism and Freedom*. In it he argued that educational vouchers were the solution to poor education; free markets make racial discrimination more costly; government regulations are the primary sources for harmful monopolies; and Social Security is an unfair and unsustainable system. At the time these weren't popular ideas, even seen as heresy, but today they are much more widely accepted.

In 1980, Professor Friedman co-authored *Free to Choose* with his wife, Rose Friedman, which was written as a follow-up to his 10-part PBS series with the same name. Among the topics discussed: The Great Depression was not a failure of capitalism, as so often claimed, but a failure of government, mainly the Federal Reserve Bank and the U.S. Congress; our welfare system creates permanent wards of the state; and we should decriminalize drugs by treating abuse as a medical problem.

Friedman made a major intellectual contribution to the formation of a voluntary army. In testimony before President Nixon's commission on eliminating the draft, General William Westmoreland said he did not want to command an army of mercenaries. Mr. Friedman interrupted, "General, would you rather command an army of slaves?" Gen. Westmoreland replied, "I don't like to hear our patriotic draftees referred to as slaves." Mr. Friedman then retorted, "I don't like to hear our patriotic volunteers referred to as mercenaries. If they are mercenaries, then I, sir, am a mercenary professor, and you, sir, are a mercenary general; we are served by mercenary physicians, we use a mercenary lawyer, and we get our meat from a mercenary butcher."

Whether one agreed or disagreed with Professor Friedman, they found him to be a friendly, witty and tolerant person. My first encounter with him occurred during the mid-1960s while I was a graduate student at UCLA and he was a visiting lecturer. I've since forgotten my statement to him during a lecture, but I recall he had patiently replied, "Walter, you don't really mean that," and proceeded to show me why.

During my guest-hosting stints on the Rush Limbaugh show, Professor Friedman was a guest on several occasions. His responses to caller questions demonstrated the real teacher in him—the ability to explain complex phenomena in a way that ordinary people can readily understand.

In terms of his scholarly output and worldwide contributions to ideas on liberty, Professor Milton Friedman was the 20th century's greatest economist.

The Productive vs. the Unproductive

Wednesday, April 27, 2005

"The Greatest Century That Ever Was: 25 Miraculous Trends of the Past 100 Years" is the appropriate title of a 1999 article authored by Stephen Moore and the late Julian L. Simon and published by the Washington-based Cato Institute. Let's highlight some of the phenomenal progress Americans made during the 20th century. During that century, life expectancy rose from 47 to 77 years of age. Deaths from infectious diseases fell from 700 to 50 per 100,000 of the population. Major killer diseases such as tuberculosis, polio, typhoid fever, and whooping cough were virtually eliminated. Infant mortality plummeted.

The 20th century saw unprecedented material gains as well. Controlling for inflation, household assets rose from $6 trillion to $41 trillion between 1945 and 1998. Today, more than 98 percent of American homes have a telephone, electricity and a flush toilet. More than 70 percent of Americans own a car, a VCR, a microwave, air conditioning, cable TV, and a washer and dryer. In 1900, no homes had the modern conveniences of today. Today's poor Americans have choices that yesterday's millionaires could have only dreamt of, such as cell phones, computers and color television sets. Added to all this progress, most adults have twice as much leisure time as their turn-of-the-20th-century counterparts.

You say, "Williams, it would take an idiot to deny the human progress Americans made during the 20th century. What's your point?" The productive people who made this progress possible are often painted as villains. I'm talking about the innovators and the risk-takers, in a word—entrepreneurs. Today's heroes are often seen as the people who attack entrepreneurs—among them lawyers, politicians, media people, leftist organizations, college professors and others who often contribute little or nothing to human progress. My colleague, Thomas Sowell, calls the entrepreneurs, scientists and inventors the "doers" and their attackers the "talkers."

The talkers who attack the doers are glib and can turn clever phrases and thereby trick the gullible and uninformed, whether it's the general public through the mass media or judges and juries. For example, even if a particular drug has massive benefits, like saving tens of thousands lives or reducing the suffering of tens of thousands of people, but a few people suffer or die, the talkers are ready to crucify the company. Their first charge is corporate greed.

The attack on the pharmaceutical industry is particularly vicious, led by lawyers looking to make a financial killing like their colleagues who sued the tobacco industry and Microsoft. One target of today's talkers is Merck drug company, the maker of Vioxx, because for some individuals it poses an increased risk of heart attack and stroke. But for other individuals, it is safe and effective for pain relief from arthritis. The operational question for any drug is whether its benefits exceed its costs—not whether some people are harmed. Moreover, some patients would willingly accept the risk of heart attack and stroke to obtain relief from painful, crippling arthritis. Why should the FDA or the plaintiff's bar prevent them from doing so?

If we developed the practice of removing products from the market because some people are harmed by them, we might starve to death. Anaphylaxis is a sudden, severe, potentially fatal reaction that some people have to foods such as milk, wheat, soy, peanuts, fish, shellfish and eggs. Each year, food-induced anaphylaxis sends about 30,000 people to hospital emergency rooms and about 200 of them die. Since many people are harmed by these food items, should they be removed from our supermarket shelves? If not, why not? The next time we hear a talker attacking a doer, we just might ask: What have you done to further human progress?

Making Intelligent Errors

Wednesday, August 10, 2005

We're not omniscient. That means making errors is unavoidable. Understanding the nature of errors is vital to our well-being. Let's look at it.

There are two types of errors, nicely named the type I error and the type II error. The type I error is when we reject a true hypothesis when we should accept it. The type II error is when we accept a false hypothesis when we should reject it. In decisionmaking, there's always a non-zero probability of making one error or the other. That means we're confronted with asking the question: Which error is least costly? Let's apply this concept to a couple of issues.

The stated reason for going to war with Iraq is that our intelligence agencies surmised Saddam Hussein had, or was near having, nuclear, biological and chemical weapons of mass destruction. Intelligence is never perfect. During World War II, our intelligence agencies thought that Germany was close to having an atomic bomb. That intelligence was later found to be flawed, but it played an important role in the conduct of the war.

Since intelligence is always less than perfect, we're forced to decide which error is least costly. Leading up to our war with Iraq, the potential errors confronting us were: Saddam Hussein had weapons of mass destruction and we incorrectly assumed he didn't. Or, he didn't have weapons of mass destruction and we incorrectly assumed he did. Both errors are costly, but which is more costly? It's my guess that it would have been more costly for us to make the first error: Saddam Hussein had weapons of mass destruction and we incorrectly assumed he didn't.

Another example of type I and type II errors hits closer to home. Food and Drug Administration (FDA) officials, in their drug approval process, can essentially make two errors. They can approve a drug that has unanticipated dangerous side effects (type II). Or, they can disapprove, or hold up approval of, a drug that's perfectly safe and effective (type I). In other words, they can err on the side of under-caution or err on the side of over-caution. Which error do FDA officials have the greater incentive to make?

If an FDA official errs by approving a drug that has unanticipated, dangerous side effects, he risks congressional hearings, disgrace and termination. Erring on the side of under-caution produces visible, sick victims who are represented by counsel and whose plight is hyped by the media.

Erring on the side of over-caution is another matter. A classic example was beta-blockers, which an American Heart Association study said will "lengthen the lives of people at risk of sudden death due to irregular heartbeats." The beta-blockers in question were available in Europe in 1967, yet the FDA didn't approve them for use in the U.S. until 1976. In 1979, Dr. William Wardell, a professor of pharmacology, toxicology and medicine at the University of Rochester, estimated that a single beta-blocker, alprenolol, which had already been sold for three years in Europe, but not approved for use in the U.S., could have saved more than 10,000 lives a year. The type I error, erring on the side of over-caution, has little or no cost to FDA officials. Grieving survivors of those 10,000 people who unnecessarily died each year don't know why their loved one died, and surely they don't connect the death to FDA over-caution. For FDA officials, these are the best kind of victims—invisible ones. When an FDA official holds a press conference to announce its approval of a new life-saving drug, I'd like to see just one reporter ask: How many lives would have been saved had the FDA not delayed the drug's approval?

The bottom line is, we humans are not perfect. We will make errors. Rationality requires that we recognize and weigh the cost of one error against the other.

Economic Lunacy

Wednesday, September 7, 2005

According to a couple of poorly trained economists, there's a bright side to Hurricane Katrina's destruction. J.P. Morgan senior economist Anthony Chan believes hurricanes tend to stimulate overall growth. As reported in "Gas Crisis Looms" (Aug. 31, 2005), written by CNN/Money staff writer Parija Bhatnagar, Mr. Chan said, "Preliminary estimates indicate 60 percent damage to downtown New Orleans. Plenty of cleanup work and rebuilding will follow in all the areas. That means over the next 12 months, there will be lots of job creation which is good for the economy."

Professor Doug Woodward, of the business school at the University of South Carolina, has the same vision. Professor Woodward said, "On a personal level, the loss of life is tragic. But looking at the economic impact, our research shows that hurricanes tend to become god-given work projects." Within six months, Professor Woodward "expects to see a construction boom and job creation offset the short-term negatives such as loss of business activity, loss of wealth in the form of housing, infrastructure, agriculture and tourism revenue in the Gulf Coast states."

Let's ask a few smell-test questions about these claims of beneficial aspects of hurricane destruction. Would there have been even greater economic growth and job creation for our nation had Hurricane Katrina not only destroyed New Orleans, Mobile and Gulfport, but other major metropolitan areas along its path, like Cincinnati and Pittsburgh, as well? Would we consider it a godsend, in terms of jobs and economic growth, if a few more category 4 hurricanes hit our shores? Only a lunatic would answer these questions in the affirmative.

Frederic Bastiat (1801–1850), a great French economist, said in his pamphlet "What is Seen and What is Not Seen": "There is only one difference between a bad economist and a good one: the bad economist confines himself to the visible effect; the good economist takes into account both the effect that can be seen and those effects that must be foreseen." What economists Chan and Woodward can see are the jobs and construction boom created by repairing hurricane destruction. What they can't see, and thus ignore, is what those resources would have been used for had there not been hurricane destruction.

Bastiat wrote a parable about this which has become known as the "Broken Window Fallacy." A shopkeeper's window is broken by a vandal. A crowd formed sympathizing with the man. After a while, someone in the crowd suggested that the boy wasn't guilty of vandalism; instead, he was a public benefactor, creating economic benefits for everyone in town. After all, fixing the broken window creates employment for the glazier, who will then buy bread and benefit the baker, who will then buy shoes and benefit the cobbler, and so forth.

Those are the seen effects of repairing the broken window. What's unseen is what the shopkeeper would have done with the money had the vandal not broken his window. He might have employed the tailor by purchasing a suit. The vandal's breaking his window produced at least two unseen effects. First, it shifted unemployment from the glazier who now has a job to the tailor who doesn't. Second, it reduced the shopkeeper's wealth. Had it not been for the vandalism, the shopkeeper would have had a window and a suit; now he has just a window.

Of course, were it the Tooth Fairy or Santa Claus providing the resources to repair the destruction of Hurricane Katrina, Mr. Chan and Professor Woodward would be correct. But what the heck, maybe we shouldn't be so harsh on these economists in light of the fact that they didn't receive their training at George Mason University's Economics Department, where there are no bad economists.

Do We Really Care about Children?

Wednesday, November 2, 2005

I cringe with disgust when I hear politicians say, "We're doing it for the children." What's worse is so many Americans mindlessly fall hook, line and sinker for the hype. Judging by our actions, Americans could not care less for future generations, and future generations will curse us for it. Let's look at it.

According to several respected authorities, including the Concord Coalition (co-chaired by former Sens. Warren Rudman and Robert Kerrey), the Congressional Budget Office, U.S. Treasury Secretary John Snow, and the Social Security Administration, the estimated present value of the unfunded liability of Social Security and Medicare ranges between $61 trillion and $75 trillion dollars.

"Williams," you ask, "what's this present value business?" Simply put, between $61 trillion and $75 trillion dollars is the money that would have to be put aside right now, at current interest rates, in order to meet future obligations of Social Security and Medicare. To put an astronomical sum like $61 trillion or $75 trillion in a bit of perspective: The value of our entire national output of goods and services (GDP) in 2004 was only $12 trillion.

Congress can't put aside $75 trillion as reserves against future liabilities of Social Security and Medicare. Therefore, according to the Dallas, Texas-based National Center for Policy Analysis (NCPA), the annual rate of Social Security unfunded liabilities is growing at a $667 billion clip and Medicare's at $4 trillion.

What does all this mean? It means little in pocketbook terms to today's Americans who are 65 years or older. They will collect their Social Security checks and their promised Medicare benefits, but not so for future generations. Here's that future according to House Ways and Means Committee testimony, given by Dr. John Goodman, president of the NCPA (May 2005). "In 2020, combined Social Security and Medicare deficits will equal almost 29 percent of federal income taxes. At that point the federal government will have to stop doing almost a third of what it does today. By 2030, about the midpoint of the baby boomer retirement years, federal guarantees to Social Security and Medicare will require one in every two income tax dollars. By 2050, they will require three in every four." And by 2070, Social Security and Medicare will consume all federal revenues.

There are some "optimists" who seek to minimize the pending disaster that will be caused by these and other federal unfunded liabilities. They argue that the federal government can always meet its obligations through its power to tax. According to some estimates, by 2030, Social Security and Medicare obligations alone will require a 50 percent increase in payroll taxes. If tax increases are off the table, 2030 will see a 30 percent reduction in promised Social Security benefits and stringent rationing of health care services promised by Medicare. There's another "solution." Even though Congress can't increase our life-expectancy, they can raise the age of Social Security and Medicare eligibility. Were Congress to make 80 as the age for Social Security and Medicare eligibility, they'd solve the problem because most of us would be dead.

Let's look at the raw politics of the Social Security/Medicare situation. Few, if any, of our 535 congressmen will be around in 2030 and later when the real crunch comes, but they are subject to today's, not tomorrow's, political pressures. Similarly, few of today's Americans 65 years of age and older will be around. Other than mouthing a concern for future generations, both have little economic incentive to be concerned about what happens in 2030. After all, what do they have at stake?

In 2030, will young people in the labor force be willing to see themselves taxed at Social Security rates of 20, 30 and 40 percent to take care of some old people? I don't think that will politically fly, and they might begin to get ideas about euthanasia. In addition to economic strife, Social Security and Medicare are laying the groundwork for intergenerational conflict. Unfortunately, the politics of today don't give us room to prevent these twin disasters.

Why We're a Divided Nation

September 13, 2004

Recent elections pointed to deepening divisions among American people but has anyone given serious thought to just why? I have part of the answer that starts off with a simple example.

Different Americans have different and intensive preferences for cars, food, clothing and entertainment. For example, some Americans love opera and hate rock and roll. Others have opposite preferences, loving rock and roll and hating opera. When's the last time you heard of rock and roll lovers in conflict with opera lovers? It seldom if ever happens. Why? Those who love operas get what they want and those who love rock and roll get what they want and both can live in peace with one another.

Suppose that instead of freedom in the music market, decisions on what kind of music people could listen to were made in the political arena. It would be either opera or rock and roll. Rock and rollers would be lined up against opera lovers. Why? It's simple. If the opera lovers win, rock and rollers would lose and the reverse if rock and rollers won. Conflict would emerge solely because the decision was made in the political arena.

The prime feature of political decisionmaking is that it's a zero-sum game. One person or group's gain is of necessity another person or group's loss. As such political allocation of resources is conflict enhancing while market allocation is conflict reducing. The greater the number of decisions made in the political arena the greater is the potential for conflict.

There are other implications of political decisionmaking. Throughout most of our history we've lived in relative harmony. That's remarkable because just about every religion, racial and ethnic group in the world is represented in our country. These are the very racial/ethnic/religious groups that have for centuries been trying to slaughter one another in their home countries, among them: Turks and Armenians, Protestant and Catholic, Muslim and Jew, Croats and

Serbs. While we haven't been a perfect nation, there have been no cases of mass genocide and religious wars that have plagued the globe elsewhere. The closest we've come was the American Indian/European conflict that pales by comparison.

The reason we've been able to live in relative harmony is that for most of our history government was small. There wasn't much pie to distribute politically.

When it's the political arena that determines who gets what goodies, the most effective coalitions are those with a proven record of being the most divisive—those based on race, ethnicity, religion and region. As a matter of fact our most costly conflict involved a coalition based upon region—namely the War of 1861.

Many of the issues that divide us, aside from the Iraq war, are those best described as a zero-sum game where one group's gain is of necessity another's loss. Examples are: racial preferences, social security, tax policy, trade restrictions, welfare and a host of other government policies that benefit one American at the expense of another American.

You might be tempted to think that the brutal domestic conflict seen in other countries at other times can't happen here. That's nonsense. Americans are not super-humans; we possess the same frailties of other people in other places. If there were a severe economic calamity, I can imagine a political hustler exploiting those frailties, just as Hitler did in Germany, blaming it on the Jews, the blacks, the East Coast, Catholics or free trade.

The best thing the President and Congress can do to heal our country is to reduce the impact of government on our lives. Doing so will not only produce a less divided country, greater economic efficiency but bear greater faith and allegiance to the vision of America held by our Founders—a country of limited government.

What's Inflation?

Wednesday, November 16, 2005

Last month, President Bush nominated Dr. Ben S. Bernanke, currently chairman of the President's Council of Economic Advisors, as chairman of Federal Reserve Board to replace the retiring Alan Greenspan. Alan Greenspan's replacement comes at a time of heightened fears of inflation resulting from the recent spike in oil prices.

First, let's decide what is and what is not inflation. One price or several prices rising is not inflation. When there's a general increase in prices, or alternatively, a reduction in the purchasing power of money, there's inflation. But just as in the case of diseases, describing a symptom doesn't necessarily give us a clue to a cause. Nobel Laureate and professor Milton Friedman says, "[I]nflation is always and everywhere a monetary phenomenon, in the sense that it cannot occur without a more rapid increase in the quantity of money than in output." Increases in money supply are what constitute inflation, and a general rise in prices is the symptom.

Let's look at that with a simple example. Pretend several of us gather to play a standard Monopoly game that contains $15,140 worth of money. The player who owns Boardwalk or any other property is free to sell it for any price he wishes. Given the money supply in the game, a general price level will emerge for all trades. If some property prices rise, others will fall, thereby maintaining that level.

Suppose unbeknownst to other players, I counterfeit $5,000 and introduce it into the game. Initially, that gives me tremendous purchasing power, whereby I can bid up property prices. After my $5,000 has circulated through the game, there will be a general rise in the prices—something that would have been impossible before I slipped money into the game. My example is a highly simplistic example of a real economy, but it permits us to make some basic assessments of inflation.

First, let's not let politicians deceive us, and escape culpability, by defining inflation as rising prices, which would allow them to make the pretense that inflation is caused by greedy businessmen, rapacious unions or Arab sheiks. Increases in money supply are what constitute inflation, and the general rise in the price level is the result. Who's in charge of the money supply? It's the government operating through the Federal Reserve.

There's another inflation result that bears acknowledgment. Printing new money to introduce into the game makes me a thief. I've obtained objects of value for nothing in return. My actions also lower the purchasing power of every dollar in the game. I've often suggested that if a person is ever charged with counterfeiting, he should tell the judge he was engaging in monetary policy.

When inflation is unanticipated, as it so often is, there's a redistribution of wealth from creditors to debtors. If you lend me $100, and over the term of the loan the Federal Reserve increases the money supply in a way that causes inflation, I pay you back with dollars with reduced purchasing power. Since inflation redistributes (steals) wealth from creditors to debtors, it helps us identify inflation's primary beneficiary. That identification is easy if you ask: Who is the nation's largest debtor? If you said, "It's the U.S. government," go to the head of the class.

So what about the president's nomination of Ben S. Bernanke as Alan Greenspan's replacement? I know little or nothing about the man. What I do know is that it's not wise for one person, or group of persons, to have so much power over our economy. Here's my recommendation for reducing that power: Repeal legal tender laws and eliminate all taxes on gold, silver and platinum transactions. That way, Americans could write contracts in precious metals and thereby reduce the ability of government to steal from us.

Basic Economics

Wednesday, December 7, 2005

With all the recent hype and demagoguery about gasoline price-gouging, maybe it's time to talk about the basics of exchange. First, what is exchange? Exchange occurs when an owner transfers property rights or title to that which is his.

Here's the essence of what transpires when I purchase a gallon of gasoline. In effect, I tell the retailer that I hold title to $3. He tells me that he holds title to a gallon of gas. I offer to transfer my title to $3 to him if he'll transfer his title to a gallon of gas to me. If this exchange occurs voluntarily, what can be said about the transaction?

One thing we know for sure is that the retailer was free to retain his ownership of the gallon of gas and I my ownership of $3. That being the case, why would we exchange? The only answer is that I perceived myself as better off giving up my $3 for the gallon of gas and likewise the retailer perceived himself as better off giving up his gas for the $3. Otherwise, why would we have exchanged?

Exchanges of this sort are called good-good exchanges, namely "I'll do something good for you if you do something good for me." Game theorists recognize this as a positive-sum game—a transaction where both parties are better off as a result. Of course there's another type of exchange not typically sought, namely good-bad exchange. An example of that kind of exchange would be where I approached the retailer with a pistol telling him that if he didn't do something good for me, give me that gallon of gas, I'd do something bad to him, blow his brains out. Clearly, I'd be better off, but he would be worse off. Game theorists call that a zero-sum game—a transaction where in order for one person to be better off, the other must be worse off. Zero-sum games are transactions mostly initiated by thieves and governments.

Some might argue that there's unequal bargaining power between me and the gas retailer. That's nonsense! The retailer has the power to charge any price he wishes, but I have the power to decide how much I'll buy, including none, at that price. You say, "Gas is a necessity, and we're forced to buy it." That too is nonsense. If I voluntarily purchase the gas, I do so because I deem it better than my next best alternative. Of course, at a high enough price, I wouldn't deem it as such.

In the wake of the spike in fuel prices, many Americans demand that politicians do something. You can bet the rent money that whatever politicians do will end up harming consumers. Despite a long history of their economic calamity, some Americans and politicians are calling for price controls or, what amounts to the same thing, anti price-gouging legislation. As Professor Thomas DiLorenzo points out in "Four Thousand Years of Price Control" (www.mises.org/story/1962), price controls have produced calamities wherever and whenever they've been tried.

Economic ignorance, misconceptions and superstition drive us toward totalitarianism because they make us more willing to hand over greater control of our lives to politicians. That results in a diminution of our liberties. Think back to the gasoline price controls during the 1970s. The price controls caused shortages. To deal with the shortages, restrictions were imposed on purchases. Then national highway speed limits were enacted. Then there were more calls for smaller and less crashworthy cars. With the recent gasoline supply shocks, we didn't experience the shortages, long lines and closed gas stations seen during the 1970s. Why? Prices were allowed to perform their allocative function—get people to use less gas and get suppliers to supply more.

U.S. Atrocities in Iraq

May 12, 2004

It's the end of the semester at George Mason University and for the past couple of weeks I've been too busy preparing final exam harassment for my students to pay much attention to all the news stories about how U.S. soldiers were torturing Iraqi prisoners at Abu Ghraib prison. Now that my spring semester's work has just about been completed, I decided to bring myself up to speed on these American atrocities.

I braced myself for the worst. Part of my 1959 Fort Jackson, South Carolina, basic training involved lessons on evasion and escape. Our drill sergeant who fought in the Korean War told us about how North Koreans tortured American prisoners of war. His graphic descriptions gave us added incentive to pay attention to what we were being taught about evasion and escape. Remembering his graphic descriptions, and given the worldwide condemnation of our soldiers, I was prepared to see pictures of American soldiers engaged in atrocities such as: eye gouging, piercing of prisoner's hands and knees with electric drills, beating soles of prisoner's feet, cigarette burns, fingernail extraction, whipping, and placing prisoners in acid baths. I also thought I might see pictures of Iraqis looking like the diseased and starved World War II American prisoners of the Japanese who were brutally marched from Bataan to Camp O'Donnell and when liberated from Japanese prisoner of war camps, many didn't weigh much over 100 pounds if that.

Much to my surprise I saw none of this. What I saw in no way could be described as torture or atrocities, at least if we stick to historical definitions of torture and atrocities. Among the pictures I saw were: Pfc. Lynndie England with a dog leash tied to a naked Iraqi. Iraqi prisoners forced to parade naked before their jeering captors. Two American soldiers—a male and a female—forcing a group of Iraqi prisoners into simulating group sex. An American female soldier playing with two naked Iraqi captives. A British soldier urinating on an Iraqi prisoner. Of the pictures I saw, the worst act was a soldier putting a rifle butt to an Iraqi prisoner's groin.

These acts aren't anything that Americans should be proud of but at the same time they don't qualify as torture and atrocities so far as those terms have been historically defined. Moreover, they are mild in comparison to the kind of prison treatment to which Iraqis have become accustomed.

Before we condemn our soldiers too much we might consider that this war is the most humane war ever fought. In toppling the Saddam Hussein regime, there were relatively few non-combatant casualties. Afterwards our troops and American and foreign civilians went to great lengths to begin to rebuild the country and much of that rebuilding has little to do with what was destroyed in war. How has this unprecedented effort been rewarded? Our soldiers have been ambushed and murdered by Hussein holdouts and Muslim fanatics. American and foreign civilians have been brutally murdered and their corpses treated in unspeakable ways. And all of this to the glee of large Iraqi mobs. We should keep in mind that our soldiers are humans. I think it's understandable that they might want revenge against perpetrators who've been involved with the murder and maiming of their comrades.

Don't get me wrong about this. Their actions are not to be condoned. But if President Bush and Congress want to know whether our soldiers' actions constitute torture, I suggest they ask former American Japanese POWs or better yet ask former Hanoi Hilton resident Senator John McCain. By the way, if our soldiers are to be court martialed for anything, it should be for stupidity—stupidity of permitting photos to be taken of what they were doing.

Will the West Survive?

June 23, 2004

The Muslim world is at war with western civilization. We have the military might to thwart them. The question is: do we have the intelligence to recognize the attack and the will to defend ourselves from annihilation? Their intent is clear but let's refresh our memories with a bit of history.

At the 1972 Olympic games in Munich several athletes were massacred. In 1979, the U.S. embassy was taken over and 52 hostages held for more than a year. In 1983, U.S. Marine barracks in Beirut were blown up killing 241 U.S. soldiers. In 1988, Pan Am flight 103 was bombed killing 270 people. In 1993, there was the first bombing of the World Trade Center and in 2001 it was reduced to rubble killing more than 3,000 Americans. In 1988, U.S. embassies in Kenya and Tanzania were bombed resulting in the deaths of 220 people and 4,000 injured. Who are the people responsible for these and other wanton murders of innocents including the recent barbaric beheading of two innocent men? They were all Muslims.

You say, "Williams, you can't make an indictment of a whole people and their religion!" I'm not and let me clearly state: By no means are all Muslims murderers. But on the other hand, I've never heard broad Muslim condemnation of their fellow Muslims' murderous acts committed in the name of their God. If anything there has been jubilation and dancing in the streets in the wake of Muslim attacks on westerners. Contrast their response to the widespread western condemnation of the, mild by comparison, behavior of a few coalition forces in Iraq's Abu Ghraib prison.

Muslim atrocities, and the collective Muslim response to those atrocities, might be better understood knowing their belief system as spelled out by a few, among many, passages from the Koran: "Fight those who do not believe in Allah" (Surat At-Taubah 9:29). "I will instill terror into the hearts of the unbelievers, Smite ye above their necks and smite all their finger tips of them" (Koran 8:12). "The unbelievers among the People of the Book and the pagans shall burn forever in the fire of Hell. They are the vilest of all creatures" (Koran 98:1-8). "Fight against those who believe not in Allah, and those who acknowledge not the religion of truth [Islam], until they are subdued" (Surat At-Taubah 9:29).

Phil Lucas, editor of the *Panama City News Herald* 4/4/04, in his editorial, "Up Against Fanaticism" asks, "Can anybody name three on-going world conflicts in which Muslims are not involved?" Mr. Lucas says, "They can't get along with their neighbors on much of the planet: France, Chechnya, Bosnia, Indonesia, Spain, Morocco, India, Tunisia, Somalia, etc., etc., etc."

My colleague Dr. Thomas Sowell observes, "Those in the Islamic world have for centuries been taught to regard themselves as far superior to the "infidels" of the West, while everything they see with their own eyes now tells them otherwise." He adds, "Nowhere have whole peoples seen their situation reversed more visibly or more painfully than the peoples of the Islamic world." Sowell adds that few people, once at the top of civilization, accept their reversals of fortune gracefully. Moreover, they don't blame themselves for their plight. For the Muslim world, it's the West who's to blame.

History never repeats itself exactly but we might benefit from knowledge of factors leading to the decline of past great civilizations. Rome was one of those advanced civilizations. Rome was so caught up in "bread and circuses" and moral decline that it couldn't manage to defend itself from invading barbaric hordes that ultimately plunged Europe into the Dark Ages. The sooner we recognize that the West is in a war for survival the more likely we'll be able to escape the fate that befell the Roman Empire.

Economics 101

August 11, 2004

Economic ignorance allows us to fall easy prey to political charlatans and demagogues, so how about a little Economics 101.

How many times have we heard "free tuition," "free healthcare," and free you-name-it? If a particular good or service is truly free, we can have as much of it that we want without the sacrifice of other goods or services. Take a "free" library; is it really free? The answer is no. Had the library not been built, that $50 million could have purchased something else. That something else sacrificed is the cost of the library. While users of the library might pay a zero price, zero price and free are not one and the same. So when politicians talk about providing something free, ask them to identify the beneficent Santa Claus or Tooth Fairy.

It's popular to condemn greed but it's greed that gets wonderful things done. When I say greed, I don't mean stealing, fraud, misrepresentation, and other forms of dishonesty. I mean people trying to get as much as they can for themselves. We don't give second thought to the many wonderful things that others do for us. Detroit assembly line workers get up at the crack of dawn to produce the car that you enjoy. Farm workers toil in the blazing sun gathering grapes for our wine. Snowplow drivers brave blizzards just so we can have access to our roads. Do you think these people make these personal sacrifice because they care about us? My bet is that they don't give a hoot. Instead, they, along with their bosses, do these wonderful things for us because they want more for themselves.

People in the education and political establishments pretend they're not motivated by such "callous" motives as greed and profits. These people "care" about us but which areas of our lives do we derive the greatest pleasures and have the fewest complaints, and which areas do we have the greatest headaches and complaints? We tend to have a high satisfaction level with goods and services like computers, cell phones, movies, clothing and supermarkets. These are areas were the motivation is greed and profits. Our greatest dissatisfaction are in areas of caring and no profit motive such as public education, postal services, and politics. Give me greed and profits and you can keep the caring.

How about the idea that if it saves just one life it's worth it? That's some of the stated justification for government mandates for child-proof medicine bottles, gun locks, bike helmets and all sorts of warning labels. No doubt there's a benefit to these government mandates but if we only look at benefits we'll do darn near anything because there's always a benefit to any action. For example, why not have a congressionally mandated five mph highway speed limit? According to the U.S. Department of Transportation, there were 43,220 highway fatalities in 2003 with an estimated cost of $230 billion. A five mph speed limit would have spared our nation of this loss of life and billions of dollars.

You say, "Williams, that's preposterous!" You're right. Most people would agree that a five mph speed limit is stupid, impractical and insane. That's one way of putting it but what they really mean is: the benefit of saving 43,200 highway deaths and the $230 billion, that would result from mandating a five mph speed limit, isn't worth all the inconvenience, delays and misery.

Admittedly, the five mph speed limit is an extreme example, a reductio ad absurdum. Nonetheless, it illustrates the principle that our actions shouldn't be guided by benefits only; we should also ask about costs. Again when politicians come to us pretending they're Santa Clauses or Tooth Fairies delivering benefits only, we should ask what's the cost and who's going to pay and why.

Economic Lunacy

November 17, 2004

Here's a couple of newspaper headlines following Florida's bout with hurricane disasters: "Storms create lucrative times," *St. Petersburg Times* (9/30/04). Then there's *USA Today*, "Economic growth from hurricanes could outweigh costs" (9/26/04). The writers, Joni James and Barbara Hagenbaugh might have been listening to economists like Steve Cochrane, director of regional economics at Economy.com, a consulting firm in West Chester, Pennsylvania who said, "It's a perverse thing ... there's real pain, but from an economic point of view, it is a plus." Why are Florida's hurricanes a "plus"? It's simple. According to *St. Petersburg Times* reporter Joni James, "Construction creates thousands of jobs, insurance provides for billions in consumer purchases and new facilities built to higher standards might help offset future storm-related losses."

This kind of reasoning, often put forth by poorly trained economists, doesn't even pass a simple smell test. Think about it this way. Using Mr. Cochrane's statement, if "from an economic point of view, it [hurricanes] is a plus," would the country have been even better off if the entire east coast shared Florida's damage and destruction? If it would have been a plus for the east coast, what about hurricane destruction for the entire nation east of the Mississippi? Almost anyone with a speck of brains would recognize that equating economic growth with destruction is lunacy.

French economist Frederic Bastiat (1801–1850) wrote a pamphlet "What is Seen and What is Not Seen," where he says, "There is only one difference between a bad economist and a good one: the bad economist confines himself to the visible effect; the good economist takes into account both the effect that can be seen and those effects that must be foreseen." In the case of Florida's hurricane disaster, what is seen is the employment associated with rebuilding. What is unseen is what Floridians would have spent the money on and the benefits there from had there not been hurricane destruction.

Bastiat wrote a parable about this which has become known as the "Broken Window Fallacy." A shopkeeper's window is broken by a vandal. A crowd forms sympathizing with the man, but pretty soon they start to suggest the boy wasn't guilty of vandalism; instead, he was a public benefactor, creating economic benefits for everyone in town. After all fixing the broken window creates employment for the glazier who will then buy bread and benefit the baker, who will then buy shoes, and benefit the cobbler, and so forth.

Those are the seen effects of the broken window. What's unseen is what the shopkeeper would have done with the money had the vandal not broken his window. He might have employed the tailor by purchasing a suit. The broken window produced at least two unseen effects. First, it shifted unemployment from the glazier who now has a job to the tailor who doesn't. Second, it reduced the shopkeeper's wealth, namely, had it not been for the vandalism the shopkeeper would have had a window and a suit; now he has just a window.

The broken window fallacy was seen in a column written by Princeton University Professor Paul Krugman after the terrorist attack on the World Trade Center, "After the Horror" *New York Times* (9/14/01). He wrote, "Ghastly as it may seem to say this, the terror attack—like the original day of infamy, which brought an end to the Great Depression—could do some economic good." He went on to point out how rebuilding the destruction would stimulate the economy through business investment and job creation. Again, do the smell test. If Professor Krugman is right, wouldn't the terrorists have done us a bigger economic favor if they had destroyed buildings in other cities?

Maybe we shouldn't be so harsh on these reporters and economists in light of the fact that they didn't receive training at George Mason University's Economics Department where there are no bad economists.

Attack on Decency

December 1, 2004

Janet Jackson's "wardrobe malfunction," Nicolette Sheridan's towel malfunction and naked leap into the arms of Philadelphia Eagle wide receiver Terrell Owens on ABC's Monday Night Football, and the recent Detroit Pistons/Indiana Pacers game melee are just the most recent signs of a new culture that has emerged among Americans and it's just the tip of the iceberg.

Years ago the lowest of lowdown men wouldn't use the kind of language that's routinely used today not only in the presence of women but often to women. To see men sitting while a woman was standing on a public conveyance used to be unthinkable. Children addressing adults by their first name was also unthinkable, not to mention the use of foul language in the presence of or to adults. How about guys and girls walking down the street whilst the guy has his hand in the girl's rear pocket?

What might explain the differences in behavior today versus yesteryear? A significant part of the explanation is seen by recognizing that society's first line of defense is not the law but customs, traditions and moral values. Customs, traditions and moral values are those important thou-shalt-nots such as: shalt not murder, shalt not steal, shalt not lie and cheat. They also include respect for parents, teachers and others in authority plus those courtesies one might read in Emily Post's rules of etiquette.

The importance of customs, traditions and moral values as a means of regulating behavior is that people behave themselves even if nobody's watching. There are not enough cops and laws can never replace these restraints on personal conduct so as to produce a civilized society. At best, the police and criminal justice system are the last desperate line of defense for a civilized society. Unfortunately, too many of us see police, laws, the criminal and civil justice systems as society's first line of defense.

For nearly a half century, the nation's liberals along with the education establishment, pseudo-intellectuals and the courts have waged war on traditions, customs and moral values. Many in this generation have been counseled to believe that there are no moral absolutes. Instead, what's moral or immoral is a matter of convenience, personal opinion, or what is or is not criminal.

During the '60s, the education establishment launched their agenda to undermine lessons children learned from their parents and the church with fads like "values clarification." So-called sex education classes are simply indoctrination that sought to undermine family/church strictures against pre-marital sex. Lessons of abstinence were ridiculed and considered passé and replaced with lessons about condoms, birth control pills and abortions. Further undermining of parental authority came with legal and extra-legal measures to assist teenage abortions with neither parental knowledge nor consent.

Customs, traditions, moral values and rules of etiquette, not laws and government regulations, are what makes for a civilized society. These behavioral norms, mostly transmitted by example, word-of-mouth, and religious teachings, represent a body of wisdom distilled through ages of experience, trial and error, and looking at what works and what doesn't.

Customs, traditions and moral values have been discarded without an appreciation for the role they played in creating a civilized society and now we're paying the price. What's worse is that instead of a return to what worked, many of us fail to make the connection and insist "there ought to be a law." As such it points to another failure of the so-called "great generation"—the failure to transmit to their children what their parents transmitted to them.

Profiling Needed

November 5, 2001

Standing in long lines to pass through airport security, I thought: Where's racial and sexual profiling now when it can benefit most, if not all passengers? You say, "What's wrong with you, Williams, everybody knows that profiling has been declared racist and sex profiling is no better?" Let's look at profiling as a principle.

Suppose you were chief of police seeking to apprehend some unknown gangsters involved in a recent drive-by shooting, would you instruct your officers to include 80-year-old women as possible suspects to be detained and questioned? You probably wouldn't and why? It's not because you have affection or special respect for the civil rights of older women. Focusing police resources on 80-year-old women, and for that matter 80-year-old men, as suspects would be stupid and a gross waste of resources because the chances that 80-year-olds would be involved in drive-by shootings is close to nil.

Criminals involved in the drive-by shooting would benefit if there were to be an anti-profiling law forcing police to view 80-year-olds just as likely to be involved in drive-by shootings as any other age group in the population. Doing so would waste police resources and give criminals greater opportunities to escape detection and apprehension.

Similar reasoning can be applied to airport security measures. Right now part of enhanced security includes forcing all passengers to wait in long lines to have their tickets and ID checked, take off outer garments, be frisked, and have their carry-on items searched for anything that might be used as a weapon—that includes fingernail files and clippers, cuticle cutters, knitting needles and you name it. Lines and passenger inconvenience could be reduced by applying profiling where less scrutiny is given to older women and men. While older women and men are not likely to be hijackers, they might be used by hijackers to carry weapons; thus, a reasonable case can be made for requiring them as well as any other passengers to pass through metal detectors.

Who should receive more scrutiny and who should receive less? This is an important question if we are to insure against hijacking. As a generality women should receive less scrutiny, after all women have never been significant players in hijacking. Black Americans of either sex should receive less scrutiny for the same reason. Most security resources should be spent scrutinizing Caucasian males, particularly those with a Middle East appearance. And why? It's simply that virtually all hijackings in the U.S. and elsewhere have been committed by men fitting that general description.

Some might say that it's unjust to single out some Americans for more security scrutiny than others. But it is also unjust, plus a waste of resources, to subject people to airport security harassment who pose absolutely no hijack threat, such as old men, women of any age and young children.

There are security measures we can take that are far more effective than anything that we're doing now. There are tens of thousands of retired policemen and active duty policemen, as well as their counterparts in the FBI and Secret Service who fly. How about a program that allows them to fly half-fare if they carry their weapons and act as sky marshals? That would create considerable uncertainty for hijackers. They wouldn't know who or how many people were on the plane who would be in the position to blow their brains out. Current government regulations give aid and comfort to hijackers. The FAA has guaranteed hijackers that no one on the plane is armed but them. That must be changed.

A Dynamite Economics Department

November 30, 2001

Reporting their findings in *Applied Economics Letters* (2/2001), a British professional journal, Professors Franklin G. Mixon, Jr. and Kamal P. Upadhyaya rank economics departments in the U.S. South. The rankings are based upon faculty research productivity. As former chairman of George Mason University's Economics Department, for the last six years, I am pleased and proud to report that our department heads the list of some 69 southern university Ph.D. granting economics departments.

You say, "How did we achieve that status? What kind of economists are you people anyway?" Everybody's heard of Keynesian economists, Austrian, neoclassical, and free market economists. I'd like to think that we're none of those. My friend and colleague Nobel Laureate Milton Friedman always reminds us there are only two kinds of economists—good economists and bad economists. We're good economists.

You say, "Nobody's going to admit that they're a bad economist so how can we tell the difference?" See if the economist suggests the possibility of a free lunch. We all know that there's no free lunch but free-lunch economists will tell you things such as: WWII got us out of the Depression; building sports arenas will stimulate employment; monopolies can charge any price they wish; government spending is good for the economy; and trade surpluses are good and trade deficits are bad. Since my colleagues are good economists, you'll hear no such nonsense from them.

George Mason University economists are leaders in economic thinking. They include scholars such as Nobel Laureate James Buchanan who, along with his colleague Gordon Tullock, pioneered the field in economics known as public choice. At the heart of their contribution is the idea that when people become politicians or bureaucrats they don't suddenly become selfless servants imbued with the public interest. Instead, they remain self-interested just as any other person but simply face a different set of restraints.

Towards the end of my tenure as department chairman, we acquired all seven members of the University of Arizona's distinguished Economic Science Laboratory. Professor Vernon Smith, its director, is widely mentioned as a likely prospect for the Nobel Prize in economics for his path-breaking work in the field of experimental economics. Along with Professor Gordon Tullock, also mentioned as a likely prospect for the Nobel Prize in Economics, it is not inconceivable that GMU's Economics Department will not only rank number one in the South but will be home to every single Nobel Laureate in the South. In addition to these three stars on our faculty, there are a number of junior and senior faculty who are also on the frontiers of the pursuit of economic knowledge.

You say, "Okay, Williams, there are good economists and bad economists but can't you give a better description of your department?" If asked to generalize, I'd say that GMU's economics department is probably the nation's, if not the world's, only completely free market department, although there's one of my colleagues whom I hold under suspicion. In other words, we accept the evidence that peaceable, voluntary exchange is not only morally superior to other forms of social organization, such as those involving force, intimidation and threats, it also provides for the highest standard of living for the ordinary man.

Some readers might accuse me of immodestly bragging. I accept the accusation and I don't mind. It was my beloved grandmother who used to say, "It's a poor dog that won't wag his own tail."

Who May Harm Whom?

December 24, 2001

Webster's Dictionary defines harm as: to hurt, damage, injure. People who don't or can't think believe that government should step in to prevent one person from harming another such as in the case of tobacco smoke. But harm is a two-way street and it's a daunting task to determine whether one harm is more important than another.

Let's list just a few instances of harms and decide whether they should be banned. When handheld calculators were invented, manufacturers of slide rules were harmed. They were run out of business. When chain hardware stores like Home Depot and Lowes opened, many neighborhood hardware stores were run out of business. When I married Mrs. Williams, other women were harmed by a reduction in the number of highly desirable men to marry. I enjoy smoking and you might find it an abomination and worry about the health effects of secondhand smoke. If I'm stopped from smoking, I'm harmed by a reduction in my pleasure and you're benefitted. If I'm permitted to smoke, I'm benefitted and you're harmed.

There are literally thousands of examples of how people harm one another. No one but an idiot would make an attempt to objectively determine which harm is more important than the other and should be banned by government. Thus, we're confronted with the question: What is it that decides what kinds of harm should be permitted? How is it decided who may harm whom? In a dictatorship it's the dictator who decides. In a democracy, it's mob rule.

How is it decided in a free society? In a free society, the question of who may harm whom in what ways is decided through private property rights. Harming another by rape, murder and robbery should be prohibited because it violates private property rights. We own ourselves. Thus, rape, murder and robbery are private property rights violations. In the case of the handheld calculator producer harming the slide ruler producer, it's property rights that decides. The calculator producer owns his materials and skills. Customers have private property rights to their money. That means they have the right to spend it purchasing calculators. The slide rule producer has no right to force customers to purchase his product. While the calculator producer has a right to harm the slide rule manufacturer by offering a more desirable product, he doesn't have the right to harm him by burning down his factory. That would violate the slide rule manufacturer's property rights.

What about cigarette smoke harming others? In a free society, as opposed to a dictatorship or mob rule, the matter is resolved through private property rights. If you own property, be it your house, restaurant, airplane or workplace, another does not have the right to smoke on your property without your permission. Alternatively, in the house, restaurant, airplane or workplace that I own, another doesn't have the right to prohibit smoking. If you don't like the fact that smoking is permitted in my restaurant, you can go elsewhere. Similarly, I can do the same if you don't permit smoking. Of course, if there's dictatorship or mob rule, and I can get the ear of the dictator or mob, a law can be written to require you to allow smoking. You say, "Williams, that would be unfair." It's no more unfair than when people get the ear of the dictator or mob and get laws written to ban smoking.

A free people will always want private property rights to decide who may harm whom. It's less arbitrary, more certain, and less subject to political whims.

Too Much Safety

August 27, 2001

There's the old admonition: It's better to be safe than sorry. The fact of life is that one can be both safe and sorry—that's if we acknowledge the consequences of having too much safety. Let's look at it.

National Transportation Safety Board (NTSB) investigators blamed a fuel tank fire for the July 17, 1996 crash of Paris-bound TWA 800 where all 230 people on board were killed. The Federal Aviation Administration (FAA) advisory committee recently heard a joint industry-agency task force report concluding that adding non-flammable gases (fuel tank inerting) would significantly reduce, perhaps eliminate, the risk of fuel tank explosions. Nonetheless, the task force recommended against a FAA fuel tank inerting mandate saying that it would "have an enormous operational impact, with costs that far exceeded the benefits." They estimated that the $10 to $20 billion cost of fuel tank modification would save a total of 253 lives.

One predictable response to the agency-industry task force recommendation was the condemnation: You can't put a price on human life. That's a frequently heard response to safety issues, often accompanied by: if it saves one life, it's worth it. Despite the emotional appeal of such pleas, intelligent, not to mention humane, public policy demands that we ask: Is it worth it to spend $10 to $20 billion dollars to save an estimated 253 lives? Of course if it's your life that's saved, you'll say, "It's worth it," but that's a callous disregard for other lives.

You say, "Williams, what in the world could you possibly mean?" Reconfiguring airliner fuel tanks will cost $10 to $20 billion. Guess how airlines will recoup that cost? If you guessed higher ticket prices, go to the head of the class. Higher ticket prices might mean that some families, who might otherwise fly to visit grandmother during the Christmas holidays, would decide to drive instead. Highway travel is many times more hazardous than air travel. So we should ask: how many people would die on the highway as a result of higher ticket prices caused by "fuel tank inerting"? It might be many more than 253 lives.

Some years ago, there were calls for mandatory airline infant seats. The FAA's analysis showed that, by forcing parents traveling with babies to purchase another ticket, instead of their infant traveling on their laps would cost an additional $1 billion in airfare expenses on families over a 10-year period. Because of the higher cost, 20 percent of the families would shift to driving. Because of the higher fatality rate associated with driving, FAA analysis concludes there would be a net increase of 82 infant and adult fatalities over the 10-year period as a result of imposing this "safety" regulation.

So what's the lesson? The first is that if we only look at the benefits of a policy, we'd do darn near anything, including stupid things such as mandating a 5 mph highway speed limit. After all there's a benefit to anything. The second is that in evaluating public policy we shouldn't only pay attention to what is seen but to what is unseen as well. Another way of putting this is: There is no free lunch. Fuel tank inerting might save 253 lives by preventing fuel tank explosions but is the $10 to $20 billion price tag the only cost? What if higher airfares led to an additional 1,000 highway deaths? Are the 253 lives saved by fuel tank inerting worth it? If more of us were familiar with Frederic Bastiat's pamphlet "What Is Seen and What is Not Seen," (available through fee.org) these questions would be a natural part of the public policy debate.

There's No Free Lunch

September 24, 2001

Each semester I spend a few minutes explaining to my students, both graduate and undergraduate, the first and second laws of thermodynamics. Why? Mother Nature permits us to do many things but she prohibits the construction of machines of the first and second kinds. The first is a something-for-nothing machine and the second is a perpetual motion machine. If students understand this, they can't be tricked into believing there's a free lunch.

Dr. Paul Krugman, Princeton University economist and *New York Times* writer, apparently believes in the machine of the first kind. In his column, "After the Horror" (*New York Times* 9/14/01), he says, "Ghastly as it may seem to say this, the terror attack—like the original day of infamy, which brought an end to the Great Depression—could do some economic good."

He suggests that the destruction will stimulate the economy through business investment in rebuilding the destruction.

We know this has to be fishy just by asking: Would there have been even greater "economic good" had the terrorists succeeded in destroying buildings in Los Angeles, San Francisco, Chicago, Philadelphia, Boston and all other major cities? Of course, you and I know that is utter nonsense. Property destruction always lowers the wealth of a nation. I hope one of Professor Krugman's students asks him, "If property destruction is good for the economy, why aren't Beirut and Belfast boom towns?"

There's another question related to both the Krugman article and measures that Congress is considering to jumpstart the economy: Where does the government or private money come from for rebuilding the destruction or bailing out the airlines? If it came from the Tooth Fairy or Santa Claus, then at least some of what Professor Krugman and politicians say has some merit. They both might benefit from reading French economist (1801–1850) Frederic Bastiat's pamphlet "What is Seen and What is Not Seen," where he says, "There is only one difference between a bad economist and a good one: the bad economist confines himself to the visible effect; the good economist takes into account both the effect that can be seen and those effects that must be foreseen."

Since the money going to rebuild the destruction or bail out the airline industry doesn't come from the Tooth Fairy or Santa, we might ask what would have been done with the money if it weren't spent rebuilding destruction or bailing out the airline industry? What is seen is the employment associated with the rebuilding and the bailout. What is unseen is what the money would have been used for. Not asking this question commits the "broken window fallacy." This is a story where a vandal smashes a baker's window. A person in the crowd that gathered (it could be Professor Krugman) tells the baker there's a good side to his misfortune. It will create a job for the glazer and when the glazer spends the $100 there will be multiplier effects that stimulate the village's economy. That's the seen. The unseen is that the baker would have spent that $100 to buy a suit and it would have created employment for the tailor. Had the vandal not struck, the baker would have had a window plus a suit; now he has just a window. Of course, there's greater employment for glazers but at the expense of less employment for tailors.

Steps Congress could take to jumpstart the economy are cuts in the capital gains tax and taxes in general and deregulation but guess what: Professor Krugman is against these steps; he calls them political opportunism. I call them sound economics.

Dopey Ideas and Expressions

May 19, 2003

How many times have we applauded those who "made a difference in the lives of others" and been admonished to do the same? On the face of it, that has to be one of the more mindless generalities of our modern era. After all didn't Hitler, Stalin, Pol Pot and Castro also make a difference in the lives of others?

A prominent politician once told me that it's up to Congress to save jobs. That's a sentiment with enormous appeal today, reflected in tariffs, quotas and other economic restrictions. Taken literally saving jobs means lower wealth and I'm against it. Let's think about it.

In 1776, farmers made up 90 percent of the labor force; today farmers are about two percent. That's a lot of jobs lost. What should an earlier congress have done to save those jobs? In my youth, icemen and milkmen delivered their wares in horse-drawn wagons. Those jobs have been lost, along with the jobs of stable keepers and wagon repairmen. Was it the responsibility of congress to save those jobs?

The destruction of jobs through natural market forces is, for example, a wonderful thing; it frees up labor resources to do other things, although a hardship on those displaced. After all if 90, 60, or 30 percent of our labor force were farming where in the world would we get workers to produce cars, computers, roads and ships? Many parents tell their children that anything worth doing is worth doing as well as possible. That's nonsense. I never tell my economic students they ought to try to get the best grade they can in my class. Why? Spending the resources to earn an A in economics means that those same resources can't be spent for other classes. For example, spending the time to earn an A in my class might mean a C in biology, D in math and a F in chemistry. That translates into a grade point average of 1.75. If by spending less time learning economics, maybe earning a C, and spending more time on other classes so as to earn a C in each of them, the student would have a higher grade point average.

What about statements like this: "It's advantageous to have reporters on the ground," or, we should "connect policy to people on the ground in developing countries." I sometimes wonder whether there's the alternative of, say, connecting policy to people in the air in developing countries. I personally grow weary of one reference or another, usually made by a reporter or politician, to people, equipment, food, this or that "on the ground."

I have generous office hours for students but not every hour in my office is open to students. Quite often during non-office hours, a student or colleague will knock on my door. When I open it, they'll often ask, "May I disturb you?" That's an incredible question to which I frequently rely, mostly in a civil fashion, "You've already disturbed me; now what do you want?"

Dr. Martin Rosenberg, my high school English teacher, having had it with my classroom antics whilst he drilled us in English grammar, told me "Williams, teaching you this material is like casting pearls before the swine." That was in 1952 before everyone became concerned about self-esteem but it was precisely the kind of dressing down that I needed to challenge me and turn my high school academic performance around. Two years later, it was Dr. Rosenberg who proudly coached me with my salutatorian address for our graduation ceremony. I thank God that I received my education before educators and psycho-babblers became concerned about self-esteem; I'm also thankful for having received it before it became fashionable for white people to like black people. It meant my grades were honest.

Different Visions, Different Policy

March 3, 2003

We're often confronted by the enigma of decent people professing identical goals but advocating polar opposite policies. Sometimes the political alignment is seen as conservative versus liberal where, for example, conservatives fight against minimum wage increases and liberals support those increases. The enigma is why is it that two groups of people, professing concern for low-skilled workers, advocate vastly differing means to help them. I think that part of the answer lies in differing visions of how the world works; but that answer only applies to honest people who don't have a self-interested hidden agenda.

Consider what might have been an argument between two Spaniards in 1300 A.D. One person's initial premise is that the earth is flat while the other's initial premise is that the earth is round. The person with the flat-earth premise would argue that it's impossible to sail west from Spain and reach India. The person with the round-earth premise would argue the opposite, while the voyage would be long, one can sail west from Spain and reach India.

The internal logic underlying both arguments, given the initial premises, are flawless. After all if the world is flat, and India lies to the east of Spain, sailing west from Spain means that somewhere along the way you're going to fall off the earth. By contrast, with the premise that the earth is round, of course one could sail west and reach India. Here's the point: Given the initial premises both arguments are flawless, internally consistent and believable to their adherents.

Let's apply this reasoning to the minimum wage debate to see how it might explain how two groups of decent and honest people can reach polar opposite conclusions. If one's initial premise is that employers must employ certain amount of labor, say ten workers, to get a job done, the logic that higher minimum wage laws would help low-skilled workers is flawless. It simply means higher wages for those ten workers coming at the expense of the employer's profits.

By contrast, if one's initial premise is that employers are sensitive to labor prices and can substitute capital for labor or move their operation to places where there's cheaper labor, the logic that the minimum wage would hurt at least some low-skilled workers is similarly flawless. After all a low wage is better than no wage as a result of having been replaced by machinery or your job has moved overseas.

Competing visions of how the world works enters many areas of our lives and generate polar opposite policies. Another example is gun control. If it's your vision that an inanimate object such as a gun can cause crime, then you'll advocate gun control as a means to reduce crime. The logic is impeccable; fewer guns means less crime. But, if it's your vision that evil people, not guns, cause crime, you might advocate more gun ownership as a means to reduce crime, namely giving law-abiding citizens greater protection and providing more uncertainty for criminals.

A way out of the conundrum of competing visions is to demand that people make their initial premises explicit so they can be challenged. Supporters of higher minimum wage law, as a means to help low-skilled workers, should be required to provide evidence that employers are insensitive to increases in labor prices and those who argue against should be required to provide evidence employers are sensitive. Gun control advocates should be required to provide evidence that guns, not evil people, cause crime and gun ownership advocates should be pressed for their evidence that it's evil people, not guns, that cause crime.

My Organs Are for Sale

The Freeman: Ideas on Liberty, *October 2002*

According to a new book, *The U.S. Organ Procurement System*, written by economists David Kaserman and A. H. Barnett, there are 80,000 Americans on the organ transplant waiting list. Twenty of them die each day as a direct result of organ shortages; that's over 7,000 each year. These lost lives are not so much an act of God as they are an act of Congress because of its 1984 National Organ Transplant Act, that prohibits payment to organ donors. Reliance on voluntary donations, has been an abject policy failure. It's noteworthy that everyone else involved in the organ transplant business is rewarded handsomely—that includes surgeons, nurses and organ procurement workers.

How might an organ transplant market work? Lloyd Cohen, a law professor at George Mason University, envisions letting people contract in advance to permit the harvesting of any usable organs when they die. The money earned would become a part of their estate. Many people are offended by the notion of human body parts becoming commodities for sale. There's at least a tiny bit of inconsistency because there is a market for human blood, semen and hair.

How many vital things in our lives do we depend on altruism or voluntary donations to provide? Food is vital, water is vital; so are clothing and housing. We don't depend on altruism and voluntary donations to provide these goods. And for good reason—there'd be massive shortages. Why should we depend on altruism or voluntary donations to provide what we may one day need more urgently than food, water, clothing or housing? All objections to organ sales reduce to either nonsense, ignorance or arrogance. Let's look at some of them.

One concern is that if organs are sold rather than donated, poor people couldn't afford them. There's a difference between methods

This article is reprinted with permission from the Foundation for Economic Education's journal, *The Freeman: Ideas on Liberty*, October 2002.

of attaining organs and methods of distributing them. For example, poor people need food but Congress hasn't mandated that food prices be zero so that poor people can eat. If Congress did that, there'd be massive shortages and poor people would probably starve. Instead of such a stupid policy, we simply allow the market mechanism to supply food and then subsidize purchases, through programs like food stamps. That same principle can be applied to organ transplants— allow the market to supply organs and if needed subsidize or provide through charity their distribution.

Won't organs be very costly? Kaserman and Barnett and others estimate that the organ shortage would be resolved at a prices of $1,000 to $3,000 per donor. To the extent that markets would eliminate organ shortages, it would significantly reduce health care costs. For example, the cost of kidney dialysis is about $44,000 per year. The cost of kidney transplant and medical care for the first year is about $90,000. After the first year, medical treatments, mostly for immunosuppressant drugs to prevent rejection are $16,000. That means after about two and a half years transplants save the medical system $27,000 per year as opposed to patients remaining on long-term dialysis.

Another concern is that if there's a market for organs, poor people will sell their organs and become ill. The proposals made so far provide monetary payments be made for only cadaver organs. But from a strictly ethical point of view, people should be able to dispose of their organs for whatever reason they please. Why? If we agree that people have property rights in themselves, i.e., own themselves, they have a right to dispose of themselves anyway they please so long as they do not violate the property rights of others. I would surely prefer a person who might be unwilling to give me his kidney find motivation to sell me his kidney rather than for me to do without.

Some people have argued that an organ transplant market will lead to murder and the sale of the victim's organs to unscrupulous organ brokers. Murder will remain illegal and punishable. However, when the sale of a commodity is illegal there's a heightened potential for illegal activity and concomitant social disorder. During Prohibition there was far more criminal activity associated with alcohol manufacture, distribution and consumption than there is now. To the extent that prohibition of organ sales reduces their supply, holding all else equal there's greater incentive for illegal activities involving organ transplants, including murder.

The medical profession has traditionally been opposed to organ sales. Their opposition would seem to be in violation of Hippocrates' admonition—primum non nocere. But they've recently taken steps, all be they timid, towards ending the day to day deaths due to organ shortages. At their July 2002 meeting, the American Medical Association voted agreement to commence trials in which payments will be made to organ donors or their families as a means to encourage cadaveric organ collections.

Parting Company Is an Option

The Freeman: Ideas on Liberty, *November 2004*

My last essay in *Ideas On Liberty*, "How Did We Get Here?," provided clear evidence that Congress, the White House, as well as the Courts, had vastly exceeded powers delegated to them by our Constitution. To have an appreciation for the magnitude of the usurpation, one need only read Federalist Paper 45, where James Madison the acknowledged father of our Constitution explained, "The powers delegated by the proposed Constitution to the Federal Government, are few and defined. Those which are to remain in the State Governments are numerous and indefinite. The former will be exercised principally on external objects, as war, peace, negotiation, and foreign commerce; with which last the power of taxation will for the most part be connected. The powers reserved to the several States will extend to all the objects, which, in the ordinary course of affairs, concern the lives, liberties and properties of the people; and the internal order, improvement, and prosperity of the State."

Short of some kind of cataclysmic event liberties lost are seldom regained but there is an outside chance to regain them if enough liberty-minded Americans were to pursue Free State Project's proposal to set up New Hampshire as a free state. Free State Project (www.freestateproject.org) intends to get 20,000 or so Americans to become residents of New Hampshire. Through a peaceful political process they hope to assume leadership in the state's legislature and executive offices and reduce burdensome taxation and regulation, reform state and local law, end federal mandates that violate the Ninth and Tenth Amendments to the U.S. Constitution and restore constitutional federalism as envisioned by the nation's Founders.

Since there is only a remote possibility of successful negotiation with Congress, the Courts and White House to obey the U.S. Constitution, it is my guess that liberty could only be realized by a uni-

This article is reprinted with permission from the Foundation for Economic Education's journal, *The Freeman: Ideas on Liberty*, November 2004.

lateral declaration of independence—namely, part company—in a word secede. While our Constitution is silent about secession, there is clear evidence that our Founders saw it as an option.

On March 2, 1861, after seven states had seceded and two days before Abraham Lincoln's inauguration, Senator James R. Doolittle (WI) proposed a constitutional amendment that said, "No State or any part thereof, heretofore admitted or hereafter admitted into the Union, shall have the power to withdraw from the jurisdiction of the United States." Several months earlier Representatives Daniel E. Sickles (NY), Thomas B. Florence (PA) and Otis S. Ferry (CT) proposed a constitutional amendment to prohibit secession. One is immediately faced with the question: Would there have been any point to offering these amendments if secession were already unconstitutional? There's more evidence. The ratification documents of Virginia, New York and Rhode Island explicitly said that they held the right to resume powers delegated should the federal government become abusive of those powers.

There's more evidence. At the 1787 constitutional convention a proposal was made to allow the federal government to suppress a seceding state. James Madison rejected it saying, "A Union of the States containing such an ingredient seemed to provide for its own destruction. The use of force against a State would look more like a declaration of war than an infliction of punishment and would probably be considered by the party attacked as a dissolution of all previous compacts by which it might be bound."

Professor Thomas DiLorenzo, in his revised *The Real Lincoln*, provides abundant evidence in the forms of quotations from our Founders and numerous newspaper accounts that prove that Americans always took the right of secession for granted. Plus, secession was not an idea that had its origins in the South. Infuriated by Thomas Jefferson's Louisiana Purchase, in 1803, the first secessionist movement started in New York, Massachusetts, Connecticut and other New England states.

The preponderance of evidence shows that states have a right to secede. The Constitution probably would have never been ratified if the states, sovereign nations as per the 1783 Treaty of Paris that ended the war of independence with Great Britain, did not believe they had a right to secede. The only barrier to secession is the brute force of the federal government as witnessed by the costly War of 1861 that produced only one decent result—the elimination of slavery. Since the issue of secession was brutally settled, it left a devastating legacy for future generations of Americans. The federal government is free to run roughshod over the restrictions and safeguards the Framers imposed on the federal government.

Self-determination is a human right we all should respect. If some people want socialism that is their right, but it is not their right to use force to make others who wish to be left alone be part of it. By the same token, liberty-minded Americans have no right to impose their will on socialist-minded Americans. A far more peaceful method is for each to simply part company.

One wonders whether the brutality witnessed in 1861 would be repeated if New Hampshire seceded—massive troops along with today's deadly modern military equipment and Americans killing Americans.

Honesty and Trust

The Freeman: Ideas on Liberty, *January 2005*

Several decades ago I used to enjoy an occasional lunch in Washington, D.C. with the late Professor G. Warren Nutter, a distinguished economist who taught at the University of Virginia. Professor Nutter had considerable expertise in comparative economic systems, particularly that of the former Soviet Union. While he had a deep understanding of economic markets, he always stressed that markets do not operate within a vacuum and we gain a greater understanding of human behavior if we paid attention to the role of non-market forces.

At one of our luncheons, just out of the clear blue sky, and maybe to get an argument, Professor Nutter said to me that if we had to stop to count our change each time we purchased something markets would grind to a halt. That's a bit of exaggeration but Professor Nutter was making the point that the institutions of trust and honesty are vital to human well-being. Honesty and trust are not simply matters of character and morality; they're crucial for efficient human interaction and a smoothly working economy.

To appreciate the significance of honesty and trust, consider what our day-to-day life would be if we couldn't trust anyone. We purchase a bottle of a hundred aspirins from our drug store. How many of us bother to count the tablets to ensure that in fact we received a hundred? We drive into a gasoline station and the meter reads that we put ten gallons of gasoline into our fuel tank. Does anyone of us bother to verify whether in fact we received ten gallons instead of nine? We paid $7.00 for a one-pound package of steak. How many of us bother to check to verify that if was in fact one pound instead of three-quarters or seventh-eighths of a pound?

Then there's, "Send me 100 diskettes and bill me." Or you call your broker telling him to purchase 50 shares of AT&T at the market price and you'll settle within seven days. A salesman says, "If you're

This article is reprinted with permission from the Foundation for Economic Education's journal, *The Freeman: Ideas on Liberty*, January 2005.

not satisfied with your order, bring it back and your money will be refunded." Or, "Mow my lawn and I'll pay you." In literally millions upon millions of transactions like these, we simply trust each other.

Imagine the costs and inconvenience we'd suffer if people were generally dishonest and we couldn't trust anyone. We would have to lug around measuring instruments to ensure, for example, that it was ten gallons of gas and one pound of steak we purchased. We'd have to bear the costly burden of writing contracts instead of relying on a buyer or seller's word and bear the monitoring expense to ensure compliance in the simplest of transactions. It's safe to say that whatever undermines trust and confidence raises costs of transactions and makes us worse off.

But generalized honesty and trust goes further than that. I live in the Main Line suburbs of Philadelphia. FedEx, UPS and other deliverymen leave packages containing valuable items on the doorstep if we're not home. A local supermarket leaves plants, fertilizer and other home and garden items outdoors overnight with no one to guard them from theft. As one enters the store, he sees merchandise unattended in the entryway. In neighborhoods, where there's less honesty, leaving merchandise on doorsteps, outdoors overnight and in the supermarket entryway would be equivalent to economic suicide. Delivery companies must bear the costs of making return trips or the customer is inconvenienced by delayed receiving. If the supermarket places goods outside, they must bear the costs of retrieving the items at the close of business, that's if they can risk to have merchandise outdoors in the first place.

Generalized honesty affects stores like supermarkets in another way that often goes unappreciated. One of the goals of a supermarket manager is that of maximizing the rate of merchandise turnover per square foot of leased space. When theft is relatively low, the supermarket can use outdoor and entryway footage thereby raising his profit potential. That opportunity is denied in localities where there's less honesty.

The fact that honesty and trust are vital should make us re-think the treatment of those who violate honesty and trust. Dishonest people impose losses that go beyond those suffered by the actual victim of the dishonest behavior. If packages are stolen from people's doorsteps, the response of delivery companies to not leave a package unless someone's home imposes costs on rest of us. If people rob bus operators and taxi drivers it requires all of us to have exact change or small bills.

Considering the large economic effects of dishonesty and not being able to trust one another, we should show little tolerance for violators. Fortunately, on the one hand we live in a society where we can generally trust and accept the word of one another, but on the other hand it's not quite the level of trust and honesty of earlier periods.

Race

Race is an area in our lives subject to many fallacies, misunderstandings, sloppy analysis, and demagoguery. Some of the problem has to do with misleading terminology, such as labeling one group or another as a minority. When one uses the term "minority," there is an inference that somewhere out there is a majority, but in the United States we are a nation of minorities. According to the U.S. Census Bureau 2000 census, when people self-indentify, the largest ethnic group is German (15.2%), Irish (10.8%), African (8.8), and English (8.7) ancestry. Of the ninety-two ethnic groups listed, seventy-five make up less than 1 percent of our population. *

Another misleading term is racial segregation, when people assert that a school or neighborhood is segregated because the black population is "underrepresented" according to their numbers in the population. But blacks are also "underrepresented," according to their numbers in the U.S. population, in South Dakota, Montana, and Idaho. They are also "underrepresented" at hockey games, opera, and dressage performances. Based on those observations, would one also claim that those activities, like schools and neighborhoods, are also racially segregated? Because a particular activity is not racially heterogeneous does not mean it is segregated. A better test for segregation, say in the case of schools, is to determine whether a black living in a particular school district is free to attend its schools. Or, if a black wishes to live in South Dakota, Montana, or Idaho, whether he is free to do so. There is no reason whatsoever to expect that people will sort themselves proportionately across any activity.

Black Americans are often portrayed as a downtrodden, discriminated against people. In my opinion, this is an insult of major proportions. Black Americans have made some of the greatest gains, over some of the highest hurdles and in the shortest span of time, than any other racial group in the history of mankind. This unprecedented progress can

*Source: U.S. Census Bureau, Ancestry: 2000, issued June 2004.

be seen through several measures. If one were to total black earnings, and consider black Americans a separate nation, one would find that in 2005 black Americans earned $644 billion, making them the world's sixteenth richest nation—that is, just behind Australia but ahead of the Netherlands, Belgium, and Switzerland. Black Americans are, and have been, chief executives of some of the world's largest and richest cities such as New York, Chicago, Los Angeles, Philadelphia, and Washington, D.C. It was a black American, General Colin Powell, appointed Joint Chief of Staff in October 1989, who headed the world's mightiest military and later became U.S. secretary of state, to be succeeded by Condoleezza Rice, another black American. Black Americans are among the world's most famous personalities and a few, among the richest. Most blacks are not poor but middle class.

On the eve of the Civil War, it is doubtful whether a slave or a slave owner would have believed these gains possible in less than a mere century and a half, if ever. As such, that progress speaks well not only of the sacrifices and intestinal fortitude of a people but of a nation in which these gains were possible.

None of this is to say that racial discrimination has been completely eliminated or that there are not major problems facing a large percentage of blacks—those 25 to 30 percent for whom these gains remain elusive. The policy-relevant question is, how much of those problems are a result of today's discrimination? As I argue in some of the columns in this section, racial discrimination cannot account for some of the most devastating problems that blacks confront, such a breakdown in the black family structure, high rates of illegitimacy, grossly fraudulent education, and unprecedented crime and social pathology in many black neighborhoods.

Many see the solution in the political arena or government programs of one kind or another. I see little evidence for such a position. For many blacks, their plight is the worst in the very cities where blacks have been mayors, city councilmen, chief of police, or superintendent of schools— cities such as Washington, D.C., Detroit, Philadelphia, Newark, and Baltimore. Trillions of dollars have been spent at the federal, state, and local levels of government on one poverty program or another. Most of what resulted is an unprecedented level of dependency. Neither blacks nor any other American is poor in the historical sense of the term; the kind of material poverty seen in the past is nonexistent today. Today's poverty is poverty of the spirit, where, for the most part people, by their personal decisions, choose to be poor.

The columns in this section shed light on a number of racial issues and question assumptions that have taken on an axiomatic status and believed to be beyond question.

Regrets for Slavery

Wednesday, March 7, 2007

Both chambers of the Commonwealth of Virginia's General Assembly passed a resolution saying government-sanctioned slavery "ranks as the most horrendous of all depredations of human rights and violations of our founding ideals in our nation's history; and . . . the abolition of slavery was followed by . . . systematic discrimination, enforced segregation, and other insidious institutions and practices toward Americans of African descent that were rooted in racism, racial bias, and racial misunderstanding." The General Assembly also expressed regret for the "exploitation of Native Americans."

Isn't that nice? I agree that slavery was an abomination, but I'm going to be even more generous than Virginia's General Assembly. I regret the murder of an estimated 61 million people whom the former USSR executed, slaughtered, starved, beat or tortured to death. I also regret the Chinese government's slaughter of 45 million Chinese; Hitler's slaughter of 6 million Jews; the Khmer Rouge's murder of 2 million Cambodians; the half a million Ugandans murdered by Idi Amin's death squads; the million Hutus and Tutsis murdered in Rwanda's genocidal bloodbath; and slavery that still exists in the Sudan and Mauritania.

All of these, and many more, are horrible injustices at least as horrible as the slavery that existed in the U.S. But after all the regrets and apologies for injustices, what comes next? Let's examine Virginia's statement of regret with an eye toward what it might mean.

I can personally relate to the Virginia General Assembly's declaration. My great-grandparents were slaves in the Virginia cities of Chase City and Newport News. The General Assembly's statement of regret for slavery means absolutely nothing to me. If anything, it's nothing less than a cheap insult and capitulation of white delegates to black hustlers. Possibly, the whites who voted in support of the declaration were mau-maued into it or they felt guilt over our history of slavery. In any case, they should know that their actions mean little in dealing with the day-to-day plight of many black Virginians—which has nothing to do with slavery.

The U.S. murder rate is 5.6 people per 100,000 of the population. In the Commonwealth of Virginia's capital, Richmond, where the General Assembly meets, the murder rate is 43 people per 100,000 of the population making Richmond the city with the third-highest murder rate in the nation, according to a 2005 FBI report.

What about black education in Virginia? According to the National Assessment of Educational Progress (NAEP), black education is a disgrace. In 2003, 51 percent of black eighth-graders scored below basic; 49 percent at or above basic; of these, only 11 percent scored proficient. For black fourth-graders, the scores were 34, 66 and 13 percent, respectively. In 2002 in reading, 38 percent of black eighth-graders scored below basic, with 62 percent at or above basic and 15 percent scoring proficient. For fourth-graders, the scores were 53, 47 and 15 percent, respectively.

Below basic is the category the NAEP uses for students unable to display even partial mastery of knowledge and skills fundamental for proficient work at their grade level. Given this extreme academic incompetence, one shouldn't be surprised by the 2002 Virginia State Education Profile showing that the median combined SAT score for black students is a disgraceful 848 out of 1600, 210 points below the white median, and the white median is nothing to write home about.

The next time the Virginia General Assembly gets into an apologetic mood and wants to pass another resolution aimed at its black citizens, here are my suggestions: The Commonwealth of Virginia apologizes to its black citizens for not protecting them from criminals who prey upon them and make their lives a daily nightmare. The Commonwealth also apologizes for our government-sanctioned school system that delivers fraudulent education, thereby consigning many of its black citizens to the bottom rungs of the economic ladder.

Do People Care?

Wednesday, July 4, 2007

Back in the late 1960s, during graduate study at UCLA, I had a casual conversation with Professor Armen Alchian, one of my tenacious mentors. Professor Alchian is among the top 20th-century contributors to economic knowledge. During our graduate student/faculty coffee hour conversation, I was trying to impress Professor Alchian with my knowledge of type I and type II statistical errors.

I told him that my wife assumes that everybody is her friend until they prove differently. While such an assumption maximizes the number of friends that she will have, it also maximizes her chances of being betrayed. Unlike my wife, my assumption is everyone is my enemy until they prove they're a friend. That assumption minimizes my number of friends but minimizes the chances of betrayal.

Professor Alchian, donning a mischievous smile, asked, "Williams, have you considered a third alternative, namely, that people don't give a damn about you one way or another?" Initially, I felt a bit insulted, and our conversation didn't go much further. That was typical of Professor Alchian—to say something profound and maybe controversial, without much comment, and let you think about it.

During the earlier years of my professional career, I gave Professor Alchian's question considerable thought and concluded that he was right. The most reliable assumption, in terms of the conduct of one's life, is to assume that generally people don't care about you one way or another. It's a mistake to assume everyone is a friend or everyone is an enemy, or people are out to help you, or people are out to hurt you.

Let's do a thought experiment applying this to issues of race. Listening to some people, one might think that white people are engaged in an ongoing secret conspiracy to undermine the welfare of black people. Evidence for those people is the large numbers of black men in prison, low black academic achievement and poverty. For some, racism is the root cause of the high black illegitimacy rate and family breakdown.

Are white people obsessed with and engaged in a conspiracy against black people? I'm guessing no, and here's an experiment. Walk up to the average white person and ask: How many minutes today have you been thinking about a black person? If the person wasn't a Klansman or a gushing do-gooder, his answer would probably be zero minutes. If you asked him whether he's a part of a conspiracy to undermine the welfare of black people, he'd probably look at you as if you were crazy. By the same token, if you asked me: "Williams, how many minutes today have you been thinking about white people?" I'd probably say, "You'd have to break the time interval down into smaller units, like nanoseconds, for me to give an accurate answer." Because people don't care about you one way or another doesn't mean they wish you good will, ill will or no will.

If Professor Alchian's vision of how the world works is correct, what are its implications? A major implication is that one's destiny, for the most part, is in his hands. In other words, how you make it in this world, for the most part, depends more on what you do as opposed to whether people like or dislike you. In order to produce a successful life, one must find ways to please his fellow man. That is, find out what goods and services his fellow man values, and is willing to pay for, and then acquire the necessary skills and education to provide it. Whether your fellow man cares about you or not is largely irrelevant.

Liberal Views, Black Victims

Wednesday, August 22, 2007

Last year, among the nation's 10 largest cities, Philadelphia had the highest murder rate with 406 victims. This year could easily top last year's with 240 murders so far.

Other cities such as Baltimore, Detroit and Washington, D.C., with large black populations, experience the nation's highest rates of murder and violent crime. This high murder rate is, and has been, predominantly a black problem.

According to Bureau of Justice statistics, between 1976 and 2005, blacks, while 13 percent of the population, committed over 52 percent of the nation's homicides and were 46 percent of the homicide victims. Ninety-four percent of black homicide victims had a black person as their murderer.

Blacks are not only the major victims of homicide; blacks suffer high rates of all categories of serious violent crime, and another black is most often the perpetrator.

Liberals and their political allies say the problem is the easy accessibility of guns and greater gun control is the solution. That has to be nonsense. Guns do not commit crimes; people do.

Up through 1979, the FBI reported homicide arrests sorted by racial breakdowns that included Japanese. Between 1976 and 1978, 21 of 48,695 arrests for murder and non-negligent manslaughter were Japanese-Americans. That translates to an annual murder rate of 1 per 100,000 of the Japanese-American population. Would anyone advance the argument that the reason why homicide is virtually non-existent among Japanese-Americans is because they can't find guns?

The high victimization rate experienced by the overwhelmingly law-abiding black community is mostly the result of predators not having to pay a heavy enough price for their behavior. They benefit from all kinds of asinine excuses, such as poverty, racial discrimination and few employment opportunities.

During the 1940s and '50s, I grew up in North Philadelphia

where many of today's murders occur. It was a time when blacks were much poorer, there was far more racial discrimination, and fewer employment opportunities and other opportunities for upward socioeconomic mobility were available. There was nowhere near the level of crime and wanton destruction that exists today. Behavior accepted today wasn't accepted then by either black adults or policemen.

Police authorities often know who are the local criminals and drug lords and where crack houses are located; however, various legal technicalities hamper their ability to make arrests and raids. Law-abiding citizens are often afraid to assist police or testify against criminals for fear of retaliation that can include murder. The level of criminal activity not only puts residents in physical jeopardy but represents a heavy tax on people least able to bear it. That heavy tax includes higher prices for goods and services and fewer shopping opportunities because supermarkets and other large retailers are reluctant to bear the costs of doing business in high-crime areas.

So here's the question: Should black people accept government's dereliction of its first basic function, that of providing protection? My answer is no. One of our basic rights is the right to defend oneself against predators. If the government can't or won't protect people, people have a right to protect themselves.

You say, "Hey, Williams, you're not talking about vigilantism, are you?" Yes, I am. Webster's Dictionary defines vigilantism as: a volunteer committee organized to suppress and punish crime summarily as when the processes of law are viewed as inadequate.

Example: A number of years ago, Black Muslims began to patrol Mayfair, a drug-infested, gang-ridden Washington, D.C., housing project. The gangs and drug lords left, probably because the Black Muslims didn't feel obliged to issue Miranda warnings. Black men should set up neighborhood patrols, armed if necessary, and if politicians and police don't like it, they should do their jobs. No one should have to live in daily fear for their lives and safety.

Insulting Blacks

Wednesday, September 12, 2007

"I don't feel no ways tired. I come too far from where I started from. Nobody told me that the road would be easy. I don't believe He brought me this far," drawled presidential aspirant Hillary Clinton, mimicking black voice to a black audience, at the First Baptist Church of Selma, Alabama. I'm wondering if Mrs. Clinton visits an Indian reservation she might cozy up to them saying, "How! Me not tired. Me come heap long way. Road mighty rough. Sky Spirit no bring me this far." Or, seeking the Asian vote she might say, "I no wray tired. Come too far I started flum. Road berry clooked. Number one Dragon King take me far."

The occasion of Mrs. Clinton's speech was the 42nd anniversary of Bloody Sunday, on March 7, 1965, when 600 civil rights marchers were attacked by police with billy clubs, cattle prods and tear gas, one of the high points in the black civil rights struggle. Commemorating a key point in American history is one thing, but a white person mimicking black dialect is demeaning and insulting. And, if it buys her votes from those in attendance, not much flattering can be said about them.

Mrs. Clinton later explained her drawl, around black audiences, to a meeting of the National Association of Black Journalists, "I lived all those years in Arkansas, and, you know, I'm in this interracial marriage." The interracial marriage bit has to do with the frequent reference to former President Clinton, by the Congressional Black Caucus and others, as the "first black president."

Mrs. Clinton is not alone in demeaning talk to black people; she's in good company with Jesse Jackson and Al Sharpton, who talk of "going from the outhouse to the White House" and "from disgrace to amazing grace" and other such nonsense. Neither Clinton nor Revs. Sharpton and Jackson address white audiences in that manner. Before a predominantly black audience, during his 2004 presidential bid, Sen. John Kerry said, in reference to so many blacks in prison, "That's unacceptable, but it's not their fault." I doubt whether Kerry would have told a white audience that jailed white people were faultless. Kerry probably holds whites responsible for their criminal behavior.

In 2004, NAACP President Kweisi Mfume said of President George Bush, "We have a president that's prepared to take us back to the days of Jim Crow segregation and dominance." During the 2000 presidential campaign, Rev. Jesse Jackson warned black audiences by telling them that a Bush win would turn the civil rights clock back to the days of Jim Crow. Now that Bush's two-term presidency is near its end, why wouldn't someone ask Jesse and Kweisi about the accuracy of their predictions?

Suppose some demagogue in 2000 told Jewish Americans that a Bush presidency would mean concentration camps, or told Japanese-Americans that his presidency would mean internment? Do you think such pronouncements would have been welcomed and applauded? I'm sure that had someone made such a stupid prediction to Jewish and Japanese-Americans, they would have had ridicule and scorn heaped upon them.

What does it say about blacks who can be taken in by pandering, alarmist nonsense from both whites and blacks as a means to get their votes? As a black man, I don't find the most obvious answer very flattering.

Betrayal of the Civil Rights Struggle

Wednesday, October 3, 2007

Five police "mini-stations" will be located in Detroit public schools this year primarily due to the merging of students from several high schools on the city's west side. According to a Sept. 1 *Detroit Free Press* article, armed police officers will patrol the hallways in an effort to stem violence.

During the 2005–06 school year, officials issued 39,318 disciplinary referrals and filed 5,500 crime reports, and that's not including truancy and property damage. Uniformed and undercover police officers ride on city buses that transport students to and from school. As of last year, according to a June 2006 *USA Today* report, Detroit's public school graduation rate is only 21.7 percent, the lowest among the nation's 50 largest school districts.

During the 2003–04 school year, only 52 of the nation's 92,000 public schools were labeled "persistently dangerous," a designation under the No Child Left Behind Act entitling students to move to an alternate "safe" school. Philadelphia had 14 schools labeled as "persistently dangerous" and Baltimore had six. The level of violence in Philadelphia schools is so high that each high school is equipped with a walk-through metal detector, security cameras and a conveyor-belted X-ray machine that scans book bags and purses.

Philadelphia and Baltimore, like Detroit, have armed police to try to stem school violence. School violence, including assaults on teachers and staff, is not restricted to inner city schools but occurs also in suburban and rural schools. However, the bulk of the violence is at schools with large black populations.

One has to ask: What happened? I graduated from Benjamin Franklin High School in 1954. Franklin had just about the lowest academic rating of all Philadelphia high schools and probably the city's lowest income students. But what goes on today in Philadelphia high schools would have been inconceivable back then. There were no policemen in or around the schools, there wasn't wanton property destruction, profanities weren't heard up and down the hallways, and the farthest thought from a student's mind was to curse or assault a teacher.

Much of what's seen today is a result of harebrained ideas and a tolerance for barbaric behavior. Kathleen Parker cited such an example in her May 16 syndicated column. The case concerned teacher Elizabeth Kandrac, who was routinely verbally abused by black students at Brentwood Middle School in North Charleston, S.C. A sample of the abusive language: white b----, white m-----f-----, white c---, white ho. Despite frequent complaints, school officials did nothing to stop the abuse. They told her this racially charged profanity was simply part of the students' culture, and if Kandrac couldn't handle the students' cursing, she was in the wrong school. Kandrac brought suit alleging a racially hostile work environment, and the school district settled out of court for $200,000.

People with such a tolerant mindset are in effect saying that blacks are not to be held to civilized standards of conduct and academic expectations that might be enforced for others. That's a disgusting and debilitating notion. I guarantee you that years ago, such nonsense would not have been tolerated, and a person making excuses for barbaric behavior by black students would have been considered a lunatic.

What has been allowed in predominantly black schools is nothing less than a betrayal of the struggle paid with blood, sweat and tears by previous generations to make possible the educational opportunities so long denied blacks that are being routinely squandered today. Blacks who lived through that struggle and are no longer with us wouldn't have believed such a betrayal possible.

There's enough blame to go around for each to have his share: Students who are alien and hostile to the education process, parents who don't give a damn, and the education establishment and politicians who accommodate and excuse this tragedy of black education.

Racial Hoaxes and the NAACP

Wednesday, December 12, 2007

Last May, firefighters at a Baltimore, Md., fire station came under scrutiny for displaying a deer with an afro wig, gold tooth, gold chain and a cigarette hanging from its mouth.

Marvin "Doc" Cheatham, president of the Baltimore chapter of the NAACP, went ballistic, charging, "There is now and has been a culture of racism and white supremacy within the Baltimore City Fire Department."

As it turns out, it was a black fireman who dressed up the critter. Cheatham refused to apologize for his accusations of fire department racism, maintaining "there is now and has been a culture of racism and white supremacy within the Baltimore City Fire Department."

On Nov. 21, a hangman's noose was found at the fire station with a note, "We can't hang the cheaters, but we can hang the failures. No EMT-1, NO JOB." The noose and note turned up on the heels of an investigation into allegations of cheating on the test that emergency medical technicians must take for certification.

Baltimore Mayor Sheila Dixon, a black, in a written statement said, "I am outraged by this deplorable act of hatred and intimidation. Threats and racial attacks are unacceptable anywhere, especially in a firehouse." Doc Cheatham said, "We're going to demand that this be handled as a hate crime. This thing really needs to end here in Baltimore city." The incident prompted a federal investigation.

Last week, Donald Maynard, a black firefighter-paramedic, confessed to having placed the noose, note and drawing depicting a lynching on a bunk in the firehouse. City officials said Maynard was recently suspended, prior to his confession, from the department Friday for failing to meet requirements for advanced life-saving training. A spokesman for Mayor Dixon said there would be no criminal charges filed.

In response to Maynard's confession, NAACP President Cheatham still blamed white racism, saying, "It really saddens us to hear that evidently things have reached a stage that even an African-American does an injustice to himself and his own people as a result of a negative culture in that department."

Doc Cheatham is a poster boy for demonstrating a much larger problem, namely that the once proud and useful NAACP has outlived that usefulness and has in some instances become an impediment to black progress. The Joint Center for Political and Economic Studies, a black liberal-to-moderate Washington-based think-tank, reported that 88 percent of blacks favored educational choice plans. A Gallup Poll found 72 percent of blacks support school choice. The NAACP, acting as handmaidens for the teachers' unions, is solidly against school vouchers. A Gallup Poll shows 44 percent of blacks are for the death penalty and 49 percent against it, but the NAACP is solidly against it.

The major problems confronting a large segment of the black community have little or nothing to do with racism—problems such as unprecedented illegitimacy, family breakdown, fraudulent education, crime and rampant social pathology. If white people became angels tomorrow, it would do nothing to solve problems that can only be solved by blacks.

But I'm somewhat optimistic. More and more blacks are seeing through race hustlers such as Al Sharpton, Jesse Jackson and Doc Cheatham. An even more optimistic note is the financial decline of the NAACP. Declining black support is good evidence that the civil rights struggle is over and won. That's not to say there are not major problems but they are not civil rights problems.

Today, most civil rights organizations get their financial support from white businesses and foundations caving in to intimidation or seeking to soothe feelings of guilt. For them, I have a cheaper alternative, "Proclamation of Amnesty and Pardon Granted to All Persons of European Descent," available at walterewilliams.com.

What's Discrimination?

Wednesday, September 6, 2006

There's so much confusion and emotionalism about discrimination that I thought I'd take a stab at a dispassionate analysis. Discrimination is simply the act of choice. When we choose Bordeaux wine, we discriminate against Burgundy wine. When I married Mrs. Williams, I discriminated against other women. Even though I occasionally think about equal opportunity, Mrs. Williams demands continued discrimination.

You say, "Williams, such discrimination doesn't harm anyone." You're wrong. Discriminating in favor of Bordeaux wine reduces the value of resources held in Burgundy production. Discriminating in favor of Mrs. Williams harmed other women by reducing their opportunity set, assuming I'm a man other women would marry.

Our lives are spent discriminating for or against one thing or another. In other words, choice requires discrimination. When we modify the term with race, sex, height, weight or age, we merely specify the choice criteria.

Imagine how silly, not to mention impossible, life would be if discrimination were outlawed. Imagine engaging in just about any activity where we couldn't discriminate by race, sex, height, weight, age, mannerisms, college selection, looks or ability; it would turn into a carnival.

I've sometimes asked students if they believe in equal opportunity in employment. Invariably, they answer yes. Then I ask them, when they graduate, whether they plan to give every employer an equal opportunity to hire them. Most often they answer no; they plan to discriminate against certain employers. Then I ask them, if they're not going to give every employer an equal opportunity to hire them, what's fair about requiring an employer to give them an equal opportunity to be hired?

Sometimes students will argue that certain forms of discrimination are OK but it's racial discrimination that's truly offensive. That's when I confess my own history of racial discrimination. In the late 1950s, whilst selecting a lifelong mate, even though white, Mexican, Indian, Chinese and Japanese women might have been just as qualified as a mate, I gave them no chance whatsoever. It appears that most Americans act identically by racially discriminating in setting up marriage contracts. According to the 1992 Census Bureau, only 2.2 percent of Americans are married to people other than their own race or ethnicity.

You say, "All right, Williams, discrimination in marriage doesn't have the impact on society that other forms of discrimination have." You're wrong again. When there is assortive (non-random) mate selection, it heightens whatever group differences exist in the population. For instance, higher IQ individuals tend toward mates with high IQs. High-income people tend to mate with other high-income people.

It's the same with education. To the extent there is a racial correlation between these characteristics, racial discrimination in mate selection exaggerates the differences in the society's intelligence and income distribution. There would be greater equality if there weren't this kind of discrimination in mate selection.

In other words, if high-IQ people were forced to select low-IQ mates, high-income people forced to select low-income mates, and highly educated people forced to select lowly educated mates, there would be greater social equality. While there would be greater social equality, the divorce rate would soar since gross dissimilarities would make for conflict.

Common sense suggests that not all discrimination should be eliminated, so the question is, what kind of discrimination should be permitted? I'm guessing the answer depends on one's values for freedom of association, keeping in mind freedom of association implies freedom not to associate.

What's Prejudice?

Wednesday, September 20, 2006

A fortnight ago, my column made a stab at applying dispassionate analysis to come up with an operational definition for discrimination. Basically, discrimination is the act of choice, and choice is a necessary fact of life. Now let's turn to prejudice, keeping in mind that for sound thinking, one should avoid confusing one phenomenon with another.

Prejudice is a useful term that's often misused. Its Latin root is praejudicium, meaning "an opinion or judgment formed . . . without due examination." Thus, we might define prejudicial acts as decision-making on the basis of incomplete information.

In a world of costly information, people seek to economize on information costs. Imagine heading off to work, you open your front door, only to be greeted by a full-grown tiger. The uninteresting prediction is the average person would slam the door or otherwise seek safety.

Why they do so is more interesting. It's unlikely that person's decision is based on any detailed information held about that particular tiger. More likely his decision is based on tiger folklore or how he's seen other tigers behave. He prejudges, or stereotypes, that tiger.

If a person didn't pre-judge tigers, he would seek more information prior to his decision. He might attempt to pet the tiger, talk to him and seek safety only if the tiger responded in a menacing fashion. The average person wouldn't choose that path, surmising that the expected cost of getting more information about the tiger is greater than the expected benefit and concluding, "All I need to know is he's a tiger, and he's probably like the rest of them." By observing this person's behavior, there's no way one can say unambiguously whether the person likes or dislikes tigers.

In the late 1990s, the Washington, D.C., taxi commissioner warned cabbies against going into low income black neighborhoods and picking up "dangerous looking" passengers whom she described as young black males dressed a certain way. A few years ago, some St. Louis, Mo., pizza deliverers were complaining about delivering pizzas to black neighborhoods. Can one say anything unambiguous about cabbies' or pizza deliverers' likes or dislikes for blacks?

In the case of the taxi commissioner's warnings, the commissioner was black and so were most of the cabbies, and 75 to 85 percent of the complaining pizza deliverers were black. Are they racists? What about Rev. Jesse Jackson who once admitted that he is often relieved when the youths he hears walking along the street behind him turn out to be white, not black? Is he a racist?

As in the tiger example, the cabbies, pizza deliverers and Jackson are pre-judging. They are using a cheaply observed physical characteristic as an information proxy for a more costly to observe characteristic. The cheap-to-observe characteristic that a person is tall, female, Asian, black or white can indicate some probability of some other more costly to observe characteristic. In the minds of cabbies, pizza deliverers and Rev. Jackson, race was associated with a higher probability of being assaulted.

No one says that all young black males, not even a majority, pose a threat, but people are assigning probabilities. Such an assignment differs little from a physician, knowing that incidences of cardiovascular diseases are 30 percent higher among blacks than whites and prostate cancer is twice as high, giving his black patients more careful screening for these two diseases. Like the cabbies, pizza deliverers and Rev. Jackson, the physician is engaging in what some have called racial profiling—using race as an indicator of something else.

For analytical purposes, it's important to correctly identify behavior. Asserting that a particular behavior reflects racial likes and dislikes, which it could, when in fact it does not, is to mislead and confound whatever problem or issue one is addressing.

Discrimination or Prejudice

Wednesday, September 27, 2006

In recent weeks, I've offered operational definitions for some of the terms used in the discussion of race. The first was discrimination, which can be broadly defined as the act of choice. When one selects one activity, good or person, of necessity he must discriminate against an alternative activity, good or person.

The second term was prejudice, which can be seen as people making decisions on the basis of incomplete information. We could call it pre-judging or stereotyping. Information is costly. To gain more information requires the sacrifice of resources, be they time, money and perhaps one's life, so people seek information shortcuts.

Imagine an employer plans to hire 20 strong people to manually unload a ship. Fifty people show up for the job, and they all appear equal, except by sex. The employer has zero information about any other attribute, and he would like to hire the physically strongest people in the group. How might he select employees?

I'm guessing the average employer's first approximation would be to select the men in the group. He does so because he surmises that sex is highly correlated with physical strength. Of course, some of the women in the group could be just as strong, or stronger, than the men, but the employer is playing the odds.

This example produces an important observation. By observing the employer's behavior, can one conclude that he doesn't like women? The fact of the matter is that by observing his hiring choices, there is nothing unambiguous one can say about his preferences. To identify a behavior as preference indulgence when it's really an effort to economize on information costs is to misunderstand the behavior.

Some might argue that the employer should seek additional information before making a choice; however, expending the additional resources might not be worth it to him. That's similar to decisions one makes when shopping. One doesn't acquire all the price information possible when he's shopping for, say, shoes. At some point,

he concludes that further searching isn't worth the additional resources of time and money, even though he guesses that somewhere
there might be a lower price.

What's a woman to do who has the physical strength to perform
just as well unloading the ship as a man? One strategy is to provide
what the employer views as reliable information about her strength.
Another alternative is to offer her services at a lower wage. There's
no better way to get people to experiment, and perhaps revise their
expectations, than by lowering prices. That's why a new, previously
unknown, supermarket, restaurant or other establishment might use
sales to attract customers.

What would be some impediments to getting an employer to experiment and take risks that might ultimately revise his expectations?
One would be legislation requiring the employer to pay everyone the
same wage. Another would be legislation making it costly to fire a
lousy worker. After all, if the employer's hunch didn't work out, he
would have to bear the costs of discrimination suits, and possibly
costly settlements, to get rid of the employee.

A few readers, in response to my discrimination discussion, said
that my argument justifies the racial segregation of the past. To explain phenomena is not the same as justifying phenomena. You could
fall off the roof of a tall building. I explain that your death is a result
of the forces of gravity that caused you to accelerate at 32 feet per
second and the sudden deceleration when you hit the ground.
Wouldn't it be silly if someone accused me of trying to justify gravity
and your death?

Discrimination, Prejudice, and Preferences

Wednesday, October 4, 2007

My previous columns have attempted to reduce confusion by suggesting operational definitions of discrimination and prejudice. Discrimination was defined as the act of choice, and prejudice was the act of decisionmaking on the basis of incomplete information. Good analytical thinking requires that we don't confuse one phenomenon with another.

The final behavioral phenomenon related to discussions of race is racial preference. We can think of preferences generally as likes and dislikes, and we all have them for many things. Some of us prefer Bordeaux wines to California wines, while others prefer the opposite. Some of us prefer jazz music while others prefer classical music. The list of differences in human preferences is endless.

There's no logically consistent argument that says to prefer one good, service or person is better, or more righteous, than another. Let's try it. Is my preference for California wines better, or more righteous, than your preference for Bordeaux? Is your preference to marry a white woman better, or more righteous, than my preference to marry a black woman? While we might like or dislike another's preferences, there are no analytical standards by which we can judge one set of preferences to be superior to another.

Preferences alone do not determine behavior. If we conducted a survey asking people which they prefer: filet mignon or chuck steak, Rolex watches or Timex, Rolls Royces or Dodge Neons, I'm guessing that filet mignon, Rolex and Rolls Royce would win hands down. Having found what people preferred the most, then watch what they actually do. You would find chuck steak outselling filet mignon, Timex watches outselling Rolex, and Dodge Neons outselling Rolls Royces any day of the week.

To fully understand behavior, we must go beyond preferences and take restrictions on choice into account, namely income and prices. That fact is very relevant to issues of race. Let's look at it. During

South Africa's apartheid era, white labor unions that would never have a black as a member were the major supporters of minimum wages for blacks. Their stated intention was to protect white workers from competition with low-wage black workers.

Gert Beetge, secretary of the Building Workers' Union, said, "There's no job reservation left in the building industry, and in the circumstances, I support the rate for the job [minimum wages] as the second best way of protecting our white artisans."

In the U.S., the Davis-Bacon Act of 1931 (still on the books), a super minimum wage law, was enacted to protect unionized white construction workers from competition with black workers. The support ran along the lines of Alabama Rep. Clayton Allgood's testimony: "That contractor has cheap colored labor that he transports, and he puts them in cabins, and it is labor of that sort that is in competition with white labor throughout the country" (Congressional Record, 1931, page 6513).

What minimum wage laws do is lower the cost of, and hence subsidize, racial preference indulgence. After all, if an employer must pay the same wage no matter whom he hires, the cost of discriminating in favor of the people he prefers is cheaper. This is a general principle. If filet mignon sold for $9 a pound and chuck steak $4, the cost of discriminating in favor of filet mignon is $5 a pound, the price difference. But if a law mandating a minimum price for chuck steak were on the books, say, $7 a pound, it would lower the cost of discrimination against chuck steak.

Minimum or maximum prices are one of the most effective ways to encourage people to indulge their preferences, be they racial or any other preference. In general, any kind of economic regulation that restricts peaceable, voluntary exchange has the capacity to lower the costs of preference indulgence. Decent people should be against such regulations.

How Much Does Politics Count?

Wednesday, November 15, 2006

Blacks and Hispanics, especially blacks, are the most politically loyal people in the nation. It's often preached and taken as gospel that the only way black people can progress is through racial politics and government programs, but how true is that? Let's look at it.

In 1940, poverty among black families was 87 percent and fell to 47 percent by 1960. Would someone tell me what anti-poverty program or civil-rights legislation accounted for this economic advance that exceeded any other 20-year interval? A significant chunk of that progress occurred through migration from rural areas in the South to big Northern cities. Between 1960 and 1980, black poverty fell roughly 17 percent and fell one percent during the '70s. Might this have been a continuation of a trend starting much earlier, or was it a miracle of the civil-rights movement or President Johnson's War on Poverty?

Dr. Thomas Sowell's research points out that in various skilled trades, the incomes of blacks relative to whites more than doubled between 1936 and 1959. What's more, the rise of blacks in professional and other high-level occupations was greater during the five years preceding the Civil Rights Act of 1964 than the five years afterward.

In 1940, 86 percent of black children were born inside marriage, and the illegitimacy rate among blacks was about 15 percent. Today, 31 percent of black children are born inside marriage, and the illegitimacy rate hovers around 70 percent.

In the mid-1960s, Sen. Daniel Patrick Moynihan sounded the alarm for the breakdown in the black family in his book *The Negro Family: The Case for National Action*. At that time, black illegitimacy was 26 percent. Moynihan said, "[A]t the heart of the deterioration of the fabric of the Negro society is the deterioration of the Negro family." He added, "The steady expansion of welfare programs can be taken as a measure of the steady disintegration of the Negro family structure over the past generation in the United States."

Moynihan's observations were greeted with charges of racism and blaming the victim. If one accepts that a weak family structure has devastating effects on well-being, pray tell us what solutions can be found by electing Republicans or Democrats to the Congress, Senate or White House. By the way, today's growing illegitimacy among whites is what it was among blacks in the 1960s.

Another significant problem for black Americans, independent of whether there are Democratic or Republican congressmen, senators or president, is the level of crime in many black neighborhoods. It's a level of crime unimaginable to most Americans and unimaginable to blacks of yesteryear. In 2005, the nationwide murder rate, per 100,000 of the population, was 5.6. Cities with large black populations had much higher murder rates, such as: Gary, Ind. (58), Richmond, Va. (43), Detroit (39), and Washington, D.C. (35).

According to Justice Department figures, blacks were six times more likely than whites to be homicide victims, and 94 percent of black victims were murdered by blacks. Again, pray tell us what solutions will be found by electing Republicans or Democrats to the Congress, Senate or White House.

Homicide is just the tip of the iceberg in terms of the level of crime in many black neighborhoods. The overwhelmingly law-abiding residents of these neighborhoods live their lives in fear of assault and battery, rape, robbery and various forms of intimidation. High crime not only turns many neighborhoods into economic wastelands, but they cause the most stable members of those neighborhoods to be the first to leave. The solutions to the major problems that confront many black people won't be found in the political arena, especially not in Washington or state capitols.

Racial Profiling

Wednesday, December 20, 2006

Charges of racial, religious and ethnic profiling swirl in the wake of US Airways' removal of six imams. According to police reports, the men made anti-American statements, were praying and chanting "Allah," refused the pilot's requests to disembark for additional screening and asked for seat-belt extensions for no obvious reason. Three of the men had no checked baggage and only one-way tickets.

According to the Council on American-Islamic Relations (CAIR), five of the men have retained lawyers and are probably going to bring a discrimination lawsuit against US Airways.

Racial profiling controversy is nothing new. For a number of years, black Americans have made charges of racial profiling by police and store personnel who might give them extra scrutiny. Clever phrases have emerged, such as "driving while black" and now "flying while Muslim," but they don't help much in terms of understanding. Let's apply some economic analysis to the issue.

God, or some other omniscient being, would never racially profile. Why? Since He is all-knowing, He'd know who is and is not a terrorist or a criminal. We humans are not all-knowing. While a god would have perfect and complete information about everything, we humans have less than perfect and incomplete information. That means we must use substitutes such as guesses and hunches for certain kinds of information. It turns out that some physical attributes are highly correlated with other attributes that are less easily, or more costly, observed.

Let's look at a few, and the associated "profiling," that cause little or no controversy. Mortality rates for cardiovascular diseases were approximately 30 percent higher among black adults than among white adults. The Pima Indians of Arizona have the world's highest known diabetes rates. Prostate cancer is nearly twice as common among black men as white men. Would anyone bring racial profiling charges against a doctor who routinely ordered more frequent blood tests and prostate screening among his black patients and more glucose tolerance tests for his Pima Indian patients? Of course, God wouldn't have to do that because He'd know for sure which patient was more prone to cardiovascular disease, prostate cancer and diabetes.

It is clear, whether we like it or not, or want to say it or not, that there is a strong correlation between terrorist acts and being a Muslim, and being black and high rates of crime. That means if one is trying to deter terrorism and in some cases capture a criminal, he would expend greater investigatory resources on Muslims and blacks. A law-abiding Muslim who's given extra airport screening or a black who's stopped by the police is perfectly justified in being angry, but with whom should he be angry? I think a Muslim should be angry with those who've made terrorism and Muslim synonymous and blacks angry with those who've made blacks and crime synonymous. The latter is my response to the insulting sounds of car doors locking sometimes when I'm crossing a street in downtown Washington, D.C., or when taxi drivers pass me by.

It would be a serious misallocation of resources if airport security intensively screened everyone. After all, intensively screening someone who had a near zero probability of being a terrorist, such as an 80-year-old woman using a walker, would not only be a waste but it would take resources away from screening a person with a much higher probability of being a terrorist.

You say, "Williams, are you justifying religious and racial profiling?" No. I'm not justifying anything any more than I'd try to justify Einstein's special law of relativity. I'm trying to explain a phenomenon. By the way, I think some of the airport screening is grossly stupid, but I'm at peace with the Transportation Security Administration. They have their rules, and I have mine. One of mine is to minimize my association with idiocy. Thus, I no longer fly commercial.

Victimhood: Rhetoric or Reality

Wednesday, June 8, 2005

If you listened to the rhetoric of black politicians and civil rights leaders, dating back to the Reagan years, you would have been convinced that surely by now black Americans would be back on the plantation. According to them, President Reagan, and later Presidents Bush I and II, would turn back the clock on civil rights. They'd appoint "new racists" dressed in three-piece suits to act through the courts and administrative agencies to reverse black civil rights and economic gains. We can now recognize this rhetoric as the political equivalent of the "rope-a-dope."

As my colleague Tom Sowell pointed out in a recent column, "Liberals, Race and History," if the Democratic party's share of the black vote ever fell to even 70 percent, it's not likely that the Democrats would ever win the White House or Congress again. The strategy liberal Democrats have chosen, to prevent loss of the black vote, is to keep blacks paranoid and in a constant state of fear. But is it fear of racists, or being driven back to the plantation, that should be a top priority for blacks? Let's look at it.

Only 30 to 40 percent of black males graduate from high school. Many of those who do graduate emerge with reading and math skills of a white seventh- or eighth-grader. This is true in cities where a black is mayor, a black is superintendent of schools and the majority of principals and teachers are black. It's also true in cities where the per pupil education expenditures are among the highest in the nation.

Across the U.S., black males represent up to 70 percent of prison populations. Are they in prison for crimes against whites? To the contrary, their victims are primarily other blacks. Department of Justice statistics for 2001 show that in nearly 80 percent of violent crimes against blacks, both the victim and the perpetrator were the same race. In other words, it's not Reaganites, Bush supporters, right-wing ideologues or the Klan causing blacks to live in fear of their lives and property and making their neighborhoods economic wastelands.

What about the decline of the black family? In 1960, only 28 percent of black females between the ages of 15 and 44 were never married. Today, it's 56 percent. In 1940, the illegitimacy rate among blacks was 19 percent, in 1960, 22 percent, and today, it's 70 percent. Some argue that the state of the black family is the result of the legacy of slavery, discrimination and poverty. That has to be nonsense. A study of 1880 family structure in Philadelphia shows that three-quarters of black families were nuclear families, comprised of two parents and children. In New York City in 1925, 85 percent of kin-related black households had two parents. In fact, according to Herbert Gutman in *The Black Family in Slavery and Freedom: 1750–1925*, "Five in six children under the age of 6 lived with both parents." Therefore, if one argues that what we see today is a result of a legacy of slavery, discrimination and poverty, what's the explanation for stronger black families at a time much closer to slavery—a time of much greater discrimination and of much greater poverty? I think that a good part of the answer is there were no welfare and Great Society programs.

Since black politicians and the civil rights establishment preach victimhood to blacks, I'd prefer that they be more explicit when they appear in public fora. Were they to be so, saying racists are responsible for black illegitimacy, blacks preying on other blacks and black family breakdown, their victimhood message would be revealed as idiotic. But being so explicit is not as far-fetched as one might think. In a campaign speech before a predominantly black audience, in reference to so many blacks in prison, presidential candidate John Kerry said, "That's unacceptable, but it's not their fault."

Betrayal of the Struggle

Wednesday, December 14, 2005

Last month, when Rosa Parks was laid to rest in Detroit, her eulogy contained well-deserved praise for her brave defiance of segregation laws that led to the 1955 Montgomery, Ala., bus boycott and later the 1956 Supreme Court ruling that banned public transportation segregation. The passing and remembrance of her generation of blacks, who made sacrifices to deliver today's opportunities, might also be an occasion for condemnation of what's no less than a gross betrayal of that generation's struggle.

Having lived just about one-third of our nation's existence, I know, as well as experienced, the uglier parts of our history. During the '30s, '40s and '50s, civil rights progress meant yearly black lynchings were down to single digits, as opposed to 50 or more in previous decades. In 1954, when I graduated from Philadelphia's Benjamin Franklin High School, rare was the opportunity for a black student to go off to college. While segregation was mostly in the South, it nonetheless existed in northern cities. There were entire Philadelphia neighborhoods where, regardless of socioeconomic status, blacks could not rent or buy. There were business establishments, including movie theaters and restaurants, where black patronage was not welcomed.

While not every vestige of racial discrimination has been eliminated, it is nowhere near the barrier it was yesteryear, but you'd think discrimination is everywhere listening to some of today's black politicians and civil rights leaders. One wonders what those blacks, who lived during the era of gross discrimination and are now deceased, would think about so much of today's behavior, rhetoric and excuses.

What would they think about black neighborhoods, once thriving economic centers that have been turned into economic wastelands by a level of criminal activity previously unknown? During my youth, walking through some of Philadelphia's predominantly white neighborhoods, one felt a sense of relief as we approached a black neighborhood. Today, it might be the other way around. What would they think about predominantly black schools where violence and intimidation are the order of the day, with police cars outside and metal detectors inside? What would they think about black students who seek academic excellence being mocked, intimidated and assaulted by their peers for "acting white"?

By any assessment, black Americans have made the greatest progress, over some of the highest hurdles and in the shortest span of time than any other racial group in the history of mankind. If one added the earnings of black Americans and thought of us as a nation, we'd be the 14th richest nation. Black Americans have held some of the nation's highest positions, such as secretaries of State, Housing and Urban Development, Health and Human Services and Education; chairman of the Joint Chiefs of Staff; and mayors of some of our largest cities. Blacks are some of the world's most famous personalities, and a few blacks rank among the world's richest people. In 1865, neither a slave nor a slave owner would have believed these gains possible in a little over a century, if ever. As such, it not only speaks well of the determination and intestinal fortitude of a people, but also of a nation in which such gains were possible.

For a large segment of the black community, these gains remain elusive. The gains will remain elusive so long as black civil rights and political leadership blame and focus their energies on discrimination. While discrimination exists, the relevant question is how much of what we see can be explained by it. A 70 percent illegitimacy rate, 60 percent of black children raised in female-headed households, high crime and poor school performance have devastating consequences. This level of pathology cannot be attributed to discrimination, considering that much of it was absent in earlier times when there was far more discrimination, greater poverty and fewer opportunities.

It's time that black people hold fellow blacks accountable for squandering opportunities won at a high cost by our ancestors. Failing to do so makes all blacks complicit in the betrayal.

Racial Profiling

Wednesday, April 26, 2004

What is racial profiling and is it racist? We can think of profiling as using cheap-to-observe characteristics as indicators or proxies for more-costly-to-observe characteristics. A person's physical characteristics, such as race, sex and height, are cheap to observe and they might be correlated with some other characteristic that's more costly to observe such as disease, strength and abilities.

Profiling examples abound. Just knowing that one person is 6'9" allows one to predict that he's a better basketball player than a 4'9" person. That might be called height profiling. While height is not a perfect indicator of basketball proficiency there is a strong association. Similarly, just by knowing the sex or age of an individual allows one to make predictions about unobserved characteristics such as weight lifting ability, running and reflex speed, and eyesight and hearing acuity because they are correlated with sex and age.

What about using race or ethnicity as proxies for some unobserved characteristic? Some racial and ethnic groups have a higher incidence of mortality from various diseases than the national average. In 1998, mortality rates for cardiovascular diseases were approximately 30 percent higher among black adults than among white adults. Cervical cancer rates were almost five times higher among Vietnamese women in the U.S. than among white women. The Pima Indians of Arizona have the highest known diabetes rates in the world. Prostate cancer is nearly twice as common among black men as white men. Would one condemn a medical practitioner for advising greater screening and monitoring of black males for cardiovascular disease and prostate cancer, or greater screening and monitoring for cervical cancer among Vietnamese-American females, and the same for diabetes among Pima Indians? It surely would be racial profiling—using race as an indicator of a higher probability of some other characteristic.

You might say that's different but using racial profiling as a proxy for potential criminal behavior is indeed racist. Just as race and ethnicity are not perfect indicators of the risk of certain diseases neither is race a perfect indicator of criminal activity but there associations and people act on those associations.

A Washington, D.C. taxicab commissioner, who is black, issued a safety advisory urging D.C.'s 6,800 cabbies to refuse to pick up "dangerous looking" passengers. She described "dangerous looking" as a "young black guy . . . with shirttail hanging down longer than his coat, baggy pants, unlaced tennis shoes." By no stretch of imagination does every young black person pose a threat to taxi drivers but in Washington, D.C. and other cities there's a strong correlation between race and robbery/murder threat. We seriously misunderstand the motives of a taxi driver who passes up a black customer if we use racism as the sole explanation for his behavior. It might be racism but it might just as easily and more probably be a fear of robbery, murder or being taken to a dangerous neighborhood. There're other examples and greater detail of this phenomena in my recent *Cornell Law and Public Policy Journal* article "Discrimination: The Law vs. Morality" at www.walterewilliams.com under "recent articles."

Needless to say the law-abiding black person who's refused a taxi ride, pizza delivery, or pulled over by the police is justifiably annoyed and offended. The rightful recipients of his anger should be those blacks who've made black synonymous with high crime and not the taxi driver or pizza deliverer who might fear for his life or the policeman trying to do his job.

God would never do profiling of any sort because God is omniscient. We humans lack that quality and must depend upon sometimes crude substitutes for finding out things.

By the way, attempting to explain profiling doesn't require one to take a position for or against it any more than attempting to explain gravity requires one to be for or against gravity.

Price Discrimination

June 14, 2004

Suppose you saw a fat, old, ugly cigar-smoking man married to a beautiful young lady, what prediction would you make about the man's income? If you're like most, you'd predict that this guy has a lot of money. In effect that fat, old, ugly cigar-smoking man is telling the woman, "I can't compete for your hand on the basis of a guy like Williams so I'm going to offset my handicaps by offering you a higher price." In the name of fairness, should that kind of discrimination be banned—namely beautiful women treating ugly old men differently from handsome young men.

Airlines typically charge half-fare for children and surely they can't justify that practice by saying that it costs twice as much to fly an adult from New York to Los Angeles. Airlines also charge business travelers higher prices than those charged tourists. Again, they can't justify the price difference by saying it costs more to fly businessmen than it costs to fly tourists. What should be done about this kind of discrimination?

Amtrak charges lower fares to senior citizens than it charges younger people and it's not because it costs less to haul older people than younger people. Amtrak is not alone with this kind of age discrimination; it's rife. Theaters do it; drugstores do it; some supermarkets do it; and some taxicab companies do it. There are numerous instances where people are charged different prices based upon some physical or behavioral characteristic.

Should price discrimination be outlawed? Yes, according to the reasoning of George Washington University law professor John F. Banzhaf. He's the lawyer who led the attack on tobacco companies and fast food chains saying they were responsible respectively for tobacco-related diseases and obesity. A recent addition to Professor Banzhaf's agenda is to outlaw ladies' night saying, "Different prices for men and women constitute illegal gender-based discrimination, and perpetrators can be sued not only for monetary damages, but in many cases also for attorney fees and punitive damages." He boasts that ladies' nights have been ruled illegal in California, Colorado, Connecticut, Iowa, Maryland, Missouri, Nebraska, New York, Pennsylvania, and recently New Jersey.

It's fruitless to attempt to convince Professor Banzhaf that price discrimination is a benign, standard and routine pricing technique; it's even practiced by his legal profession. Professor Banzhaf's true agenda is tyrannical control of our lives. Here's my question to you. Once Banzhaf finishes getting ladies' night outlawed in the other 40 states, do you think he'll be finished? I wouldn't bet the rent money on it. The reasoning Banzhaf uses in attacking night club practice of charging ladies cheaper prices is also applicable to: airlines charging children and tourists cheaper prices than adults and businessmen, businesses and other entities charging seniors cheaper prices than younger people, and theaters charging cheaper matinee prices than evening prices. I wouldn't be surprised that if Banzhaf succeeded outlawing price discrimination in these areas he'd move on to bring a class action suit on behalf of fat, old, ugly men against beautiful women. You say, "Williams, that's preposterous!" Think again; tyrants have an endless agenda. When the cigarette Nazis said they didn't care about what people did to their own lungs; they only cared about the health effects on others—secondhand smoke. I said that's a smoke screen to conceal their true agenda. In California there's a movement to outlaw smoking on beaches, many outdoor stadiums have banned smoking, there have been attempts to ban smoking on streets and parks. I'd like to see the health study pointing to the deaths and injuries stemming from secondhand smoke outdoors.

The bottom line here isn't ladies' night or smoking. It's how we Americans are allowing tyrants to attack our liberties. If we allow them to continue, once we wake up we won't have enough freedom to stop them from turning us into a nation of serfs.

Three Cheers for the Cos

May 31, 2004

May 17th saw several gatherings commemorating the 50th anniversary of the 1954 U.S. Supreme Court's school desegregation decision in *Brown v. Board of Education*. But the event held in Washington, D.C.'s Constitution Hall will be the one to be remembered because of Bill Cosby's remarks that won him scathing criticism from some in the black community.

For years I've argued that most of today's problems many black Americans face have little or nothing to do with racial discrimination. For the most part, the most devastating problems encountered by a large segment of the black community are self-inflicted. Bill Cosby mentioned several of them such as black parents who'll buy their children expensive clothing rather than something educational, poor language spoken by many children and adults, and criminals who prey on the overwhelmingly law-abiding residents of black neighborhoods. After Cosby's remarks some in the audience laughed and applauded but, according to the *Washington Post*, the black "leadership" in attendance, the head of the NAACP, the head of the NAACP Legal Defense Fund and the president of Howard University were "stone-faced."

In a recent column, my colleague Thomas Sowell explained, "Bill Cosby and the black 'leadership' represent two long-standing differences about how to deal with the problems of the black community. The 'leaders' are concerned with protecting the image of blacks, while Cosby is trying to protect the future of blacks, especially those of the younger generation."

Bill Cosby and I differ in age by one year—I'm older. We both spent part of our youth, in the 40s and 50s, growing up in North Philadelphia's Richard Allen Housing project. Being poor then was different from being poor now. My sister and I were rare among Richard Allen's residents. Our parents were separated but nearly every other kid lived in a two-parent household. Black teen pregnancy was relatively rare and just a tiny fraction of today's. During those days, many residents rarely locked their doors until the last person came home. Hot summer nights saw many people fearlessly sleeping in their yards or on their balconies.

Today, less than 40 percent of black children live in two-parent families, compared to 70 and 80 percent in earlier periods. Illegitimacy, at 70 percent, is unprecedented in black history. Between 1976 and 2000, over 50 percent of all homicides in the U.S. were committed by blacks and 94 percent of the time the victim was black. These are devastating problems but are they caused by racism and will spending resources fighting racial discrimination solve them? Don't give me any of that legacy-of-slavery nonsense unless you can explain why all of these problems were not worse during the late 19th and early 20th centuries at a time when blacks were much closer to slavery, much poorer, faced more discrimination and had fewer opportunities.

With all the opportunities available today, unavailable when Cosby and I were youngsters, black youngsters who dedicate themselves to academic excellence are attacked both verbally and sometimes physically for "acting white," being "Oreos" and "brainiacs." California Berkeley Professor John McWhorter says that, "Insidious anti-intellectualism is the prime culprit in the school-performance gap between whites and blacks, which cuts across class and income lines." He adds that the rap music culture "retards black success by the reinforcement of hindering stereotypes and by teaching young blacks that a thuggish adversarial stance is the properly authentic response to a presumptively racist society."

In at least two important ways black America is a study of contrasts. By any measure, as a group black Americans have made the greatest gains, over some of the highest hurdles, in the shortest span of time, than any other racial group in human history. At the same time for a large segment of the black community these gains are elusive and will remain so under the current civil rights vision. Bill Cosby's bold comments might be what's necessary to get an honest and fruitful discussion going within the black community, and for that we all owe him thanks.

A Usable Black History

August 20, 2001

Professor John McWhorter, linguistics professor at the Berkeley campus of the University of California, has written a compelling essay in *City Journal* (Summer 2001) titled "Toward a Usable Black History." Last year, he wrote *Losing The Race: Self-Sabotage in Black America* arguing there's a culture of black anti-intellectualism, impeding academic excellence, resulting from an ideology of victimization and separatism. The pursuit of academic excellence is seen as "acting white" and as such amounts to racial betrayal. In his *City Journal* article, McWhorter says that while it would be folly not to teach the history of the injustices of slavery, Jim Crow and gross racial discrimination, "but a history of only horrors cannot inspire."

Professor McWhorter says, "When 'Learn your history' means 'Don't get fooled by superficial changes', and 'Today's New York City Street Crimes Unit can't be distinguished from yesterday's Bull Connor', and our aggrieved despair over our sense of disinclusion from the national fabric remains as sharp as ever. Could any people find inner peace when taught to think of their own society as their enemy?"

Instead, a better, more usable history would be one that gives greater emphasis to black successes in the face of seemingly insurmountable odds. That kind of history inspires instead of breeding victimhood. McWhorter says today's education chaos is not business-as-usual but something entirely new. From the late 1800s to 1950, some black schools were models of academic achievement. Black students at Washington's Dunbar High School often outscored white students as early as 1899. Schools such as Frederick Douglas (Baltimore), Booker T. Washington (Atlanta), P.S. 91 (Brooklyn), McDonough 35 (New Orleans) and others operated at a similar level of excellence. These excelling students weren't solely members of the black elite; most had parents who were manual laborers, domestic servants, porters and maintenance men.

Professor McWhorter says that instead of "romanticizing failure" in black communities young people should be taught that successful economic communities can be had. Chicago's "Bronzeville" is a handy example. After 1875, blacks occupied a three by 15 block enclave on the South Side. During the early 1900s, Bronzeville was home to several black newspapers and 731 business establishments by 1917 in 61 lines of work. The Binga Bank opened in 1908 by its founder Jesse Binga who started out with a wagon selling coal and oil. By 1929, Bronzeville blacks had amassed $100 million in real estate holdings.

Chicago wasn't the only city where blacks established a significant business presence. Other cities would include New York, Philadelphia, Durham, Atlanta and Washington D.C., and Tulsa's Greenwood district that was destroyed by rioting whites.

Keep in mind when blacks established business successes such as those in Bronzeville and Durham it was accomplished in a harsh racial environment. No one can attribute their successes to SBA minority loans, business set asides, affirmative action and measures deemed indispensable by today's race experts. It was accomplished through hard work, sacrifice and, as my father used to say, coming early and staying late.

Ignoring or downplaying black achievement promotes the victim attitude where people believe that in order for them to be successful somebody else must perform some benevolent act. The bottom line indisputable fact of business is that black Americans have made the greatest gains, over some of the highest hurdles, in the shortest span of time than any other racial group in mankind's history. That speaks well of the intestinal fortitude of a people and it also speaks well of a nation in which such gains were possible. Today's whining and portrayal of black people as a victim class amounts to an unspeakable betrayal of the sacrifices and the successes of our ancestors.

Does Political Power Mean Economic Power?

April 7, 2003

Much of the '60s and '70s civil rights rhetoric was that black political power was necessary for economic power. In 1967, Clevelanders heeded Malcolm X's infamous "The Ballot or the Bullet" speech with the election of Carl B. Stokes who became the nation's first black big city mayor. As of 1999, blacks were mayors of 29 major cities; that includes Philadelphia, Detroit, Cleveland, San Francisco, St. Louis and Washington, D.C. In some of these cities, blacks are also city councilmen, superintendents of schools and chiefs of police. That this is a major achievement is without question and a fine commentary on America's racial progress, especially when we consider the fact that blacks are mayors in cities where blacks are a small minority such as: Des Moines, Denver, Houston, San Francisco and Dallas. By no means does it demean black political achievement to ask a more important question: What does black political power mean for the lives of ordinary black people? In other words, is political power a necessary condition for economic power? Let's look around.

Japanese and Chinese-Americans faced gross discrimination in our country, but when's the last time you heard of them worrying about how many congressmen they have or going into a tizzy worrying whether a Reagan or Bush presidency would mean the end of their handouts? By the way, Japanese and Chinese-Americans have median family incomes higher than white Americans, and in the case of Chinese-Americans 58 percent higher. Other discriminated-against minorities in America who've eschewed the political arena are: Koreans, Arabs, and Armenians.

For the ordinary person, what's more important: economic power or political power? I think it nearly goes without saying that economic power empowers the individual; it gives him the power of self-determination. Political power empowers, and even enriches, the political elite; for them getting out their constituent vote is the be all and end all. This observation has nothing to do with race. Economic power empowers people of any race and political power empowers the political elite of any race.

While black politicians have preached that political power is a means to gain economic power, whether it has done so is a testable proposition. We only have to examine the socioeconomic status of black Americans in cities where blacks hold considerable political power, cities such as Washington, D.C., Newark, Philadelphia, Detroit, Cleveland, Memphis and others. What we'll find in those cities are grossly inferior education, welfare dependency for much of the population, unsafe neighborhoods and citizens, both black and white, who can't wait for the first opportunity to get out.

Let me be clear. I am not stating a causal link between black political power and the living conditions and the welfare of many of its citizens in these cities. It's simply an argument that the expectation that political power will translate into economic power for the ordinary citizen is apt to be disappointing. But there're some political steps that black politicians can take that can create an environment for economic power.

Crime exacts a huge cost on people least able to bear it. High crime makes everything worth less whether it's houses or businesses. Among other things it means fewer neighborhood consumer choices and neighborhood employment. Black politicians should develop a ruthless zero tolerance anti-crime policy. Rotten education in these cities where blacks hold dominant political power needs to be addressed but that's more difficult. Black politicians are beholden to and serve the interests of the powerful teachers' unions and not the voters who elect them to office. Otherwise they wouldn't begin to tolerate the near systematic destruction of learning opportunities for generations of black children. A solution is to break the education monopoly through educational vouchers.

Stifling Black Students

February 14, 2002

Racial preferences, quotas, affirmative action in university admission practices have lost political and increasingly legal support. As a result states such as California, Texas and Florida have implemented a substitute practice called "percentage plans" as a means for determining who will be admitted to their flagship universities. In Texas, students in the top 10 percent of their high school class, based on grade point averages (GPA) alone, not SAT scores, are guaranteed admission; in California, it's soon to be 12.5 percent and Florida it's 20 percent. The percentage plan applies to all high schools whether it's a school where a student with an A average might achieve a 1300 or 1400 score on the SAT, or a school where A students might not be able to achieve 800 or 900 SAT score.

Let's ignore the inequities and resources misallocation that arises from the possibility that a B student at one school who might achieve a SAT score of 1100 is denied admission while his A average counterpart at another school can't score 900 is admitted. Instead, let's ask whether the policy serves the best interests of black students. From the evidence that I see, civil rights leaders, white liberals and college administrators seem to be more concerned with black student enrollment rates and the heck with whether they graduate. Black students are simply tools to keep government agencies, black politicians and civil rights organizations off their backs or to make them feel good. You say, "What's the evidence, Williams?" Nationally, only 35 percent of black freshmen, compared to 60 percent of white freshmen graduate; moreover, those who do graduate have grade point averages considerably lower than their white peers. I might add that the white graduation rate is nothing to write home about.

University of San Diego law professor Gail Heriot sheds a bit of light on this issue in her article "The Politics of Admissions in California," *Academic Questions* (Fall 2001). California's Proposition 209 ended racial admissions quotas. As a result minority student admissions at UC Berkeley, California's flagship university, fell. What went unnoticed in all the hand wringing was that at less prestigious, but respectable, California universities minority enrollment posted impressive gains. Black students were simply being admitted to universities where their academic credentials were more in line with their fellow students. For example, at UC San Diego, in the year before Proposition 209's implementation, only one black freshman had a GPA of 3.5 or better—a single black honor student in a class of 3,268—in contrast to 20 percent of white students with a 3.5 GPA.

Was this because there were no black students capable of doing honors work at UC San Diego? Certainly not. Those who might have been on the honors list at UC San Diego had been recruited, and became failures at California's flagship universities: Berkeley, and UCLA. Proposition 209 has changed UC San Diego; no longer are black honor students a rarity. In 1998, a full 20 percent of black freshman could boast of a 3.5 GPA.

Black students, and for that matter any student, will perform better, have greater graduation chances not to mention pride and self-worth by attending a university where his skills are closer to that of his peers. It's somewhat analogous to putting a young, inexperienced boxer in the ring with Lennox Lewis. That boxer might have the potential to be a world champion but he's going to have his brains beaten and his career ended before he learns how to even bob and weave. You say, "But what about diversity and multiculturalism at the nation's elite universities?" In my book, that's their problem.

Economics for the Citizen

The articles in this section are reprinted with permission from the Foundation for Economic Education's journal, *The Freeman: Ideas on Liberty*: "Economics for the Citizen," (part 1) May 2005, (part 2) September 2005, (part 3) December 2005, (part 4) April 2006, (part 5) July 2006. http://www.fee.org/publications/the-freeman/

.

Economics for the Citizen – Part I

The Freeman: Ideas on Liberty, *May 2005*

Last fall semester, I didn't teach for the first time in 37 years. No, I haven't retired. It was my semester-off reward for two terms as department chairman at George Mason University. A break is well deserved after a chairmanship—a job not unlike that of herding cats.

During fall semesters, I typically teach our first-year Ph.D. microeconomics theory course. Out of a love for teaching, I decided to not completely take off but deliver a few lectures on basic economic principles to readers. We'll name the series "Economics for the Citizen."

The first lesson in economic theory is that we live in a world of scarcity. Scarcity is a situation whereby human wants exceed the means to satisfy those wants. Human wants are assumed to be limitless, or at least they don't frequently reveal their bounds. People always want more of something, be it: more cars, more food, more love, more happiness, more peace, more health care, more clean air or more charity. Our ability and resources to satisfy all human wants are indeed limited. There's only a finite amount of: land, iron, workers and years in a lifetime.

Scarcity produces several economic problems: What's to be produced, who's going to get it, how's it to be produced, and when is it to be produced? For example, many Americans, and foreigners too, would love to have a home or vacation home along the thousand miles of California, Oregon and Washington coastline. Shipping companies would like to use some of it as ports. The U.S. Defense Department would like to use it for military installations. There's simply not enough coastline to meet all the competing wants and uses. That means there's conflict over coastline ownership and its uses. If human wants were not unlimited, or the resources to satisfy those wants were limitless, there would be no economic problem and hence conflict.

Whenever there is conflict, there must be a means to resolve it. There are several methods of conflict resolution. First, there's the market mechanism. In our land use example, the highest bidder would be the one who owns the land and decides how it will be used. Then, there's government fiat, where the government dictates who has rights to use the land for what purpose. Gifts might be the way where an owner arbitrarily chooses a recipient. Finally, violence is a way to resolve the question of who has the use rights to the coastline—let people get weapons and physically fight it out.

At this juncture, some might piously say, "Violence is no way to resolve conflict!" The heck it isn't. The decision of who had the right to use most of the Earth's surface was settled through violence (wars). Who has the right to the income I earn is partially settled through the threats of violence where our government, through the tax code, decides that farmers, businesses and poor people have rights to my income. In fact, violence is such an effective means of resolving conflict that most governments want a monopoly on its use.

Which is the best method to resolve conflict arising out the questions of what's to be produced, how and when it's produced, and who's going to get it? Is it the market mechanism, government fiat, gifts or violence? The answer is that economic theory can't answer normative questions. Normative questions are those that deal with what is better or worse. No theory can answer better or worse questions. Try asking a physics teacher which is the better or worse state: a solid, gas, liquid or plasma state. He'll probably look at you as if you're crazy; it's a nonsense question. On the other hand, if you ask your physics teacher which is the cheapest state for pounding a nail into a board, he'd probably answer that it's the solid state. It's the same with economic theory. That is, if you asked most economists which method of conflict resolution produces the greater overall wealth, they'd probably answer that the market mechanism does.

The bottom line is that economic theory is objective or non-normative and cannot make value judgments. Economic theory deals with what was, what is, and what will be. By contrast economic policy questions are normative or subjective and do make value judgments—questions such as: Should we fight unemployment or inflation, should we spend more money on education, and should the capital gains tax be 15 percent or 20 percent? Someone once said that if we took all the economists in the world, and lined them up end-to-end, they would never reach a single conclusion. Economists are just like anyone else and as such have opinions and values. Thus, much of the disagreement among economists has to do with value judgments. By contrast, there's widespread agreement in the area of core theory.

Keeping the distinction between non-normative and normative in mind is very important, so let me elaborate a bit. Take the statement: The dimensions of this room are 30 feet by 40 feet. That's an objective statement. Why? If there's any disagreement, there are empirical facts and commonly agreed to standards to which we can appeal to settle the disagreement, namely getting out a measuring instrument. Compare that statement to: The dimensions of this room should be 20 feet by 80 feet.

Say another person disagrees and argues that it should be 50 feet by 50 feet. There are no facts and commonly agreed to standards to resolve such disagreement. Similarly, there are no facts and commonly agreed to standards to which we can appeal to resolve a disagreement over whether the capital gains tax should be 15 percent or 20 percent, or whether it's more important to fight inflation or unemployment.

The importance of knowing whether a statement is non-normative or normative is that, in the former, there are facts to settle any dispute, but in the latter, there are none. It's just a matter of opinion, and one person's opinion is just as good as another. A good clue to telling whether a statement is normative is whether it contains the words should and ought.

At the beginning of each semester, I tell students that my economic theory course will deal with positive, non-normative economic theory. I also tell them that if they hear me making a normative statement without first saying, "In my opinion," they are to raise their hands and say, "Professor Williams, we didn't take this class to be indoctrinated with your personal opinions passed off as economic theory; that's academic dishonesty." I also tell them that as soon as they hear me say, "In my opinion," they can stop taking notes because my opinion is irrelevant to the subject of the class—economic theory.

I conclude this part of my first lecture by telling the students that by no means do I suggest that they purge their vocabulary of normative or subjective statements. Such statements are useful tools for tricking people but in the process one needn't trick himself. You tell your father that you absolutely need a cell phone and he should buy you one. There's no evidence whatsoever that you need a cell phone. After all, George Washington managed to lead our nation to defeat Great Britain, the mightiest nation on Earth at the time, without owning a cell phone.

I personally believe that economics is fun and valuable. More than anything else, economics is a way of thinking. People who say they found economics a nightmare in college just didn't have a good teacher-professor. I became a good teacher-professor as a result of tenacious mentors during my graduate study at UCLA. Professor Armen Alchian, a very distinguished economist, used to give me a hard time in class. But one day, we were having a friendly chat during our department's weekly faculty/graduate student coffee hour, and he said, "Williams, the true test of whether someone understands his subject is whether he can explain it to someone who doesn't know a darn thing about it." That's a challenge I love: Making economics fun and understandable.

The next in the series Economics for the Citizen discussion will be a bit more interesting. We'll talk about what kinds of behavior can be called economic behavior.

Economics for the Citizen – Part II

The Freeman: Ideas on Liberty, *September 2005*

There are four classes of behavior that can be called economic behavior. They are: production, consumption, exchange and specialization. Production is any behavior that creates utility, that is, raises the want satisfying capacity of something. When a mill smelts iron ore, it raises the want satisfying capacity of the material by changing its form. The metal's want satisfying capacity is raised further when it's made into steel and the steel into rails, girders and the like. Production also includes changing the spatial characteristics of a good. Navel oranges have no want satisfying capacity for Philadelphians, if the oranges are in California. The person sometimes called the middleman or wholesaler changes the spatial characteristics of the oranges by moving them from California to Philadelphia thereby raising their want satisfying capacity to Philadelphians.

Consumption is easy. Consumption is simply the reduction of utility, the want satisfying capacity of something. When I eat a hamburger, I reduce its want satisfying capacity. When I drive my car, I reduce its capacity to satisfy wants. By the way, if production is greater than consumption the result is called saving. If it's the opposite, we call it dissaving.

Exchange is a bit more complicated; misunderstanding it leads to considerable confusion and mischief. The essence of exchange is the transfer of property rights. Here's the essence of what happens when I buy a gallon of milk from my grocer. I tell him that I hold property rights to these three dollars and he holds property rights to the gallon of milk. Then I offer: If you transfer your property rights to that gallon of milk, I will transfer my property rights to these three dollars.

Whenever there's voluntary exchange the only clear conclusion that a third party can reach is that both parties, in their opinion, not yours or mine, perceived themselves as better off as a result of the exchange; otherwise, they wouldn't have exchanged. I was free to keep my three dollars and the grocer was free to keep his milk.

growers produce more coffee than they consume or plan to
me.

here are requirements for specialization. There must be an un-
endowment of resources and trade opportunities. The unequal
wment part means that an individual has the skills, a region or
n has a resource endowment of land, labor, capital and entre-
urial talent whereby it can produce certain things more cheaply
can another individual, region or nation. For example, while it's
ble to grow wheat and corn in Japan, it would be an expensive
osition. Why?

Because crops like wheat and corn use a lot of land and Japan is
ively land poor. That means Japanese land is relatively expensive.
ontrast the U.S. is land rich hence grain production is relatively
p. Therefore, it makes sense for the U.S. to take advantage of
it can do more cheaply—specialize in grain production, and Ja-
specialize in what it might produce more cheaply—say camera
es.

In order for specialization to occur there must be trade oppor-
ties. It wouldn't make sense for U.S. farmers to produce more
n than they consume or plan to consume if they couldn't trade it.
her would it make sense for Japanese producers to produce more
era lenses than they consume or plan to consume if they couldn't
e. That's why trade opportunities are necessary in order for people
ake advantage of wealth-enhancing specialization.

Imagine that the Japanese government imposed trade restrictions
U.S. grain imports. Japanese farmers could charge monopoly prices
enjoy higher income and Japanese consumers would pay higher
es. Would you deem it an intelligent response for the U.S. gov-
ment to retaliate against Japan's trade restrictions by imposing
le restrictions on Japanese camera lenses allowing American lens
ducers to charge monopoly prices and American consumers suffer
her prices? Put another way, is it a smart response for the U.S.
ernment to harm American consumers because Japan harmed its
nsumers?

Specialization and trade make people dependent upon one an-
er for their everyday wants. How many of us make our own eye-

If you think it's obvious that both parties exchange, then why do we hear pronounceme ploitation? Say you offer me a wage of $2 an h accept or reject your offer. So what can be a working for you at $2 an hour? One clear con have seen myself as being better off by taking ye best alternative. I must have perceived that all c less valuable or else why would I have accepte appropriate is it to say that you're exploiting m me my best offer? Rather than using the term e say you wish I had more desirable alternatives.

While people might characterize $2 an hour wouldn't say the same about $50 an hour. The part, when people use the term exploitation in re exchange, they simply disagree with the price. If agreement with exploitation, then exploitation is not only disagree with my salary, I also disagree Gulfstream private jets.

By no means do I suggest that one purge hi term exploitation. It's an emotionally valuable term ers but in the process of tricking others one nee I'm reminded of charges of exploitation Mrs. Will early on in our 45-year marriage. She'd charge, "V me!" I'd respond by saying, "Honey, sure I'm usir use for you, I wouldn't have married you in the first of us would marry a person for whom we had no u fact, the problem of the lonely hearts among us is t someone to use them.

Specialization is said to occur when people p commodity than they consume or plan to consume. occur on an individual, regional or national basis. F of each.

Detroit assembly line workers produce more they consume or plan to consume. Californian citrus more navel oranges than they consume or plan to co glasses, cars, houses, clothing and food? We get all those goods by specializing in what we do well, get paid, and trade with others for what they do well. Through specialization and trade, we might call it "outsourcing," we enjoy goods as if we actually produced them. In fact, specialization is an alternative method of production. By the way, anyone calling for independence individually, regionally or nationally is asking us to be poorer. It makes no difference whether they're calling for energy independence, clothing independence or coffee independence.

Let's look at just a few misleading statements about international trade. The U.S. trades with Japan. Does anyone really think that it is the U.S. Congress that trades with their counterparts in the Japanese Diet? It's really individual Americans trading with individual Japanese through intermediaries. What about fair trade? If you purchase a Japanese-made camera lens on voluntary and mutually agreeable terms, you'd probably conclude that it was a fair trade or else you would have kept your money. An American camera lens producer might call that trade unfair because he couldn't sell you his lens at a higher price. Economic theory can't answer a subjective question like whether it would be fairer if you had to pay a higher price; it can say that a higher price would result in your having fewer dollars for other things.

The next installment of this series will focus on one of the most important economic concepts—costs.

Economics for the Citizen – Part III

The Freeman: Ideas on Liberty, *December 2005*

Someone might have made you a gift of Ideas on Liberty. Does that mean reading this article is free? The answer is a big fat no. If you weren't reading the article, you might have watched television, talked to your wife, or worked on your homework. The costs of having or doing anything is what had to be sacrificed. While reading this article might have a zero price, if it was a gift, it most assuredly doesn't have a zero cost.

To reinforce the idea that price is not the full measure of cost, imagine that you live in St. Louis. The barber who cuts your hair charges $20. Suppose I told you that a barber in Charleston, S.C. would charge you $5 for an identical haircut, would you consider the Charleston haircut cheaper? While it has a lower price, it has a much greater cost. You'd have to sacrifice much more in terms of time, travel and other expenses in order to get the Charleston haircut.

People often erroneously think of costs as only material things but that which is sacrificed when a particular choice is made can include clean air, leisure, morality, tranquility, domestic bliss, safety or any other thing of value. For example, a possible cost of a night out with the boys might be the sacrifice of domestic bliss.

Costs affect our choices in many ways and for the purposes of this discussion we're going to assume that all of the costs associated with a given choice are borne by the chooser.

Just about the most important generalization that we can make about human behavior is that the higher the cost of a particular choice the less of it will be chosen and the lower the cost the more of it will be chosen. This generalization underlies the law of demand. For simplicity let's assume price measures cost while we hold everything else influencing choice constant. The law of demand can be expressed several ways: the lower the price of something, the more will be taken; and the opposite is true the higher price. We can also say, there exists a price whereby one can be induced to take more or less of something. Finally, there's an inverse (reverse) relationship between the price of a good and the quantity demanded.

Why do people behave this way? The answer, in a word or two is that people try to be as happy as they can. For example, if, when the price of oil rises, people simply ignored the price increase, they'd have less to spend on other things and be less happy. If they sought substitutes for the higher priced oil, they'd have more money left over and they'd be happier. That's why higher oil prices give people incentive to purchase more insulation, buy better windows, wear sweaters and maybe move to a warmer climate. These choices, and many more, are substitutes for heating oil allowing you to use less oil.

When people say a certain amount of one thing or other is an absolute must, that's like saying the law of demand doesn't exist and there are no substitutes. That's untrue—consider a diabetic. Can he do without 50 units of insulin a day? The law of demand says that at some price, say at a $1,000 a unit, he can. There's always at least one substitute for any good and that's doing without the good all together. In the diabetic's case no insulin. While going without insulin has unpleasant consequences, it's a likely substitute at $1,000 a unit. You say, "Williams, that kind of economic analysis is cruel!" It's no more cruel than the law of gravity that predicts that if you jump off a skyscraper you're going to die. Both outcomes are unattractive but it's reality. Indeed, tragically millions of our fellow men around the globe are forced to endure the unpleasant substitute for insulin.

There's a complexity to the law of demand that states: The lower price the more people will take of something and the higher the price less will be taken. It's crucial to recognize that it's relative prices that determine choices not absolute prices. Relative price is one price in terms of another price. Here's an example; actually it's a trick I pull on freshman students. Suppose your company offered to double your salary if you'd relocate to their Fairbanks, Alaska office. Would you consider it a good deal and accept the offer? Some students thoughtlessly answer yes. Then I ask what if upon arrival you find out that rents are more than double what you're paying now and the prices of food, clothing, gasoline and other items are three and four times more expensive. The end result is that while your absolute salary has doubled, your salary, relative to other prices, has fallen.

A bit trickier example of how it's relative prices, not absolute prices, that influence behavior comes with the observation that married couples, with young children who can't be left alone, tend to choose more expensive dates than married couples without children. The couple's income and tastes have little to do with their decision; it's relative prices. Keeping the numbers small, say an expensive date, dinner and concert, has a $50 price tag and a cheap date, a movie, $20. The choice of the $50 dinner and concert date requires that the married couple without children sacrifice two and a half movies that they could have otherwise enjoyed.

The married couple with children must pay a babysitter $10 whether they go on the expensive or cheap date. With the cost of the babysitter figured in, the dinner and concert will cost them $60 and the movie $30. In choosing the dinner and concert date, they sacrifice only two movies. The dinner and concert date is relatively cheaper for the married couple with children since they sacrifice only two movies compared to the married couple with children's two and a half. Since it's cheaper we can expect to observe married couples with children to take more expensive dates when they go out. It doesn't take economic analysis to come up with this. A husband might suggest, "Honey, let's hire a babysitter and take in a movie." The wife explains, "That doesn't make sense. Since we have to pay $10 for a babysitter, whether we go on a cheap or expensive date, why not get our money's worth and take in a dinner and concert!"

How about another example of relative prices? Suppose today's coffee price is $1 a pound and you typically purchase two pounds per week. You hear news that a freeze in Brazil destroyed much of its coffee crop and coffee prices are expected to soon rise. What would you do and why? I'm guessing you'd make larger coffee purchases now, but why? The average person would answer, to save money. That's an okay answer but it doesn't tell the whole story. Once again it's the law of demand working. If coffee prices are expected to rise next week, that means coffee prices this week have fallen relative to those next week and the law of demand says that when a price of a good falls people will take a larger quantity. It works in reverse as well. If coffee prices are expected to fall next week, you'd buy less coffee this week. Why? Coffee prices have risen this week relative to next week.

You might be tempted to ho-hum this coffee analysis as oversimplification but it is the basic principle underlying the complexities of futures markets such as the Chicago Mercantile Exchange where people, as speculators, become rich, sometimes poorer, guessing about the future prices of commodities.

Our next lecture will see what the law of demand says about discrimination and other choices we make.

Economics for the Citizen – Part IV

The Freeman: Ideas on Liberty, *April 2006*

There's a reggae song that advises "If you want to be happy for the rest of your life, never make a pretty woman your wife." Mechanics have been accused of charging women higher prices for emergency road repairs. Airlines charge business travelers higher prices than tourists. Car rental companies and hotels often charge cheaper rates on weekends.

Transportation companies often give senior citizen and student discounts. Prostitutes charge servicemen higher prices than their indigenous clientele. Gasoline stations on interstate highways charge higher prices than those off the interstate. What are we to make of all of this discrimination? Should somebody notify the U.S. attorney general?

The fact that sellers charge people different prices for what often appears to be similar products is related to a concept known as elasticity of demand, but we won't get bogged down with economic jargon. Think about substitutes. Take the reggae song's advice about not taking a pretty woman as a wife. Pretty women are desired and sought after by many men. An attractive woman has many substitutes for you, and as such, she can place many demands on you. A homely woman has far fewer substitutes for you and can less easily replace you. Hence, she might be nicer to you, making what economists call "compensating differences."

It's all a matter of substitutes for the good or service in question and the buyer's willingness to pay a higher price. Business travelers have less flexibility in their air-travel choices than tourists. Women generally see themselves as having fewer alternatives for emergency auto repairs. A man might have more knowledge about making the repair or be more willing to risk hitchhiking or walking. A prostitute might see a sailor on shore leave as having fewer substitutes, not to mention pent-up demand, for her services than the area's residents.

Motorists traveling from city to city are less likely to have information about cheaper gasoline prices than local residents.

Politicians seem to ignore the idea of substitutability, namely, when the price of something changes people respond by seeking cheaper substitutes. New York City raised cigarette taxes, thereby making a pack of cigarettes $7. What happened? A flourishing cigarette black market emerged.

In 1990, when Congress imposed a luxury tax on yachts, private airplanes and expensive automobiles, Senator Ted Kennedy and then-Senate Majority Leader George Mitchell crowed publicly about how the rich would finally be paying their fair share of taxes. But yacht retailers reported a 77 percent drop in sales, and boat builders laid off an estimated 25,000 workers. What happened? Kennedy and Mitchell simply assumed that the rich would behave the same way after the imposition of the luxury tax as they did before and the only difference would be more money in government coffers. They had a zero-elasticity vision of the world, namely that people do not respond to price changes. People always respond, and the only debatable issue is how much and over what period.

This elasticity concept is not restricted to what are generally seen as economic matters; it applies to virtually all human behavior. When a parent asks his child, "How many of your privileges must I take away to get you to behave?," that's really an elasticity question. In other words, how great must the punishment be for the child to misbehave less? It's easy to see how the elasticity concept applies to law enforcement as well. What must be done to the certainty of prosecution and punishment to get criminals to commit less crime?

Economic theory is broadly applicable. However, a society's property rights structure influences how the theory will manifest itself. It's the same with the theory of gravity. While it, too, is broadly applicable, attaching a parachute to a falling object affects how the law of gravity manifests itself. The parachute doesn't nullify the law of gravity. Likewise, the property rights structure doesn't nullify the laws of demand and supply.

Property rights refer to who has exclusive authority to determine how a resource is used. Property rights are said to be communal when government owns and determines the use of a resource. Property rights are private when it's an individual who owns and has the exclusive right to determine how a resource is used. Private property rights also confer upon the owner the right to keep, acquire, sell and exclude from use of property deemed his.

Property rights might be well defined or ill defined. They might be cheaply enforceable or costly to enforce. These and other factors play a significant role in the outcomes we observe. Let's look at a few of them. A homeowner has a greater stake in the house's future value than a renter. Even though he won't be around 50 or 100 years from now, the house's future housing services figure into its current selling price. Thus, homeowners tend to have a greater concern for the care and maintenance of a house than a renter. One of the ways homeowners get renters to share some of the interests of owners is to require security deposits.

Here's a property-rights test question. Which economic entity is more likely to pay greater attention to wishes of its clientele and seek the most efficient methods of production? Is it an entity whose decision makers are allowed to keep for themselves the monetary gain from pleasing clientele and seeking efficient production methods or, is it entities whose decision makers have no claim to those monetary rewards? If you said it is the former, a for-profit entity, go to the head of the class.

While there are systemic differences between for-profit and non-profit entities, decision makers in both try to maximize returns. A decision maker for a non-profit will more likely seek in-kind gains such as plush carpets, leisurely work hours, long vacations and clientele favoritism. Why? Unlike his for-profit counterpart, the monetary gains from efficient behavior are not his property. Also, since a non-profit decision maker can't capture for himself the gains and doesn't suffer losses, there's reduced pressure to please clientele and seek least-cost production methods.

You say, "Professor Williams, for-profit entities sometimes have plush carpets, have juicy expense accounts and behave in ways not unlike non-profits." You're right, and again, it's a property-rights issue. Taxes change the property rights structure of earnings. If there's a tax on profits, then taking profits in a money form becomes more costly. It becomes relatively less costly to take some of the gains in non-monetary forms.

It's not just businessmen who behave this way. Say you're on a business trip. Under which scenario would you more likely stay at a $50-a-night hotel and eat at Burger King? The first scenario is where your employer gives you $1,000 and tells you to keep what's left over. The second is where he tells you to turn in an itemized list of your expenses and he'll reimburse you up to $1,000. In the first case, you capture for yourself the gains from finding the cheapest way of conducting the trip, and in the second, you don't.

These examples are merely the tip of the effect that property rights structure has on resource allocation. It's one of the most important topics in the relatively new discipline of law and economics.

Economics for the Citizen – Part V

The Freeman: Ideas on Liberty, *July* 2006

We're all grossly ignorant about most things that we use and encounter in our daily lives, but each of us is knowledgeable about tiny, relatively inconsequential, things. For example, a baker might be the best baker in town, but he's grossly ignorant about virtually all the inputs that allow him to be the best baker. What is he likely to know about what goes into the processing of the natural gas that fuels his oven? For that matter, what does he know about the metallurgy involved in oven manufacture? Then, there are all the ingredients he uses—flour, sugar, yeast, vanilla and milk. Is he likely to know how to grow wheat and sugar and how to protect the crop from diseases and pests? What is he likely to know about vanilla extraction and yeast production? Just as important is the question how do all the people who produce and deliver all these items know what he needs and when he needs them? There are literally millions of people cooperating anonymously with one another to ensure that the baker has all the necessary inputs.

It's the miracle of the market and prices that gets the job done so efficiently. What's called the market is simply a collection of millions upon millions of independent decision makers not only in America but around the world. Who or what coordinates the activities of all these people? Rest assured it's not a bakery czar.

There are a number of ways to allocate goods and services—deciding the who, what, how and when of production and consumption. They include: first-come-first-served, gifts, violence, dictatorship or lotteries. When it's the price mechanism that performs the allocation function, we realize efficiency gains absent in other methods. The price mechanism serves as a signaling function. Prices rise and fall, reflecting scarcities and surpluses. When prices rise as a result of higher demand, this acts as a signal to suppliers to expand output. They do so because whenever the price exceeds the costs of production, they stand to gain. They ship the goods to those with the highest willingness to pay.

Let's look at just one of the baker's needs—flour. How does the wheat farmer know whether there's a surge in demand for bakery products? The short answer is that he doesn't. All he knows is that millers are willing to pay higher wheat prices, so he's willing to put more land under cultivation or reduce his wheat inventory. In other words, prices serve the crucial role of conveying information. Moreover, prices minimize the amount of information that any particular agent involved in the process of getting flour to the baker needs in order to cooperate.

What if politicians thought that flour prices were too high and enacted flour price controls in the wake of a surge in demand for bakery products? Would wheat farmers put more land under cultivation? Would millers work overtime to produce more flour? The answer is a big fat no because what would be in it for them? The result would be flour shortages, but the story doesn't stop there because mankind is ingenious about getting around government interference. If there were flour price controls, we'd see black markets emerging—people buying and selling flour at illegal prices. That's always one effect of price controls. Another would be the corruption of public officials who know about the illegal activity but for a price look the other way.

In 302, the Roman emperor Diocletian decreed "there should be cheapness," declaring, "Unprincipled greed appears wherever our armies . . . march . . . .. Our law shall fix a measure and a limit to this greed." The predictable result of Diocletian's food price controls were black markets, hunger and food confiscation by his soldiers. Despite the disastrous history of price controls, politicians never manage to resist tampering with prices—that's not a flattering observation of their learning abilities.

In five short articles, there's no way to even scratch the surface of economic knowledge. I'll simply end the series highlighting a few popular sentiments that have high emotional worth but make little economic sense. I use some of these sentiments as a teaching tool in my undergraduate classes.

Here's one that has considerable popular appeal: "It's wrong to profit from the misfortune of others." I ask my students whether they'd support a law against doing so. But I caution them with some examples. An orthopedist profits from your misfortune of having broken your leg skiing. When there's news of a pending ice storm, I doubt whether it saddens the hearts of those in the collision repair business. I also tell my students that I profit from their misfortune—their ignorance of economic theory.

Then, there's the claim that this or that price is unreasonable. I used to have conversations about this claim with Mrs. Williams early on in our 46-year marriage. She'd return from shopping complaining that stores were charging unreasonable prices. Having aired her complaints, she'd ask me to go out and unload a car trunk loaded with groceries and other items. Having completed the chore, I'd resume our conversation, saying, "Honey, I thought you said the prices were unreasonable. Are you an unreasonable person? Only an unreasonable person would pay unreasonable prices."

The long and short of it is that the conversation never went over well, and we both ceased discussions of reasonable or unreasonable prices. The point is that whatever price a transaction is made, it represents a meeting of the minds of both buyer and seller. Both viewed themselves as being better off than the next alternative—not making the transaction. That's not to say that the seller wouldn't have found a higher price more pleasing or the buyer wouldn't have been pleased with a lower price.

How about your parents' admonition that "Whatever's worth doing is worth doing as well as possible."? Taken at face-value, that's not a wise admonition. I tell my students, often to their surprise, that it might not be worth it to try to get the best grade possible in economics. Let's look at it. Say they have biology, physics, English and economics classes. They work their butts off in economics, earning an A, but spending so much time studying economics takes time away from other classes, and they wind up earning an F in biology, a C in physics and a D in English. That makes for a semester grade point average of 1.75. They'd be better off, in terms of grade point average, if they spent less time studying economics, maybe earning a C, and allocating more time to biology and English and thereby earning a C grade in all their subjects. They'd have a higher grade point average (2.0) and wouldn't be on academic probation.

Another example: You ask your wife to have the house as neat and clean as possible when you return from work. You return, and the house is immaculate. You compliment her, saying, "That's a great job, honey. What's for dinner, and where are the kids?" She responds, "I don't know where the kids are, and there's no dinner prepared, but the house is immaculate." Just as getting the best possible grade in economics is non-optimal, so is your wife's doing the best job possible cleaning the house.

Then, there's "You can never be too safe." Yes, you can. How many of us bother to inspect the hydraulic brake lines in our cars before we start the engine and head off to work? Doing so would be safer than simply taking for granted that the lines were intact and driving off. After all, prior to launching a space vehicle, the people at NASA make no similar mechanical assumptions. They go through extensive multiple checks of all systems, taking nothing for granted. Erring on the side of over-caution is costly, and so is erring on the side of under-caution, though for a given choice, one might be costlier than the other.